George T. Wolz

May 31, 1974

W9-BQI-466

INVITATION TO THE TALMUD

INVITATION TO THE
TALMUD

A TEACHING BOOK

JACOB NEUSNER

1817

HARPER & ROW, PUBLISHERS

NEW YORK, EVANSTON, SAN FRANCISCO

LONDON

INVITATION TO THE TALMUD. Copyright © 1973 by Jacob Neusner. All rights reserved. Printed in the United States of America. No part of this book may be used or reproduced in any manner whatsoever without written permission except in the case of brief quotations embodied in critical articles and reviews. For information address Harper & Row, Publishers, Inc., 10 East 53rd Street, New York, N.Y. 10022. Published simultaneously in Canada by Fitzhenry & Whiteside Limited, Toronto.

FIRST EDITION

Designed by Sidney Feinberg

Library of Congress Cataloging in Publication Data

Neusner, Jacob, 1932–
   Invitation to the Talmud.
   Bibliography: p.
   1. Talmud—Introductions. I. Title.
BM503.5.N48   296.1'206'6   73-6343
ISBN 0-06-066098-8

In Memory of
Max Richter
1896–1973
—*my wife's father,
our children's grandfather,
and loyal, beloved friend
to us all*

Contents

Preface

My thanks go to my friends and colleagues, undergraduate and graduate students at Brown University, who share in exploring the place of Talmudic learning within the curriculum of the humanities, in general, and of the study of religions, in particular. It is my happy privilege to participate in the academic community formed by these teachers and friends. The following read the manuscript in various stages of its preparation and gave valuable criticism, though none of course bears the onus of errors or other failures: Professors Ernest S. Frerichs, Horst R. Moehring, and Wendell S. Dietrich, Brown University, Baruch A. Levine, New York University, David Goodblatt, Haifa University, Gary G. Porton, University of Illinois, William Scott Green, University of Rochester, Wayne A. Meeks and Brevard S. Childs, Yale University, Paul Ritterband, City University of New York, Jonathan Z. Smith, University of Chicago, Jakob J. Petuchowski, Hebrew Union College-Jewish Institute of Religion, Cincinnati, Rabbi Baruch M. Bokser, Rabbi Joel Zaiman, Mr. Joel Gereboff, Mr. Stuart Himmelfarb, Mr. Tom Tisch, and Mr. Charles Primus.

J. N.

Brown University

Foreword

THIS BOOK invites the reader to try to get into the Talmud. Nowadays, and for some time past, especially in America, young Jews are scarcely able to try. They do not know how to begin or where. Getting into the Talmud is no easy matter, even for those Jews who are ardent to recover for themselves what their ancestors once knew. This invitation is to join a community of learning men and women, for Talmudic learning is collective. You do not "read" the Talmud, you "learn" it, preferably with a *haver,* or a fellow student, and always with a rabbi. Here I shall be your rabbi. In the traditional *yeshivah,* the Talmud is not "learned" in a monotone. The Talmud is the music for a choir of voices; it is sung, and the music conveys the thrust and parry, the give and take of argument, which is what is truly Talmudic about the Talmud.

The Talmud is a compendium of religious laws, wise sayings, and stories. These, obviously, preserve a particular idiom and present a unique viewpoint, that of the rabbinical sages of Babylonia and Palestine in late antiquity, from the first through the seventh centuries A.D. But the Talmud's laws, sayings, and stories are, as individual units of literature, not strikingly different from those produced within other religious communities. They are, however, put together differently, in a literary form quite without parallel in world literature. They are so related to one another that they constitute a whole which is more than the sum of its parts. That "whole" not only relates the parts in theme but uncovers their underlying principles and harmonies, and shows how remote elements relate to one another. The Talmudic method consists in rigorous, abstract argument about fundamentally practical, mostly trivial matters, an argument thoroughly articulated and tested against all possible objections.

The Talmudic inquiry is phrased as a singing conversation among open and rational minds, united by a devotion to reason and commitment to unobstructed criticism, and dedicated in common to the cause of applying reason to the mundane issues of the workaday world. So the Talmud represents a sustained effort to apply to secular, mostly trivial and ordinary affairs the disciplines of thoughtful analysis and order. Its fundamental building block is the self-contained analysis of a law and all materials pertinent to that law. But "building block" is a false metaphor, for it obscures the Talmud's vigorous movement, the dialectic of its argument, the suppleness of its analytical capacities—its melodic line.

But you must not think that the Talmud is simply another document of law, not much different, except in detail, from Roman or Canon law. You must not suppose your rabbi's apologetic for the Talmud consists in the claim that the Talmud is an interesting document in the history of practical and applied reason. The Talmud is a document of faith, passionate and vivid. Its faith, which I shall spell out in the first chapter, is in the revealed will of God.

What makes that faith interesting is the capacity of the rabbis to discover, in both ordinary and extraordinary conduct, matters of interest to God and the divinely revealed Torah. The rabbi's logical and rational inquiry is not mere logic-chopping. It is a most serious and substantive effort to locate in trivialities the fundamental principles of the revealed will of God to guide and to sanctify the most specific and concrete actions in the workaday world. Reason and logic therefore serve as the vehicle, so to speak, to carry Torah—revealed teaching—from heaven down to earth, and, conversely, to make the profane sacred. They are modes of religious expression. In other religions of the Talmud's day, the pious served God, achieved holiness or sainthood, through prayer, or sacrifice, or celibacy, or martyrdom. Just as the last-named, martyrdom, is essential to the understanding of the early Christian and his imitation of Christ, so reason and logic are essential to the understanding of the rabbi and his imitation of Moses "our rabbi" —that is to say, of classical, Talmudic Judaism. What God does in heaven, as we shall see, is to study Torah. He taught the Torah to Moses, just as a rabbi teaches Torah to his disciple. In this setting, the mode of piety, the imitation of God, and the focus of sanctity—these are therefore the use of your mind. In context we are not talking about wonder-working philosophers, but about fully revealed religious men, within their setting, saints—but whose sainthood consisted in critical intelligence!

The importance of Talmudic faith therefore is not that it is rational. The contemporary interest of Talmudic Judaism is not that it is another form of reasonable, amiable, liberal intellectualism. The rabbis are not represented here as forerunners of good-natured, professorial *illuminés,* able to speak to contemporary men and women because all that they have to say is what we already hear, in any case, from reasonable people. If that were so, we should not need to hear from the rabbis at all. I should not ask you to accept me as your rabbi.

To be sure, a well-established apologetic argument, deriving from nineteenth-century Reform Judaism, stresses the ways in which "Judaism" of biblical or Talmudic times was already saying what we now want to hear, whether what we want to hear is about democracy in politics, or equity in economic life, or an open and just society. "Judaism" is a good thing, this argument holds, because it conforms more or less to the good hopes of our own age. The prophetic tradition taught the primacy of justice and morality over "ritual," and, living in an age incapable of entering into and being transformed by rite, people were glad to learn they had good precedent for their spiritual incapacities as much as for their social aspirations.

But if all to be heard from the prophets or the rabbis were what we already learn from the politics, economics, and social philosophy of our own day and of our own sector, generally on the leftward wing, of modern life, why listen at all to prophets or rabbis of old? What need do we have to make over into our own image the saints of ancient times? What moral authority is left to them if their message is supplied to them by us, and if in doing so, we distort, misinterpret, or simply obscure their particular meanings? Is this not a peculiarly sophisticated kind of fetishism, something that, for us, is a dishonest ritual? It is false because, if honest, we know we have made the prophets and the rabbis over into what we want them to be, rather than making ourselves over so as to be able to perceive what they were and mean even now. Like the carpenter described by II Isaiah (44:9-17), who plants a cedar and raises it, then chops it down and uses part for fuel, and part for a graven image, who roasts meat over part and turns the rest into a god, his idol, then prays to it and says, "Deliver me, for thou art my god," so are those who turn the prophets into liberal democrats and say, "These are our authorities." "*We* were right all the time." They make the rabbis into paragons of rational and liberal intellectuality and say, "These are our precedent. Nothing mysterious here, only sweet reason, 'justice' and 'mercy,' made over for our own solace."

I shall repeatedly insist, to the contrary, the rabbis of the Talmud are not third- and fourth-century college professors or social reformers or liberal, rational philosophers of a mildly religious, benign spirit. They were holy men—saints in an age which took sanctity seriously. But, as I just said, they were not like other saints of their day, whose holiness was expressed through ascetic, flesh-suppressing disciplines—through sitting on pillars or dwelling in caves, through eating only wormwood and dressing only in rags. Their sainthood consisted in the analysis of trivial and commonplace things through practical and penetrating logic and criticism. Their chief rite was *argument*. To be sure, they prayed like other people, but to them, learning in Torah was peculiarly "ours," praying was "theirs"—that of ordinary folk. Their heroes were men of learning, and they turned their biblical heroes, beginning with Moses, into men of learning. When we read their writings closely, we shall see exactly what that learning consisted of, and how they carried on their religious life and sought sanctity through arguments.

What we shall find out is a curious thing. We can, on the whole, follow and even participate in those arguments. They are not spun out within a private or esoteric logic. They center upon arcane matters, but are wholly public and remarkably open to our involvement. The modes of thought turn out to be not much different from those which shape our own intellects. The importance of this fact is not to be missed. It is not, as I have stressed, that the rabbis' mode of thought is worthwhile because it is like our own. The point is that, since ours is like theirs, we may talk with them about *their* ultimate convictions.

What I find strange and awesome is that the rabbis, unlike us, were able to conceive of practical and critical thinking as holy. They were able to claim sainthood in behalf of learned men, to see as religiously significant, indeed as sanctified, what the modern intellectual perceives as the very instrument of secularity: the capacity to think critically and to reason. Here is the mystery of Talmudic Judaism: the alien and remote conviction that the intellect is an instrument not of unbelief and desacralization but of sanctification. That conviction is the most difficult aspect of the Talmud to comprehend, because it is so easy to misunderstand and misrepresent. The external form of the belief—our ability to think clearly, to be mindful—is readily accessible to us. But the meaning of the belief, its substance, its place in the shaping of the religious imagination and the formation of the religious and traditional culture of the Jewish people—these are not so obvious. Explaining these things will, I contend, account also for the whole of the history and character of Judaism from the first century A.D. onward. It will provide the key for everything else, make sense, too, of much that has happened to the Jews in the nearly two centuries since so many of them parted company with the classical modes of Judaic spirituality.

What has happened is that the secular Jews, continuing in the momentum of the tradition behind them, remained within the conviction that the intellectual life was the most important expressive mode of humanity, but lost touch with the mythic and religious sources which relate that conviction to the fundamental structure of reality and impart to it cosmic meaning and metaphysical grandeur. The mind remained holy, but without the faith which made holiness matter, distinguishing the sacred from the common. This persistence within secularity of the effects of sanctity accounts for the former apologetic in behalf of Talmudism or biblical prophecy or anything that might plausibly be represented as "Judaism." The appeal from within the borders of the religious camp—though from people on its fringes, for above all the apologist seeks and needs to persuade himself—was that, on our side of the line of religious sensibility also, may be found the virtues you, on your side of the line, prize so dearly. Those outside the camp did not, for a long time, heed this invitation, or, if they did, declined it for the obvious reason: We already have, without myth, rite, faith, and mystery, what you offer us along with that unclaimed baggage.

Yet Jewish intellectualism without Judaic faith proves wanting, for, divorced from the soul of Talmudic being, secular reason among Jewish intellectuals remained formless and formal, producing, on the one side, the grotesque and the absurd, and an empty formalism, on the other. The Jewish intellectual without roots in Judaic intellectualism was seen (by his enemies) to be a creature of mere clever words, a polished, glistening surface covering nothing. But if the enemies said so, some among the intellectuals told themselves something strikingly similar, for they went in search of "faith" or "roots" wherever these might be found, except in the one sure place, the very ground on which they had all the time been standing. But that ground seemed hard and intractable, not to say infertile. And it was and would remain so, as long as the secret of its cultivation was not perceived. In its stead would come the lush growths of mysticism, in place of substantive conviction, and faddism, in place of steady, enduring commitment.

I do not see how matters could have been otherwise, so long as Talmudic intellectualism was represented either by its enemies as desiccated logic-chopping, or by its friends as nothing other than the tired academicism everyone knew about and no one found sufficient. But wherein lay the soul which had been lost and now was so much missed? Where, if not in the very texts which to begin with had given it permanence? But these too seemed closed, for those able to open them could not then give an account of what was to be found. They reported, chiefly in addressing other scholars, about the meanings of words and the variations in manuscript readings, perhaps—in a primitive way—about history and sociology. But they seldom spoke about the religion—the life of piety and spirituality—expressed within the very study of the ancient books. For the books had once been holy books; the words sacred words, spoken as prayers were spoken; the sentences had expressed a craving for sanctity and a thirst after God. And now they were reduced to their syntax alone, to the examination of logic or philology. Or, as I said, they were presented as peculiarly modern and therefore "relevant," as though people seeking a way beyond the modern, who already knew the emptiness of relevance without a criterion for importance and meaning, should be impressed. People rich in reason were told the Talmud was rich too, as indeed is so.

But the rationally rich lived in the poverty created by the deprivation of meaning, of purposeful living. The Talmud's wealth for such people remained a hidden treasure. They might perceive in the lives of classical Jews of their own day resources of the spirit, of trust, confidence, meaning, which they did not perceive within themselves. They might even lavish nostalgia upon a lost, blessed life within the tradition. But, never confronted by the specific, uncompromising claims of Talmudic Judaism—claims about what is important in life, what is sacred in man—they took for granted that for modern Jews, the holy tradition had come to an end.

And they were surely right, for the Talmud divorced from its mythic context, its larger meanings for the construction of reality and the interpretation of life, was nothing else than a mere tradition. And a tradition perceived as traditional is also conceived as passed. But the Talmud understood as a document of religion, as the expression of the soul and of the inner world of saints, becomes a vivid alternative. For ultimate meanings are not bound to a particular place or time, and a way to the sacred, once discovered, remains forever open. What is sought, and I think what is acutely required, is not what we already have, but what we realize we do not have: a mythic context for our being, a larger world of meanings for our private and individual existence. These have been found by seekers of mystic experience in the suppression of the intellect and the willful suspension of unbelief. Within the Talmud we are able to seek them by the cultivation of the intellect and the criticism even of belief.

The mystery of the Talmud is its capacity to sanctify the one thing I do not propose to abandon, which is my capacity to doubt, my commitment to criticize, above all, the beautiful, reasoned, open-ended discourse created among contentious learning men and women. The wonder of the Talmud is its tough-minded claims in behalf of the intellect, not in search, but in the service, of God. I wrote this book to try to unravel that tangled knot, composed of strands of rationality, religiosity, and mythic perception alike: How is it possible to serve God through the life of the mind? Why is "study" the holy act within the Judaic way of life? How did the religious culture of the Jewish people come to express itself through arguments and debates, more than through prayers or asceticism? Why does the Judaic tradition find God in the thrust and parry of argument, as it does when it claims God himself studies Torah? How is the exercise of the mind, and not the suspension of its function, a sacred act?

The answers to these questions are found only within the direct encounter with the Talmudic text. The purpose of this book, therefore, is twofold. First, it offers the concrete experience of Talmudic study. Second, it proposes to explain not its relevance to today, but the judgment of Talmudic modes of thought upon contemporary culture.

I shall set forth the first part of the invitation by presenting a single chapter of Talmudic law. That chapter of law occurs in four closely interrelated documents: first, the *Mishnah,* the law code of Judah, Patriarch of the Jewish Community of Palestine in the last quarter of the second century A.D.; second, the *Tosefta,* a corpus of supplementary traditions associated with the Mishnah; third, the *Babylonian Talmud,* a commentary on the Mishnah and Tosefta, produced in Babylonian rabbinical circles between the third and the seventh centuries A.D.; and fourth, the *Palestinian Talmud,* the equivalent, produced in Palestinian rabbinical circles from the third through the fifth centuries A.D. Laws on the same themes, in some instances identical in intent and even in language, thus produce a weave of rigorous literary and legal analyses. We shall first study the elements of the chapters of the four documents, then, in the case of the Mishnah and the Babylonian Talmud, we shall ask how these elements have been put together into a coherent corpus of legal literature.

The second part of this invitation to get into the Talmud is mostly concentrated in the concluding chapter, though in expounding the text much is suggested. Granted, there is more to be said than I am able even to propose. But I am not free to desist from the task of dealing with the larger issue: What does the Talmudic mode of critical thought and persistent, skeptical argumentation mean for contemporaries? My answer cannot be exhaustive, but it may at least propose both how those who will may appropriate part of the Talmud's achievements, and how Talmudic values of inquiry even may alter contemporary sensibility. The answer really is found in the chapters devoted to a close reading, line by line, of a significant specimen of Talmudic literature and thought. All I have done at the end is to bring to the surface what I believe is contained and hinted at within the antecedent pages. For me concreteness, the actual texts, the specific details of complex arguments—these are more important than generalizations about modernity and culture, for they contain whatever is worthwhile in the consequent abstractions. The reader may well compose his own answer to the question of relevance, long before he reaches mine. To do so, he owes the text a measure of patience with arcane details and alien laws, restraint at the superficially petty problems raised and solved by the masters of the Talmud. All that is of ultimate, enduring importance lies in the details.

I have not repeated the information conveniently available in Hermann L. Strack, *Introduction to the Talmud and Midrash.**
Strack seems to me to say almost everything worth knowing *about* the Talmud. He defines technical terms, tells about the several components of the Talmud and describes their contents, supplies the facts about Talmudic hermeneutics and the more important teachers. He gives exceptionally thorough, critical bibliographies (to 1925) on all aspects of Talmudic studies. Then he does the same for the biblical-exegetical literature, known as Midrash, produced by the Talmudic rabbis. His book has full notes, indices, appendices. Nothing is lacking except one thing, which my teacher, Abraham Heschel, of blessed memory, called "the spirit of the Talmud." And that spirit can be found, quite naturally, only within the Talmud's pages. Since the English reader will need some guidance in opening and studying those pages (nothing remotely Talmudic can be merely "read"), I took upon myself the tasks just now outlined. But this book may be read without reference to any other, though, if it succeeds in engaging the reader's interest in its subject, later on one will make reference to many further works on Talmudic literature, religion, and history.

This invitation is traditional. It must take its humble place at the end of a very long line, beginning over a thousand years ago, of works introducing the Talmud. Clearly, the character of these efforts depends upon the nature of the reader to whom the Talmud is to be introduced. None of them took for its reader the ordinary educated person, whether Jewish or otherwise, who wants to know

* N.Y., 1965: Harper & Row. The Temple Library.

what, if anything, the Talmud has to do with the life of the mind and its current concerns. Before modern America, it is difficult to find a situation in which gentiles took an interest in Judaism, in particular in the Judaism which flourished after the first century A.D. On the other hand, before modern times it also is difficult to find a Jewish community so remote from the classical sources of the faith of Israel as that found in this country. Curiously, one may address Jew and gentile in the same language, with the same expectations about what is and is not known in advance, because nowadays there is not much difference between them.

That ignorant and indifferent sameness, Jewish and gentile, seems to me to present advantages which outweigh the obvious disadvantages. The rabbis who produced the Talmud exhibit little "ethnic self-consciousness"—these words would have no meaning for them—for they legislated for a community of ordinary folk living commonplace lives, not much different in the fundamental ways from other groups. The Talmud is not an ethnic document. When it raises an ethical question, it speaks of "the good way in which a *man* should walk," not "in which a *Jew* should walk." When it treats dilemmas of social conflict, all parties to the conflict normally are assumed to be plain men and women—Jewish men and women, to be sure—whose claims to a cow or a palm tree are adjudicated by principles of justice everywhere pertinent and invariably right. While, admittedly, questions of mercy and of how God is to be served are referred to, and answered within, the disciplines of the Torah, the revealed will of God given to the people of Israel, and while the rabbis are well aware that some people are Jews and many are not, the Talmud is essentially interested in ordinary folk, not exclusively in Jews.

The reason is that many of its issues are not ethnic at all. Its modes of thought and argument invariably are rational and logical, therefore useful to anyone and any group, not limited to a single community, however distinguished by possession of divine revelation. The Talmud contains no special language, no esoteric or capricious logic, no private, uniquely "Jewish" forms of reasoning. If, therefore, the Talmud has to be introduced to a society exhibiting remarkably little substantive cultural and ethnic differentiation, that is appropriate and advantageous, because it is to the generality of man in society that the Talmud, in the first place, is addressed.

Earlier invitations, or introductions, to the Talmud, described by Jacob Schachter,* fall into three periods of development, the ninth through the twelfth centuries, the thirteenth through the eighteenth, and the nineteenth. Naturally, all introductions focused upon the discovery of general principles of Talmudic inquiry. The earliest tended to stress historical and biographical questions, the classification of the masters by generations and the assignment to them of approximate dates. In the twelfth century Maimonides offered guidance on how to study the Talmud systematically, not merely episodically. The second period continued the earlier historical and biographical work and added an interest in the analysis of Talmudic method and modes of interpretation and argument. The "modern period," which began in the nineteenth century, was marked by a wholly new range of questions, derived from modern philology, text criticism and the recovery of manuscript evidences as to the exact reading of the document, a critical approach to historical questions, and the illumination of specific passages by comparative studies of Greek and other cultures cognate to Jewish culture.

Before now no one recognized the necessity to introduce the literary and logical traits of the text itself. Anyone interested in an introduction to the Talmud already knew considerable parts of the Talmud. Anyone who had not already studied the Talmud was not likely to want to be introduced to it. As I said, we face a different situation. That is why I have tried to do what aforetimes was either unnecessary or unwanted.

---

* *The Student's Guide through the Talmud by the Eminent Teacher, Z. H. Chajes, Translated from the Hebrew, Edited, and Critically Annotated* (N.Y., 1960: Philipp Feldheim, Inc.), pp. xv ff.

INVITATION TO THE TALMUD

CHAPTER

I

The Talmud in Context

THE TALMUD is the single most influential document in the history of Judaism. It therefore must be read not as a historical source or a law code, though it is both, but as fundamentally and deeply religious literature. And we must come to it, if we are to learn anything about its meaning, in the spirit of anthropologists, whose questions are not of faith but of understanding.

We cannot today pay a visit to a distant community or tribe to study the classical Judaic religious tradition. All forms of contemporary Judaism, though deriving from Talmudic teachings and values, stand at too great a distance to testify to the religious world of the rabbis who created the Talmud. Too much has happened between the seventh and the twentieth centuries for any movement in contemporary Judaism to claim today exactly to represent and replicate the classical, formative tradition of the first seven centuries A.D. To pay our visit to the Talmud and through that visit to come to an understanding of the modes of faith and understanding characteristic of the men who created it, we have therefore to stand back. We must set aside, for the moment, the question of what the Talmud means to us, though at the end I shall argue it can mean a great deal.

Since I have alleged the Talmud is a document of religion, I owe at the outset a definition of religion. It comes from Clifford

Geertz*: "What a given religion is—its specific content—is embodied in the images and metaphors its adherents use to characterize reality. . . . But such a religion's career—its historical course—rests upon the institutions which render these images and metaphors available to those who thus employ them."

First of all we shall survey the central images of Talmudic Judaism. At the same time we shall attend to the organized movement of rabbis which produced the Talmud. That movement constitutes the institutionalization of Talmudic images, is responsible for making available to the Jews of its times—as of ages afterward—the Talmud's beliefs, ideals, and metaphors. Here we shall describe the context of the Talmud, and afterward shall proceed to the literature itself.

The Talmud is the product of a small group of Jewish sages, men who lived in the land of Israel, which they called "the holy land," and in Babylonia, from the first to the seventh centuries of the Common Era. What is important about them, however, is not the historical events of their day. What we want to describe is their context, their situation as men.

Four facts about them emerge even in this simple opening sentence.

First, they saw themselves as sages—men of wisdom. That means they stressed the importance of two things, learning what already is known and understanding the new in terms of the old. Right and wrong, folly and sense—these are not things decided moment to moment. To the sage they are determined within the accumulated experience of the ages. Wisdom is the deposit, the residuum of insight refined from the practical experiments of centuries.

Second, I said the sages (among others) perceived that a land could be holy—of which more later.

Third, we notice that they lived in a time of religious ferment,

* *Islam Observed: Religious Development in Morocco* (New Haven, 1968: Yale University Press; Chicago, 1971: University of Chicago Press), pp. 2–3.

in which religions were coming into being and fading away. The "first" century, after all, is *first* because it marks the beginning of one great religion, Christianity. The Talmud took shape, therefore, in a time in which men faced alternatives and made enduring and influential choices. The rabbis of the Talmud made choices which became normative for the Jews and therefore came to constitute "Judaism."

Finally, we refer to "their situation as men," and this accurately reflects the exclusively male composition of the rabbinic movement. That fact should not surprise us. The men of antiquity held a low opinion of women. Paul thought women in the church should shut up and behave themselves. Philo, the Jewish philosopher of first-century Alexandria, though sexual relations permissible only because they produce children. Eliezer ben Hyrcanus, a first-century rabbi, said one should not teach his daughter "Torah" —that is, rabbinic lore and law. We thus learn that the rabbis were very much men of their own time. What makes them interesting is their capacity to speak to men and women for a long time thereafter.

Let us abandon the historical mode of discourse. We have to, if we insist that the rabbis are interesting. I do not come merely to report that they once lived and therefore should be described as objects of historical curiosity. The rabbis are interesting because they and the literature they produced constitute alternatives for people interested in how societies take shape, how life is to be lived, and, especially, how the issues of human existence may be thoughtfully analyzed and decided. Therefore, I am going to use the present tense, even though my sources derive from men dead more than sixteen centuries.

Furthermore, in contemporary Judaism are many believing men and women for whom the ancient rabbis live, just as they live for me. Their vitality for the believers (and in some ways, I too am one with them) comes out of the rabbis' faith that their words are part of the revealed will of God, as we shall see. But for me their vitality, their intellectual interest, come because I think they testify in the formation of religion as a cultural system. They adumbrate ways in which religious belief and rite express the religious imagination, the perception and interpretation, of the community as a whole, and so form a construction of reality. As I just said, we study the rabbis of the Talmud, therefore, as an anthropologist would study a community—literate or otherwise—and not as a historian approaches the literary evidences of an ancient civilization. Our question is not, Exactly what happened? Our question is, What *is* happening within this group, and what does this teach us about ourselves and our potentialities? That is not a historical question at all.

The first thing we want to know about the rabbis is, What is their role within the larger community? The negative answer is of greatest consequence. The rabbis are not the men who ultimately hold power within the community. The Jews live under two other, coordinated governments.

First is the empire which controls the land in which they live. The land of Israel is under Rome, part of its considerable possessions. Babylonia is a province within the Iranian empire, which extends from the Euphrates eastward into central Asia and serves as the intermediary, in trade and culture, between Rome on the west, and China and India on the east.

The two empires, moreover, leave the day-to-day governance of the Jews in the hands of Jewish authorities. But these are not rabbis. In Babylonia the state-supported Jewish authority is called the exilarch, the ruler of the Jewish community "in exile from the holy land." In the land of Israel he is called the patriarch (*nasi* in Hebrew). He is recognized by the Romans not because of his learning in the Judaic traditions, though the rabbis before the third century conceded it, but because he serves the purpose of Rome. The Romans want to keep the country at peace. The patriarch wants to run the country and claims he can keep the peace and so serve the interests of the empire. It is a fair trade and produces a stable administration from the end of the first century to the beginning of the fifth.

What do the exilarch and the patriarch have in common? Both claim to descend from the biblical king, David. This claim is not a matter of genealogy. It means that the claimant supposes he comes from the family which will produce the king-messiah. Indeed, anyone who wants to govern the Jews is going to claim he either is the messiah or may be the progenitor of the messiah. Everyone knows this genealogy was alleged in behalf of Jesus. But it also was the claim of the Maccabees, who governed the Jews from 160–150 B.C., and even of King Herod, son of an Idumean convert to Judaism in the first century B.C. In other words, the established convention to legitimate and justify your rule of the Jews is that you are, or will father, the Messiah.

Now the rabbis, for their part, form a religious and political movement, a group of men who possess particular beliefs and aim at particular social goals. The one thing they cannot claim to be is—*the* Messiah! For a collectivity may lay claim to keep the messianic promise. But it cannot personify the Messiah, and this is by definition. So it is on an unequal basis that the rabbis have to compete with important and powerful individuals, backed by the force of the great empires, on the one side, and by the inertia of their established bureaucracies, on the other. Not only so, but they will not achieve their goals if they oppose the established authorities. They can hope to accomplish them only by subverting, or taking over for their own purposes, the established authority.

The rabbis do so by serving in the autonomous administrations of exilarch and patriarch, respectively. They regard the former as "ignorant" and accuse him of being "unobservant." This tells us the exilarch is not part of their movement. For what he does not know or observe is not the religion of the ordinary Jews, but the mode of living of the rabbi. But institutional control will serve no substantial purpose without something more, a symbolic message— an ideology—as forceful, an image as powerful, as that of the Messiah. What does the Messiah promise? He inaugurates the perfect age, the end of time; he heals the sick, cures the insane, drives out the evil spirits, rids the people of all the things that bother them. He restores the exiles to their land and rebuilds the Temple. If people believe that such wonders come of their ruler, whether he does miracles or not, he is going to have a strong hold upon their imagination and loyalty.

What can the rabbi promise instead? Several things. First, the rabbi will teach that when all the Jews do what he now does, then the Messiah will come. The way to that great day lies not through the court of the exilarch, but within the circle of the sages. So, for example, one of them said, "If all Israel will keep the Sabbath for one time only, the Messiah will come." It should be clear that "all Israel," that is, the Jewish community, do keep the Sabbath, more or less. People do not ordinarily work on that day or violate the other biblical rules which make the day holy. We know this because the rabbis seldom, if ever, complain about outright violation of the biblical commandments respecting the Sabbath as a day of rest. The complaint is, therefore, against people who do not keep the Sabbath the way *the rabbis* say it should be kept.

To take another example, the rabbis, believing they receive communications from the prophet Elijah, say he told one of them, "You ask, Why has not the Messiah come? Now today is the Day of Atonement, and yet how many virgins have been embraced this day in your town!" Modern Judaism knows the Day of Atonement—Yom Kippur—as a day of fasting and solemn reflection. But before the Temple was destroyed, in A.D. 70, the day called forth a great celebration. After the sin-offering was completed in the Temple, people felt themselves free of sin and guilt. It was a time of tremendous spiritual exultation and excitement. Then young people—we are told—would go out and dance in the fields. Evidently they did more than dance. And the pre-70 spirit of the Day of Atonement continues to prevail among ordinary folk, so the rabbis do not approve. They have another conception of the meaning of the day, of the requirements of atonement, than a mere animal sacrifice.

We observe, therefore, that the rabbis stand apart from the larger community of Israel, but not wholly so. They share the way of living of the ordinary folk, but differ in some important ways. Similarly, some of them serve in the government of the community, though they do not fully accede to the basis on which the head of the government claims to be legitimate. Who, then, are the rabbis and what are the beliefs and practices which set them apart?

The encompassing myth revealed in the pages of the Babylonian Talmud centers upon the figure of Moses and tells the story of the Moses-piety—spirituality centered on Moses—of the rabbis. That story relates God's disclosure to Moses of a dual revelation, or Torah, at Mount Sinai—one in writing, the other handed orally from master to disciple. The whole Torah—oral and written—contains the design for the universe, the divine architect's plan for reality. It is to be studied, therefore, not merely for information, but as an act of piety and reverence for the divine lawgiver. Just as God taught Torah to Moses, so the rabbi, modeling his life after Moses "our rabbi," teaches his own disciple. In "studying Torah," and even more so in effecting it in the lives of Israel, the rabbi thus imitates God. Following the model of the "school" in heaven, the schools for Torah-study bring together masters and disciples and preserve the ancient traditions.

The most striking aspect of these schools is the rabbis' conception that in them live holy men, men who more accurately than anyone else conform to the image of God conveyed by divine revelation through the Torah of Moses "our rabbi." The schools are not holy places only or primarily in the sense that pious people make pilgrimages to them or that miracles are supposed to take place there. The schools are holy because there men achieve sainthood through study of Torah and imitation of the conduct of the masters. In doing so, they conform to the heavenly paradigm, the Torah, believed to have been created by God "in his image," revealed at Sinai, and handed down to their own teachers. Thus obedience to the teachings of the rabbis leads not merely to ethical or moral goodness, but to holiness or sainthood. Discussion of legal traditions, rather than ascetic disciplines or long periods of fasting and prayer, is the rabbis' way to holiness.

If the masters and disciples obey the divine teaching of Moses our rabbi, then their society, the school, replicates on earth the heavenly academy, just as the disciple incarnates the heavenly model of Moses our rabbi. The rabbis believe that Moses was a rabbi, God dons phylacteries, and the heavenly court studies Torah precisely as does the earthly one, even arguing about the same questions. These beliefs today may be seen as projections of rabbinical values onto heaven, but the rabbis believe that they themselves are projections of heavenly values onto earth. The rabbis thus conceive that on earth they study Torah just as God, the angels, and Moses our rabbi do in heaven. The heavenly schoolmen are even aware of Babylonian scholastic discussions, so they require a rabbi's information about an aspect of purity taboos.

So the rabbis believe that the man truly made in the divine image is the rabbi; he embodies revelation—both oral and written—and all his actions constitute paradigms that are not merely correct, but holy and heavenly. Rabbis enjoy exceptional grace from heaven. Torah is held to be a source of supernatural power. The rabbis control the power of Torah because of their mastery of its contents. They furthermore use their own mastery of Torah quite independent of heavenly action. They issue blessings and curses, create men and animals, and master witchcraft, incantations, and amulets. They communicate with heaven. Their Torah is sufficiently effective to thwart the action of demons. However much they disapprove of other people's magic, they themselves do the things magicians do.

The rabbis furthermore want to transform the entire Jewish community into an academy where the whole Torah is studied and kept. This belief aids in understanding the rabbis' view that Israel will be redeemed through Torah. Because Israel had sinned, it was punished by being given over into the hands of earthly empires; when it atones, it will be removed from their power. The means of this atonement or reconciliation are study of Torah, practice of commandments, and doing good deeds. These transform each Jew into a rabbi, hence into a saint. When all Jews become rabbis, they then will no longer lie within the power of history. The Messiah will come. So redemption depends upon the "rabbinization" of all Israel, that is, upon the attainment by all Jewry of a full and complete embodiment of revelation or Torah, thus achieving a perfect replica of heaven. When Israel on earth becomes such a replica, it will be able, as a righteous and saintly community, to exercise the supernatural power of Torah, just as some rabbis are already doing. With access to the consequent theurgical capacities, redemption will naturally follow. The issues of Talmudic analysis, while rationally investigated, thus are transcendent and cosmic in significance.

Rabbinic theology includes two important elements. First are secret doctrines pertaining to the being and essence of God, the mysteries of history and redemption, and the like. These doctrines are studied in the schools and rarely, if ever, taught or even alluded to outside of them. Second, the rabbis publicly offer a self-consistent and comprehensive view of man's relationship to God. Man has to submit to God's will, and he demonstrates his submission through observing the commandments. If he sins by not doing so, he will be held responsible. Punishment follows in this world through suffering, but the suffering has to be gladly accepted, for it insures that one has at least begun atonement here, and hence may worry less about the world to come. If people sin and nonetheless prosper, or if they do not sin and yet suffer, an easy explanation is available. The wicked might enjoy this world, but in time to come they pay a terrible penalty. Similarly, the righteous suffer now, but in time to come they enjoy a great reward. This neat account suffices for the orderly conceptions of the schools, although probably not for the disorderly life of the streets.

Other elements of rabbinic theology cannot be ignored. Demons, witchcraft, and incantations; revelations through omens, dreams, and astrology; the efficacy of prayers and magical formulas; rabbinical blessings and curses; the merit acquired through study of the Torah and obedience to both the commandments and the sages —all these constitute important components of the rabbinic world view. A comprehensive account of the rabbis' beliefs about this world and those above and below and about the invisible beings that populate space and carry out divine orders would yield a considerably more complicated theology than that briefly given here. Its main outlines, however, would not be much modified, for magic, angels, demons, and the rest represent the way the rabbis think matters work themselves out—all these elements constitute the *technology* of the rabbis' theological world view.

The spiritual attitude of both rabbis and the masses may be described in the following way: "We are absolutely worthless, and are now deprived even of the former ways of finding favor with You. Once there was a Temple, and we could offer sacrifice there, but now it is no more, so we must give the sacrifice of our flesh and blood. But who are we to propitiate, we who are of no consequence and on our own have no future? We are nothing, except that we are *Israel,* the children of men You loved, and bearers of the revelation You delivered.

"Even in the most private moments of life, therefore, we are not alone, but are surrounded by the merits of the fathers and the presence of memories of the sacred moments of our history. Nor are we hopeless, because we look forward to the fulfillment of the promises made to the prophets in olden times. We are sanctified in all which we do out of love and loyalty to You. In the hour of our greatest private joy, at the marriage canopy, we remember both the public sorrow and the coming joy of Zion, and recall not only its destruction, but what was said by Jeremiah when it was destroyed, that it *will* be rebuilt.

"So if we are sinners, we lie in the hands of a God of great mercy. The passage of the seasons, which we witness regularly month by month, testifies to Your enduring sovereignty. Just as the moon keeps Your laws, so do we, and just as it testifies to the greatness of its Maker, so would we. When we find ourselves in a time of danger, we turn to You and beseech Your blessing."

The ordinary people comprehend and believe in the faith of the rabbis as it is here expressed. The spiritual situation revealed in the rabbis' prayers is precisely congruent to theirs. They too are "Israel," and they revere the Scriptures and remember its lessons. They too long for the coming of the Messiah, and although unable to express their yearnings in the evocative and noble language of the rabbis, they adopt the rabbinical liturgies without difficulty.

The more narrowly academic concerns include the precise and detailed discussions of laws on how and when to pray, the proper blessings to say over one thing or another, the conditions for interrupting prayer, and the like. We shall see how these rules are formulated. It is doubtful that ordinary people are much bothered by liturgical issues posed to the masters or that the instruction imparted to the disciples reaches a broad audience. To learn the proper way of saying grace proves terribly difficult even for many students, and outsiders scarcely comprehend all the rules. Indeed, knowing and keeping these rules is one of the important significations that a person has entered the rabbinical estate. Yet the issues of the common faith are not divorced from the rabbinical discussions. It is precisely *because* they believe in prayer as fervently as do ordinary people that they think one should pray with at least the decorum and respect shown to an earthly king of kings; therefore, they seriously inquire into the proper and improper procedures for praying. In this sense the rabbis' laws represent the continuation of popular faith: If the people believe that prayer matters, then the rabbis—who are, after all, lawyers—set out the rules of conduct and procedure which conform to such a belief.

Prayers composed by rabbis center upon four major themes: (1) the Temple and its cult, (2) the wrath of God, which is revealed in an hour of crisis, (3) the humility and helplessness of man, and (4) the corpus of ideas and symbols embodied in the sacred history of Israel. Above all, however, one is struck by the intensity of rabbinical prayers concerning the Messianic kingdom. In the liturgy for the marriage ceremony the center of attention focuses upon the coming joy of Zion, prefigured by the delight of bridegroom and bride. Just as one loves the other, and rejoices in that love, so in time would God again espouse Israel in Zion, and rejoice in her. The private joy of life is thus seen to be paradigmatic for the public event of coming history. It is the Messianic hope which becomes vivid in times of difficulty. The deep and abiding longing for the Messiah's coming characterizes master, disciple, and outsider alike.

While they might accommodate themselves to the conditions of the current life, the Jews see this world as merely transitory and impoverished. In time to come the advent of the true and permanent age will inaugurate a time of fulfillment and completion. Although the prayers and discussions of the rabbis seem private, personal, and ahistorical, they must be seen against the broader framework of faith in which they find meaning. Within the humble affairs of Israel's life at that time one discerns though darkly the shadowed reflections of the great illumination that is to come.

It therefore would be a gross error to overestimate the differences separating the way of life of the ordinary Jews from that of the rabbinical estate. In general the rabbis' merely conventional social manners or customs are deepened into spiritual conceptions and magnified by their deeply mythic ways of thinking. In the villages the ordinary people regard the rabbi as another holy and therefore exceptional man, but still heart and soul at one in the community with other Jews. The rabbinical ideal is antidualistic; the rabbis believe that all Israel, not just saints, prophets, and sages, stood at Sinai and therefore now bear common responsibilities. No one conceives of two ways of living a holy life—two virtues or two salvations—but of only one Torah to be studied and observed by all. The cutting edge of rabbinical separateness thus is blunted.

The inevitable gap between the holy man and the layman is further reduced by the deep concern felt by rabbis for the conduct of the masses. This concern leads them to involve themselves in the everyday affairs of ordinary people, and it produces considerable impact upon daily life.

Only two really substantial, differentiating characteristics are observable. First is the relationship between master and disciple.

The rabbis' social life follows forms wholly alien to those of outsiders. The disciple reveres the master as a living Torah and humbles himself before him as before God. The outsider honors the master as a learned man, fantasizes about his magical powers, submits to his judicial authority, and accepts his communal influence. These reflect basically different attitudes: on the one hand stands a living myth; on the other, the superficial effects of that myth. Furthermore, the disciple of the sages conforms to personality traits and behavior patterns quite unnatural for ordinary folk. He forces himself into a posture of abject humility with implications far beyond what outsiders comprehend or accept. We shall see stories expressing such humility. His reverence for the master is only a little lower than his fear of the Lord. His imitation of the master's deeds and his preservation of the memory of those deeds shapes a religious discipline quite alien to the workday life of common people. The humility shown to God and to the master is supposed to extend to the disciple's behavior with everyone else.

The second characteristic separating rabbis from common Jews is study. Obviously, the reasons are not that ordinary people do not understand the need for information, that they are entirely ignorant of the world and its way, or that they know nothing of traditions. The people know the Scriptures. They listen to the reading of the Torah in the synagogues. Prophetic writings and passages of wisdom literature are also regularly read to them. The masses observe the Sabbath, the festivals, the holy days, and food and sex taboos. All these observances require knowledge, and the constant exposure to Scriptures and to the sages produces a considerable amount of it. Therefore, the "learning" of the rabbis cannot be spoken of in total contrast to the "ignorance" of the masses. Unless you accept the rabbinical belief in the rabbis' sole possession of the oral Torah, the people cannot be regarded as "ignorant" at all.

What the ordinary Jews do not know and the rabbis always do know is the one thing that makes a common man into a rabbi: *"Torah" learned through discipleship.* It begs the question to speak of the ordinary people as "ignorant of Judaism." One does not have to exaggerate the educational attainments of the community as a whole to recognize that learning in the rabbinical traditions does not by itself separate the rabbi from other people. What is important is the rabbi's attitude toward his *own* study. Extrinsic qualities deriving from the mythic context transform the natural actions of learning facts or ideas or memorizing sayings—which anyone might do—into the ritual actions unique to the rabbi.

The "Judaism" of the rabbis at this time is in no degree either normal or normative, and speaking descriptively, the schools cannot be called "elite." Whatever their aspirations for the future and pretensions in the present, the rabbis, though powerful and influential, constitute a minority group seeking to exercise authority without much governmental support, to dominate without substantial means of coercion. What they want to accomplish is the formation of the kingdom of priests and holy people demanded at Sinai, and to do so according to the revelation of Sinai as they alone possess it. Admittedly, this description of the rabbinical schools is hardly a portrait of the religious life of Jewry. Yet, in my view, the rabbis do tend more and more to set the standard, the golden measure, the royal way.

The Talmudic chapter before us is going to focus upon one small aspect of the law, and the specific law involves very minor details of commonplace behavior. Yet within the chapter are four of the greatest themes of Talmudic Judaism. These have now to be set forth and explained.

First, the law itself involves eating a meal. Who is supposed to keep this law? In Talmudic times the laws about conduct at a meal are observed chiefly by disciples of rabbis, and then especially when they are in the presence of the master. So we are about to consider one detail in the larger "ritual of being a rabbi" we have alluded to. Yet it goes without saying that nothing in the chapter before us is going to suggest such a limited focus of law observance. On the contrary, everything is phrased in terms of what any-

one should do. Indeed, subjects are rarely, if ever, given for predi-
cates, which are simply, "[he] does . . ." or "[they] do . . ." or
"[one] blesses . . ." Thus while the law may practically concern
only a small group, the formulation of the law conceals that fact
and announces a much wider intention, to speak to everyone and
about what all are supposed to do.

To understand why meals should be subject to rabbinic legislation, we have to turn to the Hebrew Scriptures, the Torah. There
we find numerous laws about food which is clean, animals which
are unclean. One may eat only the clean, never the unclean. Not
only so, but biblical literature tends to equate the clean with the
holy, the unclean with the profane or unholy. The land of Israel
is holy. Zechariah 14:20–21 holds that in the end of days, the
land will also be clean. The Temple is holy—set apart, sanctified.
It therefore has to be kept clean.

But what is this "cleanness" to which we refer? It is not a matter of removing dirt from your hands, of hygienic antisepsis. On
the contrary, when we speak of "clean" or unclean, we are far
from a concern with the physical presence of dirt. We are rather
confronted with the legacy of concerns left over from pre-Mosaic
Israelite culture.

That culture, like many others, regarded some things as taboo,
therefore to be kept out of the holy community. Various crucial
periods in life—childbirth, or the menstrual period—were regarded as dangerous. Various diseases were particularly feared,
regarded as the mark of the presence of an evil spirit or demon.
Chief among these was leprosy. Mildew, mysteriously appearing
on the wall of a house, was feared.

When we reach the biblical legislation contained in the books
of Leviticus and Numbers, we enter a world in which demons,
who can do things independent of the will of God, or terrors outside of the divine power, are unknown. The biblical law comes
long after the revolution effected by the concept of one, unique,
all-powerful God, transcendent over the world, not subject to any
of its laws. It cannot take account, therefore, of evil forces, de-

mons, that work their will outside of God's purpose. But the law must and does take account of the archaic remains of those old conceptions—the taboos associated with certain animals, certain periods of life, certain natural phenomena.

These are neutralized, first by being subsumed under the Torah's laws, therefore made to express the will of God. The laws which designate as impure certain animals, excretions, or diseases know nothing of these as malignant enemies operating independent of the divine will. Uncleanness is merely hateful to God and must be avoided by all who have anything to do with the divinity. All biblical views of purity and impurity represent an *interpretation* of taboos which must in their origins have been perceived quite differently. The taboos are not wholly neutralized; they retain the independent, antecedent, autonomous power of evil.

In biblical literature what also happens is the transformation of purity and impurity into metaphors for moral and immoral living. "Pure" and "impure" or clean and unclean to begin with connote a condition entirely lacking in ethical or moral traits. They assign to the status of impurity a bodily state or an animal, or a corpse. But they do not thereby impute a negative ethical or moral valuation, nor stand for something else. They represent the equivalent of the good or morally right, of the evil or immorality.

But the very treatment of purity in the biblical *laws,* made by the priests, accomplishes a correlative purpose. The priestly laws take for granted that whatever its cause, impurity has one constant effect: You cannot go to the Temple. Purity functions solely as the requirement of entering into and participating in the cult. The multiform world of impurities thus is homogenized. While treating purity primarily in the context of the cult may not seem so imaginative as regarding it as a metaphor for moral uprightness, in fact the force of the consequent limitation of the fear of impurity as a cause or mark of evil is enhanced. For if purity and impurity are made relative to the cult, they are, while not emptied of intrinsic power, at least limited in the locus of that power's effects. One who is impure is not everywhere a bearer of a malevolent, autonomous power. The menstruating woman or the leper is not dangerous outside of the cult. These people are unclean—which means *only* that they cannot come to the Temple until purified. Focusing the matter upon the Temple therefore begins to convert purity into a matter of relationship or status. It eventually will remove from impurity any sort of independent, material, nonrelative significance. In Talmudic law this process of neutralization is completed. Purity and impurity constitute a set of highly complex relationships, but these have nothing to do with the physical world. All things depend upon intention and purpose, circumstance and time.

The reason we have had to review these facts is that one central issue of the chapter before us is going to concern purity in the ritualistic sense in which we have just treated it. This at the outset is surprising. For the meal of which we shall speak is not in the Temple. The participants—ordinary folk or rabbis—are not priests. But the rabbis believe exactly this: The ordinary meal of an ordinary person in his own home has to be eaten *as if* he were a priest, as if his home were the Temple, and as if he were engaged in the act of sacrifice to God. It is not merely that his food has to conform to the biblical laws of what may or may not be eaten. The man himself, his wife and family and all present also must be in a state of purity in accord with the requirements of the biblical code of the priesthood. The utensils with which he eats, the pots and pans in which the food is prepared, have likewise to conform to those requirements.

For example, a corpse is a source of "uncleanness." For students of nonliterate cultures that is not going to be surprising; in few cultures is a corpse entirely free of taboo. In biblical law the building in which a corpse is lying spreads the "uncleanness of the corpse" to all the objects under its roof. So the pots and pans of our meal must not have been in a building in which a corpse is located. They cannot have been touched by a menstruating woman, or by a leper, or by a man or woman who suffers a genital flux. So we are far from the simple requirement not to eat pork. The range of "purity" and "impurity" is, as I said, drawn from the setting of the Temple cult, on which the Scriptures had focused the application of the purity rules to begin with.

By this point you must surely wonder why I have chosen a chapter centered upon ritual, upon such a remote and arcane matter as the purity and impurity of food and of the setting of a meal. Before I explain, let me introduce the other important themes of the laws before us.

A second major theme is the prayers you say at a meal.

A third is prayers you say at a meal on the Sabbath or on a festival.

This brings in its wake, fourth, concern for the differences between one time and another, between sacred time—a holy day, on which one behaves in accord with various rules—and ordinary days, to which such rules do not apply.

So the interrelated laws before us concern the most commonplace and fundamental concerns of the religious person: eating, praying, the awareness of the passage of time, and "ritual." "Ritual" here covers not liturgy, to which it is commonly applied nowadays, but actions or concerns subject to rules extrinsic to their normal, everyday, or "natural" character and explained by reference to a myth, in this case a story about God and his Torah.

Eating is not a ritual. It may be made so if the way in which you eat, or the words you recite before or after eating, or the foods you eat—if any of these is subject to considerations extrinsic to the actual need to prepare and put food into your mouth, eating is set within a ritualistic context. And it would be difficult to find a religious tradition without rituals of eating. Take, for example, the Christian instance, in which are involved specific ritual foods made to represent something quite other than their own substance (wine as the blood of the new covenant).

Anyone familiar with Jewish religious observance will notice that food plays a considerable part throughout. For example, even today particular sorts of food are associated with specific holy days. You have to eat in the *Sukkah*—a frail hut—on Tabernacles. You are supposed to eat a particularly fine meal on the eve and afternoon of the Sabbath. You observe the Atonement rite and commemorate the destruction of the Temple by fasting. A Jewish wedding ceremony must be concluded with special prayers composed as part of the Grace after Meals. Purim is observed by eating a large meal and getting drunk. Passover is laden with food rites and taboos. You must eat unleavened bread and must not eat leavened bread. You eat dairy products on Pentecost (*Shavu'ot*). The list could easily be extended. That this originally religious consideration persists in the secular setting of Jewish culture goes without saying—for instance, the lavish Bar Mitzvah banquet divorced from any religious meaning, or the popularity of "*kosher*-style" delicatessens.

So the Talmud's treatment of food and eating suggests how it will deal with many other important concerns of everyday life. It provides a glimpse into the Talmudic mode of defining, of thinking about, of analyzing the most fundamental actions of ordinary people. At the same time, as I said, the meal will introduce important theological concerns. Because of the importance of praying before, after, and on the occasion of eating and drinking, the meal allows us to review important elements in Talmudic theology as expressed by prayers associated with food. At the same time, the way in which the Talmud deals with such prayers is going to tell us a great deal about its authors' conception of what praying means, how one relates to and addresses God.

Our fourth important theme—the distinctions among various days or hours, the experience of the natural course of time—recurs throughout the laws. The reason is that for the Talmud (as for biblical literature), time is not one and unchanging, but highly differentiated; the setting of the sun, on Friday, the sixth day of the week, is a tremendous event. It differentiates the profane from the holy time.

One final question remains: On what basis do the rabbis incorporate the Temple purity laws into the meal? What lies behind the rules, everywhere taken for granted, that you eat your meal like a priest in the Temple—free of contact with a corpse, or with a creeping thing, or with a woman in her menstrual period, careful not to touch unclean objects, thoughtful about what you have done all day long and about what has been done to your food and your dishes? This is a far cry from the biblical priests' interpretation of purity, which limited purity to the Temple. For the rabbinic rule raises purity to a level of consciousness and importance without parallel in the ordinary life of Jewry in pre-Talmudic times, introduces purity and impurity into every aspect of the common life, above all, into the everyday meal.

The answer is that the Talmudic rabbis are heirs of the Pharisaic group which flourished one hundred fifty years before the destruction of the Temple in 70. And the Pharisees' interest in purity was one significant part of their legacy to the post-70 rabbis, their continuators.

The Pharisees before the destruction were those Jews who believed that one must keep the purity laws outside of the Temple. Other Jews, following the plain sense of Leviticus, supposed that purity laws were to be kept only in the Temple, where the priests had to enter a state of ritual purity in order to carry out the requirements of the cult, such as animal sacrifice. They also had to eat their Temple food in a state of ritual purity, but lay people did not. To be sure, everyone who went to the Temple had to be ritually pure. But outside of the Temple the laws of ritual purity were not observed, for it was not required that noncultic activities be conducted in a state of Levitical cleanness.

The Pharisees held to the contrary that even outside of the Temple, in one's own home, one had to follow the laws of ritual purity in the only circumstance in which they might effectively apply, namely, at the table. They therefore held you must eat secular food, that is, ordinary, everyday meals, in a state of ritual purity *as if you were a Temple priest*. The Pharisees thus arrogated to themselves—and to all Jews equally—the status of the Temple priests and did the things which priests must do on account of that status. The table of every Jew in his home was seen to be like the table of the Lord in the Jerusalem Temple. The commandment, "You shall be a kingdom of priests and a holy people," was taken literally. The whole country was holy. The table of every man possessed the same order of sanctity as the table of the Temple cult. But at this time, before 70, only the Pharisees held such a viewpoint, and eating unconsecrated food as if one were a Temple priest at the Lord's table thus was one of the two significations that a Jew was a Pharisee, a sectarian.

The other was meticulous tithing. The laws of tithing and related agricultural taboos may have been kept primarily by Pharisees. Pharisees clearly regarded keeping the agricultural rules as a chief religious duty. But whether, to what degree, and how other Jews did so, is not clear. Both the agricultural laws and purity rules in the end affected table fellowship: *How, with whom, and what you may eat.* That is, they were "dietary laws."

The commonplace setting of Pharisaic table fellowship is striking. The sect ordinarily did not gather as a group at all, but in the home. All meals required ritual purity. Pharisaic table fellowship took place in the same circumstances as did all nonritual table fellowship: common folk eating ordinary meals in an everyday way, among neighbors who were not members of the sect. They were engaged in workaday pursuits like everyone else. The setting for law observance was the field and the kitchen, the bed and the street. The occasion for observance was set every time a person picked up a common nail, which might be unclean, or purchased a bushel of wheat, which had to be tithed—by himself, without priests to bless his deeds or sages to instruct him. Keeping the Pharisaic rule required neither an occasional exceptional rite at, but external to, the meal, as in the Christian sect, nor taking up residence in a monastic commune, as in the Dead Sea sect in Judaism. Instead, it imposed the perpetual ritualization of daily life, on the one side, and the constant, inner awareness of the communal order of being, on the other.

The role of purity in the response of the Pharisees to the destruction of the Temple is known to us only from rabbinic materials, which underwent revisions over many centuries. A story about Yohanan ben Zakkai and his disciple, Joshua ben Hananiah, tells us in a few words the main outline of the Pharisaic-rabbinic view of the destruction:

Once, as Rabban Yohanan ben Zakkai as coming forth from Jerusalem, Rabbi Joshua followed after him and beheld the Temple in ruins.

"Woe unto us," Rabbi Joshua cried, "that this, the place where the iniquities of Israel were atoned for, is laid waste."

"My son," Rabban Yohanan said to him, "be not grieved. We have another atonement as effective as this. And what is it? It is acts of loving-kindness, as it is said, 'For I desire mercy and not sacrifice' " [Hos. 6:6].

(Avot de Rabbi Natan, Chap. 6.)

How shall we relate the arcane rules about ritual purity to the public calamity faced by the heirs of the Pharisees at Yavneh, the rabbinic center founded in 70? What connection joins the ritual purity of the "kingdom of priests" to the atonement of sins in the Temple?

To Yohanan ben Zakkai, preserving the Temple was not an end in itself. He taught that there was another means of reconciliation between God and Israel, so that the Temple and its cult were not decisive. What really counted in the life of the Jewish people? Torah, piety. (We should add, Torah as taught by the Pharisees and, later on, by the rabbis, their continuators.) For the zealots and messianists of the day, the answer was power, politics, the right to live under one's "own" rulers.

What was the will of God? It was doing deeds of loving-kindness: "I desire mercy, not sacrifice" (Hos. 6:6) meant to Yohanan, "We have a means of atonement as effective as the Temple, and it is doing deeds of loving-kindness." Just as willingly as men would contribute bricks and mortar for the rebuilding of a sanctuary, so they ought to contribute renunciation, self-sacrifice, love, for the building of a sacred community. Earlier Pharisaism had held that the Temple should be everywhere, even in the home and the hearth. Now Yohanan went a step further. He taught that sacrifice greater than the Temple's must characterize the life of the community. If one were to do something for God in a time when the Temple was no more, the offering must be the gift of selfless compassion. The holy altar must be the streets and marketplaces of the world, as, formerly, the purity of the Temple had to be observed in the streets and marketplaces of Jerusalem. Just as the prophets treated purity as a metaphor, so now did Yohanan interpret the Temple and its sacrifice. In a sense, therefore, by making the laws of ritual purity incumbent upon the ordinary Jew, the Pharisees already had effectively limited the importance of the Temple cult. The earlier history of the Pharisaic sect had thus laid the groundwork for Yohanan ben Zakkai's response to Joshua ben Hananiah. It was a natural conclusion for one nurtured in a movement based upon the priesthood of all Israel.

The Pharisees determined to concentrate on what they believed was really important, and that was the fulfillment of all the laws of the Torah, even ritual tithing, and the elevation of the life of the people, even at home and in the streets, to what the Torah had commanded: You shall be a kingdom of priests and a holy people. A kingdom in which everyone was a priest, a people all of whom were holy—such a community would live as if it were always in the Temple sanctuary of Jerusalem. Therefore, the purity laws, so complicated and inconvenient, were extended to the life of every Jew in his own home. The Temple altar in Jerusalem would be replicated at the table of all Israel. The biblical limitation of purity is reversed.

We return to our rabbis. We see that in taking over the legacy of Pharisaism as of the much older biblical inheritance, the rabbis face the task of continuing to deal with issues originally raised in quite other circumstances and with the response, now archaic, of much different times. Purity ought not to mean much to them. After all, there now is no Temple to go to. For the Babylonian part of the rabbinic estate, purity is impossible, for one cannot be pure in an unholy land. Yet the rabbis doggedly work out rules based upon the purity laws of olden times. They persist in assigning meaning in terms of those ancient laws to rather humble details of the meal.

It is an extraordinary act of loyalty to the long-ago past and its long-impertinent teachings. But, as we saw, once the purity laws are taken over for ordinary life, the Temple might fall, but the Temple's mode of holiness will endure. The historical event of the destruction of Jerusalem is rendered of little everyday importance for those who keep the Temple's laws wherever they may be, who view their table as the Temple altar, and who see themselves as priests carrying on the ancient cult.

What has happened, therefore, is a curious thing. The rabbis preserve the historical Pharisaic legacy and make it timeless. That legacy consequently frees the rabbis and their followers from the single most important and tragic historical event of their age—thus, from "history." Once the Temple may be everywhere and every man may be a priest, the rabbis preserve the Temple's sanctity. The belief that people are close to God and are able to serve him, the certainty that the small and private actions of men and women retain transcendent importance to God and may be holy—these things will go on and on. No longer is the holy life limited to one place, one time, subject to the exigencies of the politics in one state, and disposed of within the affairs of nations. Given the precarious context of the Jews' life on earth, in history, I think this no small achievement.

So much for the context of our particular chapter of the Talmud. Let us now turn to the document itself.

CHAPTER

II

Introducing the Talmud

BECAUSE of its vastness and depths the Talmud is aptly compared to an "ocean." It is a compilation of law and lore created by Palestinian and Babylonian rabbis between the late first and seventh centuries A.D. From that time onward it has been studied partly as a source of practical law but mainly for the pleasure of joining in the discussions commenced within its pages. Commentaries laid open and added to its complexities; codes systematized and updated its laws. What is remarkable is devotion to the study of the Talmud not only by legal specialists and religious virtuosi, but by ordinary Jews living commonplace lives. Knowledge of Talmudic literature and ability to enter into the issues first raised in arguments of the Talmud furthermore served as the measure not only of intellect but of piety and virtue, of holiness. This invitation to learning how to live and why extended over twenty centuries. The entire tradition rested on the Hebrew Scriptures and other sacred literature going back for another ten—what a short time it takes to lose so much, so long considered! In less than half a century ordinary Jews in the West and in the State of Israel have forgotten what thirty centuries observed and thought, argued and wrote down.

What made the Talmud so engaging as to retain the interest of one generation after another, so fascinating as to form the focus of interest for ordinary men, not merely learned specialists?

The answer is the Talmudic argument and its mode of inquiry, an applied and yet suspecting, modest rationality. The Talmud compelled interest because its problems were worldly and accessible, its mode of argument open to participation by any person willing to reason, and its logic relevant to, and persuasive in, many and varied circumstances. People studied the Talmud because they could themselves join fully—in both intellect and feeling—in its arguments. They could attempt first to master and unravel them, then to reshape and revise them, and, perhaps, finally even to improve upon them, and in consequence, repair the conduct of their own lives. Study of the Talmud therefore supplied the opportunity for reason to do its work, for the mind to be stretched and to move, and for the disciplined intellect to exercise itself through clean, sustained, and rigorous argumentation. Nor should the aesthetic pleasure of Talmudic learning be ignored. For those to whom beauty consists in order, architectonic clarity, and elegant structure, the Talmudic argument, with its balance, brilliance, clarity, completeness, and frequent elegance, constitutes a thing of splendor.

This invitation is for myself too. I am not a "Talmudist." I do not engage in the classical disciplines of Talmudic study. I have not mastered the medieval commentaries. Although I study the laws and engage in the exegesis of specific passages, it is not my main activity in life to participate in, and add to, the great Talmudic tradition. A historian, a positivist, and seeker after facts about religious and social history, I make use of the Talmud for purposes quite separate from its own. The Talmud is not meant as a historical source, but that is what I make it. What I lack in the received virtuosities of Talmudic learning, however, I hope to make up in passionate interest. I first discovered the Talmud at the age of twenty-two, when I entered the Jewish Theological Seminary. It then seemed to me, and thereafter continued to be, the most interesting thing I had ever encountered. Scarcely a day has passed from then until now in which I did not spend most of my time in study of, and reflection on, Talmudic literature. If the study of the history of the Jews and Judaism in antiquity, not of the Talmud itself, supplied me with the primary agendum for my inquiries, discovering the Talmud nonetheless constituted something of a religious experience, for to me the luminous came to be numinous. I choose to convert the Talmud, to make it my own, rather than to be converted to its discipline. But perhaps that is a real Talmudic option, a way through, nowadays, to iron discipline, and not simply to mumbling learnedness. To make the Talmud my own is not to escape being possessed by it.

This "confession" is meant to suggest that the Talmud is not an ordinary document from antiquity, interesting primarily to historians or lawyers (in Jewish courts) or theologians, but not pertinent to people without scholarly concerns. On the contrary, like other great and abiding literature, the Talmud, for all its remoteness, its alien idiom and arcane data, has the capacity to win attention because of its timelessness, therefore its permanent pertinence to one generation after another. It lies open to the participation of minds with concerns quite different from those of its original authorities and with interests shaped by a world remote from that in which it was created. Because of its mode of critical thought and argumentation, the Talmud therefore preserves enduring intellectual vitality. The argument and counterargument, thesis and refutation, which constitute Talmudic dialectic—these are the ongoing foci of personal interest. So long as new minds reflect upon the old issues in new ways, but within the ancient disciplines of practical reason, the argument never ends.

To understand the Talmud, therefore, it is not enough to quote its stories and sayings, to survey its laws and cases, to praise its wisdom. Were the Talmud merely a series of compilations of stories and laws, it would not warrant study in its own terms and language. Scholars of history, law, and philology, not to mention theology and the history of religions, might recover and present in the contemporary mode of learned discourse whatever is worthwhile in its pages. Because the Talmud is essentially a set of highly disciplined arguments effected through sustained criticism, it is to be confronted in its own language; its mode of thinking remains apposite to contemporary ways of reasoning and reflection. Introducing the Talmud requires mapping out the arguments, not merely citing the conclusions. It cannot be learned except by a deeply personal engagement to its inner movements, by a love of its learned meanings—and, moreover, by an effort to reconstruct those meanings for oneself and not merely to repeat them. Here I try to invite you into the Talmud, there to go your own way—in a way generations of others before have gone. There is no end to Talmudic argument; it is part of the unending life, a maze of continuities. The Talmud is an astonishing variety of links in the chain of Jewish wisdom.

Yet, as I stressed at the outset, what is important in the Talmud is not simply the elegance and beauty of its mode of argument. What is remarkable is that, for many generations, people could perceive not mere beauty, but holiness, in the criticism and arguments of the Talmudic authorities. And that is what requires attention. The rabbis are not forerunners of merely rational professors, but are holy men. But what is it about rational inquiry that is holy? This is the question to confront us on every page. The answer is that the working of the intellect in man is perceived to be the counterpart of the divine. What makes man human is his mind, his ability to be mindful and thoughtful, different from animals, which lack consciousness. But man is most mindful when he takes seriously the ideas of his fellow man, when he exercises his power of concentration to take account of, to criticize, and to respond to ideas held by others. Reason joins man to man and men to God. It establishes the tie between heaven and earth.

This is an extraordinary conviction, expressed to begin with in the mythic picture of God's studying Torah along with Moses and the heavenly academy, of the rabbi's imitating God through his learning of the law. But the myth speaks of a deeper reality. It is not merely a pious fable. It conveys the stubborn conviction of the rabbis that the give-and-take of argument represents man at his most human and speaks to God at his most accessible. This conviction makes the Talmud more than a document in the history of rationality. It renders it an open book for those seeking a faith through understanding, yet surpassing understanding. And to the contemporary intellectual, it is a peculiarly pertinent and strangely open mode of faith—belief in the one thing intellectuals vividly perceive and cultivate, their minds, but belief, too, in the *sanctity* of the exercise of the intellect. Surely without the Talmud the intellectual knows this: All that is worthwhile derives from the active intellect, in the curious communication of people who take one another seriously enough to engage in argument.

Talmudic faith is accessible precisely because it is experienced even before articulation. Yet what makes that experienced faith *Talmudic* is the apprehension of the transcendent, the view that sustained criticism bears otherworldly meanings. I shall claim, without apology, that those meanings constitute the vindication of the intellect, its consecration. People able to give their lives to thought and its expression cannot remain indifferent to the ways in which, within the Talmud, their devotion constitutes an adumbration of the sacred.

Where to Begin?

Every Talmudic tractate—there are thirty-seven of them in the Babylonian Talmud—begins on page 2; there are no page 1's because there is no beginning. Wherever you start your study, you will feel you have joined a conversation which began long before you came along. A great many facts will be taken for granted, and these have to be learned before a discussion begins to make sense. Principles established somewhere else are always assumed within a given argument; you have to master those principles. Information not fully articulated is going to be cited. Finally, Talmudic argument presupposes modes of thought which are everywhere present but never wholly explained. Distinctions and rational considerations have to be assimilated. We might, to be sure, begin with a generalized discussion of the fundamentals of an argument, but such an analysis would produce useless abstractions. Since the Talmudic structures exhibit thoroughgoing consistency, you may apply to nearly every page what you have learned on nearly every other page of your study. The best way to study, therefore, is inductively, to proceed from one concrete problem to the next, carrying forward the generalizations and modes of argumentation already mastered, certain that they will recur time and again. That is how we shall proceed, for no Talmudic passage is better than any other; all passages are both constructed in a consistent pattern and equally typical and suggestive of the whole. Since there is no beginning—or ending—we may just as well jump into the middle.

A Page of the Talmud

A page of the Talmud is called a folio (Hebrew: *daf* from the Akkadian word for tablet), of which the obverse is designated A, the reverse, B (Hebrew for a side: *amud,* column). The pages (32–33) before us are Babylonian Talmud, Tractate of Blessings (*Berakhot*) 51b and 52a; the next side is 52b. The section marked I contains the Mishnah; II, the *Gemara,* the text of the Talmud which we shall study verbatim. Section III contains the phrase-by-phrase commentary of Rabbi Solomon bar Isaac, known as Rashi (R[abbi] Sh[elomo] Y[ishaq]), who lived, mainly in Troyes, France, from 1040 to 1105.

Rashi is one of the towering figures in the history of Judaism because he composed immensely influential commentaries for nearly the whole of the Hebrew Bible and the Babylonian Talmud. His commentaries exhibit such lucidity and pedagogic deftness that the texts which they serve are not to be approached except through Rashi. But everyone may study them with Rashi. The commentary to the Pentateuch is popular, addressed to the ordinary pious man. That to the Talmud is wide-ranging and sophisticated, written for the scholar, but still a paradigm of effective pedagogy. So Rashi had the ability to find appropriate language for many audiences. His unexcelled mastery of the whole of rabbinic literature, moreover, meant that he could bring to bear in the elucidation of a given problem virtually all available information. His step-by-step commentary on the dialectic of the Talmudic argument stresses the importance of the course of argument itself, not simply the practical conclusions. Finally, his pedagogical sense told him what was important for the student at any particular point and what could be omitted. The comments always are adequate, never excessive; they are glosses, not separate monographs; precise, subtle, remarkably concise, tasteful and selective, they are always appropriate to the context. Many later authorities wrote commentaries on his commentaries, both in Scripture and in Talmud; none improved on his style or replaced him.

The most important of these supercommentaries, designated as IV, is the *Tosafot,* supplements or additions to Rashi's commentary (not to be confused with the Tosefta, the supplement to the Mishnah). The *Tosafot* are printed on the outer margin, opposite Rashi's commentary. The work of the Tosafists, of addition and criticism, began when Rashi completed his; the first ones in fact were his sons-in-law and grandsons. Their work was chiefly to gloss Rashi. But the project of commenting on antecedent comments gradually was superseded by another task: the active criticism of any and all authority—including Rashi's—and the development of the law through the extension to new problems of established principles. This work took the form not of continuous commentary, but of essays on specific problems. While the first Tosafists were French, many of the later ones lived in the German Rhineland. Their work ended in the early fourteenth century. The writing of *Tosafot* in France ceased with the destruction of the Talmud in the reign of Louis IX ("Saint Louis"), regarded in the history of Talmudic texts as an exceptional calamity for his systematic destruction of Talmuds found in the libraries, Jewish and otherwise, in his kingdom.

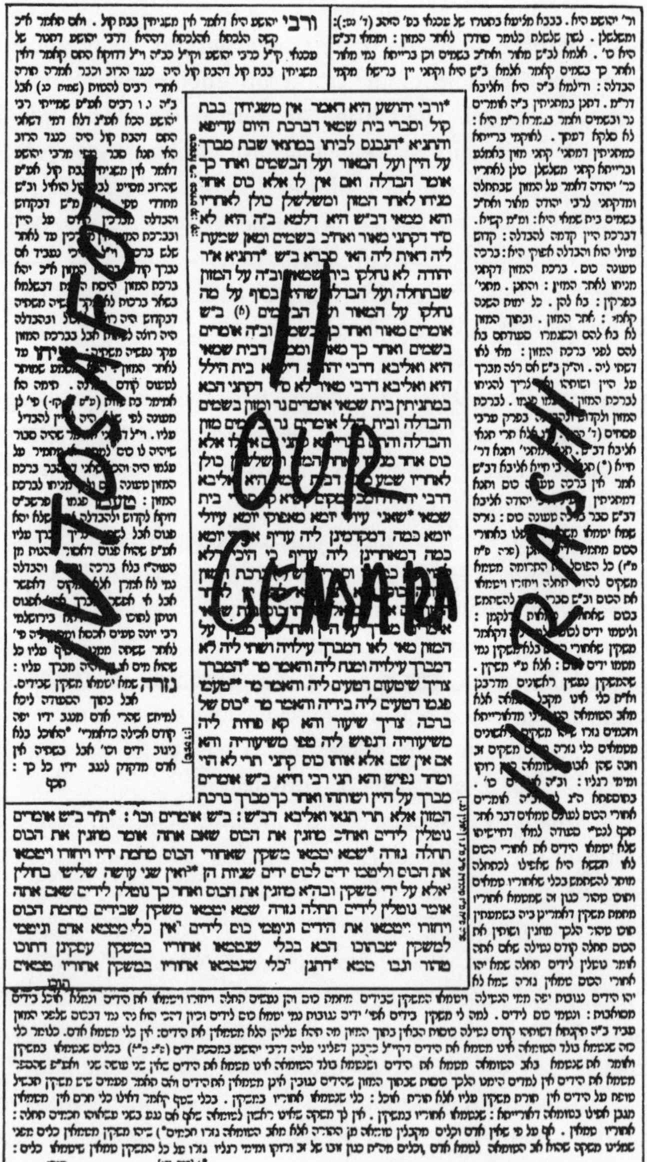
TOSAFOT
OUR GEMARA
RASHI

[The page reproduces a standard Vilna-edition Talmud page (Tractate Berakhot), with the central Gemara text surrounded by Rashi and Tosafot commentaries. An artistic graffiti overlay reading "IN ISRAEL — PASHA II — OUR GEMARA — I — OUR MISHNAH — U — OUR GEMARA" is painted across the page, obscuring much of the Hebrew.]

הדרן עלך שלשה שאכלו

הדרן עלך שלשה שאכלו

אלו דברים שבין בית שמאי ובית הלל בסעודה ב"ש אומרים מברך על היום ואח"כ מברך על היין ובה"א מברך על היין ואח"כ מברך על היום

These are the four main components of a page of the Babylonian Talmud. Printed texts today include numerous other commentaries and aids to understanding; most are printed as appendices to the several tractates. The work of nearly fifteen centuries and countries from the Euphrates to the Atlantic and from the Sahara to the Baltic Sea and as far east as the Dnieper—all will be contained within the standard printed texts. We shall concentrate, however, on the Talmud as explained by Rashi.

We shall study together (the right word is "learn") the eighth chapter of the tractate of Blessings, which in the Babylonian Talmud covers two and a half folios. Our task is simply to read the chapter in its entirety, step by step and line by line. We shall ask for information external to the analysis and argument only so far as it is intrinsic to the task of "learning." Our primary problem is not what the chapter teaches us about history of the Jews or of Judaism, theology, history of religions, philology, or related sciences. We simply want to know, What does the chapter say? How does it go about its business? and What is "talmudic" about the Talmud? For history or philology the Talmud is a source among other sources. For us the Talmud's the thing. At the end we shall read the chapter as a whole, secure in our understanding of its parts. Our chapter consists of two parts, a pericope of *Mishnah,* and its accompanying, Babylonian *Gemara.* The Mishnah is a law code. The *Gemara,* as we shall soon see, is essentially a wide-ranging, but tightly organized, commentary on that law code.

CHAPTER

III

The Mishnah

THE HEBREW WORD *Mishnah* comes from the root *shanah,* to repeat; the word for the ordinal, second, *sheni,* has the same root.
As the title of the law code of Judah, the Patriarch of Jewish Palestine in the beginning of the third century A.D., it means, "that
which is to be learned by repetition," therefore by memory. The
further implication is that the Mishnah contains materials which
had been memorized and not written down for a very long time.
For the Talmudic sages claimed that to Moses had been revealed
two Torahs, or revelations, at Mount Sinai. One was contained in
the Scriptures—that is, in written books—and the other in oral
traditions learned by repetition and handed on in that manner for
many centuries. So the Mishnah was represented by the authority
behind it as the second, essential part of the whole Torah of Moses.

The Mishnah is divided into six large sections, or orders (Hebrew: *Seder*), which deal with, first, agricultural law (called *Zera
'im,* seeds); second, Sabbath and festival law (*Mo'ed,* season);
third, family law, vows and oaths, marriages, divorces, inheritances
(*Nashim,* women); fourth, civil law, torts, damages, criminal law,
the structure of the ideal government, penalties and punishments
(*Neziqin,* damages); fifth, sacrifices and things devoted to the
Temple in Jerusalem, the order and rules of the cult of animal
sacrifice (*Qodashim,* holy things); and sixth, rules of ritual purity

and impurity, how purity is acquired and how it is removed, sources of impurity and objects which are susceptible to becoming impure (*Toharot,* purities). There are subdivisions in each order of the Mishnah, and these are further divided into chapters; a subdivision is called a tractate (*Massekhet*), of which there are sixty-three in all. The six orders are divided as follows: *Zera'im,* eleven tractates, with 74 chapters; *Mo'ed,* twelve tractates with 88 chapters; *Nashim,* seven tractates with 71 chapters; *Neziqin,* ten tractates with 73 chapters; *Qodashim,* eleven tractates with 91 chapters; *Toharot,* twelve tractates with 126 chapters.

Our chapter in a general way deals with blessing food at meals. But very rapidly we shall find ourselves in the midst of technicalities, which take for granted a considerable number of further generalities. Indeed, while we shall be told at the outset that the law concerns a meal, it is not a routine meal that is under study at all, but the Sabbath meal in particular. Furthermore, the issues of blessing food before and after a meal are subordinated. More prominant are problems of ritual purity and impurity, on the one hand, and the proper way in which to say the prayers at table for the advent of the Sabbath and for the conclusion of the Sabbath, on the other. We therefore have to begin by describing the general context in which the specific rules are laid forth.

The Mishnah As Law Code

First, we have to take most seriously the fact that the ancient rabbis of Israel produced, as their major, enduring documents, collections of law codes, commentaries, rulings of sages about practical affairs. The founders of Talmudic tradition—they were called "fathers of the world"—who flourished in the first six centuries A.D., believed that their task was to realize in everyday life the precepts of the revealed Torah. "To do justice, love mercy, and walk humbly with God"—to the rabbis these were not abstractions. They had to be effected in the world, and nothing is so difficult in secular affairs as to find exactly what is justice or mercy here and now—and what is to be done that is just and merciful. Since the Torah contained rules on many subjects, and since these rules had to be interpreted to apply to wholly new matters and to issues important only long after Sinai, we should not be surprised to find the sages' concentrating on the minutiae of daily life.

Second, we have to revise our understanding of the word *law,* not only because in the Talmud specific laws apply to matters today not regarded as subject to societal, legal regulation at all, but also because *law* in English is not an accurate representation of its Hebrew equivalent, *halakhah. Halakhah* derives from the root *halakh,* to go, to walk, and denotes "the *way* things are done." In this sense *halakhah* is descriptive as well as prescriptive. It describes how one normatively does things. The laws are phrased in present-tense participles: "One does this, one does not do that." They are not given as commandments, "Do" or "Don't do" or "You *will* do this." They are not expressed in the form of cases, "If you do this, that will be the result." The laws (Hebrew plural: *halakhot*) and the language in which they are phrased therefore should be taken as something different from what their equivalents mean in contemporary usage.

The difference is that through *halakhah* the rabbis described the way they thought life should be lived, society should be organized, God should be served. True, they tried to guide ordinary folk to live life, form society, and serve God in the ways they thought right. Their description of what was correct did not depend upon what is in fact now. It was meant to stand as the measure and criterion for reality. *Halakhot* dealt with many matters over which, in fact, the rabbis had no control. For one instance, the fifth order of the Mishnah concerns the Temple cult, which by A.D. 200 had been in ruins for more than a century; the sixth deals with purities in the Temple, rules no more relevant to everyday life than the foregoing. For another, the rabbis described, in tractate *Sanhedrin,* the constitution of the government of the Jewish state, although there was no such state. The laws in *Sanhedrin* furthermore had nothing whatever to do with the organization of any Jewish state that had existed before A.D. 70. The Romans, who ruled the country in the first century, Herod, who reigned in the last half of the first century B.C., and the Maccabees, who governed from ca. 150 to ca. 50 B.C.—none of the antecedent authorities had organized the government as the rabbis responsible for Sanhedrin claimed they should, and the rabbis did not say they had. Nor should these historical limitations be taken as exhaustive. The enforcement of many laws lay beyond the power accorded to the Jewish authorities of Palestine and Babylonia by the respective imperial authorities, the Romans and the Iranians; at least some laws had to be enforced in ways different from those prescribed by the rabbis; or they were different from rabbinic law entirely.

What kind of law, therefore, do we approach? It cannot be called utopian, but it also cannot be called entirely practical. It is a kind of "platform" for the future: In the ideal world, this is how things are to be done. Meanwhile, we shall effect as much of the law as we are able. But if this description is accurate, then we must wonder whether *law* is the right word for "teachings" which neither describe nor prescribe, yet do not exhort or threaten. Here is neither prophecy nor history. That is why I warned that we have to revise our understanding of the word *law;* yet the revision is not of one word, but of how we understand the materials before us.

Some Essential Facts

Our chapter consistently refers to the House of Shammai and the House of Hillel. Who were they?

Shammai and Hillel were Pharisaic masters at the beginning of the Common Era (Christian usage: A.D.). The Houses, or schools, named after them constituted groups of their followers within the Pharisaic sect. Their differences concerned minor matters of detail, within a considerable area of agreement on basic questions. The Houses flourished in the first century; eventually, after 70, the Hillelites prevailed over the Shammaites. Specifically, as we saw, the Pharisees believed, first, one should tithe his food according to the biblical requirements and otherwise give to the priests all the dues Scripture had assigned to them; ordinary folk gave some, but not all the tithes. Second, they believed that one should eat his ordinary meals in the state of ritual purity required of priests both in the Temple and in the time in which they consumed the priestly gifts, such as Heave-offering of the crops. In other words, the Pharisees held that everyone at his own table at home was like a Temple priest at the table of the Lord in the holy sanctuary: "You shall be a kingdom of priests and a holy people" (Ex. 19:6) was understood by them literally to mean that the people should act as if they were priests in the Temple. Most, though not all, of the differences between the two Houses pertained to these two fundamental considerations, tithing and purity. The laws before us involve the latter; they exhibit differences about purity rules. These rules, it should be remembered, fell into disuse during the second and third centuries. Since, moreover, foreign countries were impure to begin with, the purity laws never could be kept outside of the holy land, and so for Babylonian Jews had no practical meaning. But, as we now understand, that does not mean the Babylonian sages were indifferent to, or refrained from studying, these laws and ruling on difficulties pertaining to them, as if they would be kept.

Three further facts are necessary.

First, we shall hear much about "blessing the day" and "saying a blessing over the wine." "Blessing the day" refers to the Prayer of Sanctification of the Sabbath. After the recitation of Genesis 1:31 and 2:1–3, it begins, in today's liturgy, as follows:

Blessed are you, Lord, our God, king of the world, who has sanctified us by his commandments and taken pleasure in us and in love and good will given us as an inheritance, his holy Sabbath, a memorial to the creation of the world. For it is the first day of the holy convocations, a memorial to the exodus from Egypt. For you have chosen us and sanctified us above all peoples, and given us as an inheritance, in love and good-will, your holy Sabbath. Blessed are you, Lord, who sanctifies the Sabbath.

The Sanctification is said with a cup of wine in hand. The issue is, Which comes first? Does a man say the Sanctification of the day and then recite the requisite blessing over the wine, "Blessed are you, Lord our God, king of the world, who creates the fruit of the vine," or vice versa, the blessing over the wine and then the Sanctification? What principles set the correct order?

Second, the laws speak of "light, food, spices, and *Havdalah*." What are these?

At the end of the Sabbath, after the sun has set, you say a prayer marking the conclusion of the sacred day and the beginning of the secular week. This prayer, called *Havdalah,* or division, is as follows:

Blessed are you, Lord our God, king of the world, who divides between holy and profane, between light and darkness, between Israel and the peoples, between the seventh day and the six days of work. Blessed are you, Lord, who divides between sacred and profane.

Before saying the above prayer, which is recited with a cup of wine in hand, you also recite a blessing over spices or incense and light: "Blessed are you, Lord our God, king of the world, who creates various kinds of spices," and ". . . who creates the lights of fire." Thus we shall have repeated references to (1) light, (2) spices, and (3) *Havdalah*.

Now what do these things mean? Why do they matter to the men who discuss them? The rabbis discuss prayers everyone is expected to say. We cannot suppose they here express a different view of God and the world from that held by other Jews. Everyone believed in the Sabbath. Saying blessings—words of thanks—over food was commonplace. We may take for granted, also, that the prayers at the end of the Sabbath were old and accepted. Why, to be sure, you should say a blessing over light at the end of the Sabbath is not explained here. The Talmud will tell us a story about that. The meal at the end of the Sabbath surely would have to be blessed. The *Havdalah* prayer, marking the distinction between holy time and the ordinary week, expresses a belief of the community as a whole: The people itself is holy, like the land; the course of the natural world is to be interpreted in terms of the historical realities of the life of the holy people. Just as the week consists of the six ordinary days and the holy Sabbath, so mankind consists of the peoples and Israel, made holy by God and divided by him from the rest. So the natural order and the historical life of men and of Israel correspond to each other. Nothing in these prayers speaks only for the rabbinical movement. But the Talmud's concern for them does.

The Talmud wants to know exactly what is the proper way to do things, the right order for prayers. Its creators, first of all, are lawyers. They take very seriously indeed the forms of life, correctly supposing that the form cannot be distinguished from the function and meaning of what a man does. They are, second, religious men, who conceive that the service of God must call forth, is expressed through, man's most thoughtful reflection. As religious men they see themselves like suppliants before a king. They call God the king of kings of kings—for the Roman and Iranian emperors were kings over many kings, but God is king of them all. When the Israelite approaches God in prayer, he comes before the ruler of the universe, the king of the world—and the Talmud will make use of that metaphor many times. Now a man does not approach a king lightheadedly or thoughtlessly, but in accord with the protocol and procedures of the court. This is how you honor the king, express your submission to him. So the careful consideration of the order of prayer expresses through the close analysis of the traditions and reasons of that order an attitude of profound reverence for God and of seriousness in prayer.

To be sure, nowadays people who pray at all tend to show impatience with the concept that there may be rules and regulations in the matter. To pray however one feels, wherever, whenever, and by whatever means—these kinds of spontaneous prayer are more highly valued than the ancient, formal, measured prayers, stately processions, hoary gestures, and dignified music of synagogues or churches. Worship called creative, because someone has made it up on the spot, seems to matter more, is called more sincere, than following the forms of worship created over centuries. The rejection of discipline in favor of perfect spontaneity has not, to be sure, produced more praying or greatly enhanced the liturgical life of synagogues or churches, though enthusiasts think otherwise. It has to be clear that formlessness of prayer, like the formlessness of music, of art, of education and other things, is something the rabbis before us could not have understood. Their world was orderly, well-regulated, and structured, so too their approach to God. You do not have to enter into their world, but to understand and appreciate their seriousness and interest in detail, in form and movement, in dignity and appropriateness, you have to leave ours.

What about references to "food," which occur throughout our chapter? These allude to "blessing the food," that is, to the prayers of thanks, or Grace after Meals. The three important elements in the Grace are as follows (in the translation of Judah Goldin):

1. Blessed art Thou, Lord our God, King of the Universe, who nourishes all the world by His goodness, in grace, in mercy, and in compassion: "He gives bread to all flesh, for His mercy is everlasting." And because of His great goodness we have never lacked, and so may we never lack, sustenance—for the sake of His great Name. For He nourishes and feeds everyone, is good to all, and provides food for each one of the creatures He created.

Blessed art Thou, O Lord, who feeds everyone.

2. We thank Thee, Lord our God, for having given our fathers as a heritage a pleasant, a good and spacious land; for having taken us out of the land of Egypt; for having redeemed

us from the house of bondage; for Thy covenant, which Thou hast set as a seal in our flesh; for Thy Torah which Thou hast taught us; for Thy statutes which Thou hast made known to us; for the life of grace and mercy Thou hast graciously bestowed upon us; and for the nourishment with which Thou dost nourish us and feed us always, every day, in every season, and every hour.

For all these things, Lord our God, we thank and praise Thee; may Thy praises continually be in the mouth of every living thing, as it is written, "And thou shalt eat and be satisfied, and bless the Lord thy God for the good land which He hath given thee."

Blessed art Thou, O Lord, for the land and its food.

3. O Lord our God, have pity on Thy people Israel, on Thy city Jerusalem, on Zion the place of Thy glory, on the royal house of David Thy Messiah, and on the great and holy house which is called by Thy name. Our God, our Father, feed us and speed us, nourish us and make us flourish; unstintingly, O Lord our God, speedily free us from all distress.

And let us not, O Lord our God, find ourselves in need of gifts from flesh and blood, or of a loan from anyone save from Thy full, generous, sanctifying, wide-open hand; so we may never be humiliated, or put to shame.

O rebuild Jerusalem, the holy city, speedily in our day. Blessed art Thou, Lord, who in mercy will rebuild Jerusalem. Amen.

This is what is meant by "food," the blessing after a meal.

The Elements of the Chapter

Usually, the Mishnaic parts of a chapter of the Talmud will be quoted discretely, paragraph by paragraph, so that the *Gemara's* comments follow each element in the Mishnah. Here, however, the entire chapter is given at the outset, and we shall therefore consider it as a unit. I translate following the Kaufmann manuscript of the Mishnah, which is found in the library of the Hungarian Academy of Sciences in Budapest. This is universally regarded as the best manuscript of the Mishnah; it dates from some time before 1500. The best printed text of the Mishnah is that edited by C. Albeck* together with a simple commentary; it does not greatly differ from the readings of the Kaufmann and other manuscripts, though in other parts of the Mishnah the differences are considerable and may be important.

We shall first examine each element of the chapter and afterward consider how the whole has been put together. At the same time we shall not seek on our own the "reasons" for the laws. These are supplied in later documents—the Tosefta and the *Gemara*—and in turn will be analyzed and criticized. Our purpose is to consider the Mishnah entirely in its own terms, to point up problems to be dealt with in later strata of the Talmud, thus to participate in the dynamic of the growth of Talmudic literature by experiencing in our own study the process of commentary, exegesis, elaboration, and development.

8:1.A. These are the things which are between the House of Shammai and the House of Hillel in [regard to] the meal:

B. The House of Shammai say, "One blesses [says the blessing for] the day, and afterward one says the blessing over the wine."**

And the House of Hillel say, "One says the blessing over the wine, and afterward, one blesses the day."

The chapter begins with a superscription, A, which announces the subject and identifies the authorities whose opinions are to be given. No one can suppose that the only laws "in regard to the meal" derived from the Houses, or that no one thereafter raised issues or formulated opinions on the same subject. Nor are these

---

* *Seder Zera'im* (Jerusalem and Tel Aviv: 1957).
** The difference between "blessing wine" and "reciting a blessing over wine" has important theological implications.

the only points about meals on which the Houses differed. The *Gemara* lists others. What we have are elements of a much larger tradition which have been chosen for redaction and preservation. What we do not have, by and large, are the items omitted or passed over by those editors responsible for the document in our hands. To some measure these omitted materials are preserved in other compilations of rabbinical traditions, or occur as singletons, not in collections, in the *Gemara;* they will be signified as deriving from the authorities of the first and second centuries, called Tannaim ("repeaters"—the Aramaic root, TNY, is equivalent to the Hebrew SHNY, thus Mishnah-teachers), masters whose opinions were formulated and included in the Mishnah, or in the stratum of materials from which the Mishnah was finally selected.

We have already observed that the superscription, A, is misleading. We expect differences in regard to the meal in general, but then, in B, we have a specific, and special, meal, that of the evening of the Sabbath Day, Friday night.

The first difference concerns the order of blessing the wine and saying the Sanctification of the Sabbath Day. The House of Shammai say the Sanctification comes first, then the blessing for the wine. The House of Hillel rule contrariwise. The Mishnah explains nothing about these requirements and their meaning. We are supposed to know that "day" means reciting the Sanctification, "wine" means saying a blessing over the wine. So "meal" is not only misleading, but confusing, for it does not hint at the real issue before us at all. That first occurs later on.

8:2.A. The House of Shammai say, "They wash the hands and afterward mix the cup."

And the House of Hillel say, "They mix the cup and afterward wash the hands."

With this law we begin the consideration of the details of purity at meals. This is not an abstract concept, but rather a concrete and detailed problem. How do you remove the impurity which will prevent your eating the meal like a Temple priest? That depends upon the normal status accorded to your hands—impure, but in what ways and in what degrees? As we shall see, there are several very important considerations.

First comes the food itself. Some food is more susceptible of impurity than others. The priests are given various gifts. The most important of these is called "Heave-offering"—that which is "raised up" ("heaved") out of the food for the priesthood's use. Heave-offering is highly susceptible to uncleanness. Ordinary food, never brought to the cult or to the cultic functionary, the priest, is less susceptible.

Second are the degrees of uncleanness, which I shall explain in detail later on. Something unclean in the first degree is more capable of rendering food unclean than something unclean in the second degree of uncleanness—and so on, down to the fourth degree. That which is unclean in the first degree will, therefore, make more things unclean than something unclean in the second. Something unclean in the first will affect ordinary food as well as the priests' food, the Heave-offering. What is unclean in the second degree will not affect ordinary food, but it will affect the priests' food. And so on.

Again, I remind you, we are in the hands of lawyers, and to them detail is important. They are not interested in a general rule, which might assert that "we are all priests and all holy." To them such an assertion lacks all meaning until it is accompanied by details to give it effect, laws to give it body and substance. If we are all priests, therefore we must *do* such and so. And I think these lawyers are right, for merely asserting you are in the priestly status can carry little weight, until you actually *do* the things priests do, or, at least, pretend to. You are what you do, not merely what you claim to be or say about yourself.

Now we go back to the laws with which we started. They seem out of order. First we spoke of saying a blessing. But now we move back a step, to the preparation for eating at any meal. Two things need to be done before blessing the bread.

First, a man has to wash his hands. This is not for hygienic

reasons, but for ritual purity. As we observed, the Pharisees and
their rabbinic continuators believed that ordinary, noncultic meals
had to be eaten in a state of ritual purity, in accord with the laws
of Leviticus about the purity of the Temple cult. Washing the
hands made them incapable of rendering something else unfit or
impure, so was a prophylactic for the ritual purity of the food.
(This point will be sharpened later on.)

Mixing the cup of wine with water was necessary, second, because the wine itself, undiluted by water, was too thick to drink.
This mixing was done before the meal.

The issue is, Which comes first? To understand the reasons we
have to know another law about making a vessel unclean. A vessel
is not made unclean if it is dry, or if it is touched by clean hands.
But if it is wet, and unwashed hands touch it, the hands will make
the liquid on the vessel unclean. And the liquid does render the
cup unclean.

Now we may understand the Shammaites' ruling, which takes
this law for granted. The Shammaites first have the hands washed,
since during the mixing of the wine, liquid may fall on the outer
side of the cup. If then the man touches the cup with unwashed
hands, he will make the liquid unclean. The liquid then will render
the cup unclean.

The House of Hillel differ, for reasons we shall examine later.

8:3.A. The House of Shammai say, "He dries his hands on
the cloth and lays it on the table."
And the House of Hillel say, "On the pillow."

After washing the hands, you dry them on a towel, then leave
the towel for use as a napkin during the meal. The House of
Shammai say you lay it on the table, but not on the cushion on
which you are sitting. For the cushion may be unclean and render
unclean the liquid in the cloth, which will then make the hands
unclean again. This consideration is parallel to the one operative
in the foregoing law.

The House of Hillel say you put the napkin on the cushion. Even if the cushion makes the hands unclean, it is not a severe (first grade) uncleanness. Only a first grade uncleanness will affect the food. So this one will not make food unclean. But you should not put it on the table, lest the table be unclean and render the water in the napkin unclean, which in turn will make the food unclean.

The House of Shammai say that in the first place one cannot make use of a table which is unclean. So the consideration important to the Hillelites does not apply.

The stress on rendering the liquid unclean, rather than the hands themselves, is for the following reason: Unclean hands are in a secondary level, or second grade, of uncleanness. At the second degree of uncleanness one may render Heave-offering *unfit,* that is, if unclean hands touch clean Heave-offering. But second grade uncleanness does *not* render food or vessels *unclean.*

On the other hand, liquids made unclean by a second level source of uncleanness, such as the hands, then forthwith enter the primary level, or first grade, of uncleanness. Something unclean at the first grade indeed does render vessels unclean.

So here the napkin will not be made unclean by the cushion. An unclean vessel cannot render unclean either another vessel or man. But it does render the liquid unclean, and the napkin is assumed to contain some liquid. We shall say more about the cleanness laws later on.

To summarize: We distinguish between liquids and dry substances. The former are always unclean in the first degree. The latter are not. Dry, unclean hands are unclean in the second degree. So they will not make dry food unclean. Only something unclean in the first degree can do that. If the unclean hands touch dry food, the food is not unclean.

But if they touch liquids or something wet, they forthwith make the liquids unclean in the first degree. And if the liquids then touch food, they render it unclean. That is the basis of the problem before us. To be sure, in order to make sense of the dispute we have to suppose the Houses are talking about different circumstances, because we take for granted they agree about the principles of the law. So, as we noticed, the House of Shammai take for granted the table has to be insusceptible to uncleanness. The Talmuds are going to have difficulties sorting out the disputes.

8:4.A. The House of Shammai say, "They clean the house and afterward wash the hands."
And the House of Hillel say, "They wash the hands and afterward clean the house."

"Cleaning the house" means sweeping the floor. A second washing of hands is required after the meal, before the recitation of Grace. The House of Shammai say that first of all the person sweeps up the crumbs of food, then washes his hands, so that the remaining crumbs will not be spoiled by the water. The position of the House of Hillel remains to be explained.

8:5.A. The House of Shammai say, "Light, and food, and spices, and *Havdalah*."
And the House of Hillel say, "Light, and spices, and food, and *Havdalah*."
B. The House of Shammai say, " '[The blessing of light is] [Blessed are you, Lord our God] Who *created* the *light* of the fire.' "
And the House of Hillel say, " '[Blessed are you, Lord our God] Who *creates* the *lights* of the fire.' "

Two further disputes are before us, both concerning *Havdalah*. The first (A) involves the order of the liturgies at a meal which takes place at the end of the Sabbath Day. During the meal, the sun has set and the Sabbath ended. Thus you have to bless light and spices, say *Havdalah,* and also recite the Grace. What is the appropriate order? The Houses agree light comes at the outset, *Havdalah* at the end. The House of Shammai place the Grace before the blessing of spices; the House of Hillel give the opposite order. A cup of wine is blessed for the Grace; here it will also be used for *Havdalah,* and that accounts for the difficulty about which prayer takes priority.

Clearly, the man starts with the light, for it is used as soon as it is kindled, so its blessing is to be said immediately. Afterward one completes Grace, then spices, finally, *Havdalah,* so say the Shammaites. The House of Hillel say the blessing of the light and spices are to be said together; both are brief sentences, as we observed above.

The second dispute (B) concerns the blessing of the light. The issue is whether one refers to the creation of the light of the flame at the creation of the world, or whether one regards the flame as constantly re-created as new lights in the preexistent flame. The larger issue—which is not made explicit here—is the nature of creation: perpetual or one-time only, and of flame: is it a completed substance or constantly renewed? Did God complete his activity of creation at the beginning, or does he continue to exert a creative force in the world perpetually? Is he—by extension— solely transcendent, outside of the created world, or is he immanent and involved daily in the maintenance of creation? So too, is the flame complete? Or is it renewed as it burns? What constitutes the flame *itself,* if it consumes its fuel and so is composed of ever-changing elements? This kind of "philosophical" issue about continuity and change is introduced only and always in concrete terms, never in the abstract.

8:6. They do not bless over the light or the spices of gentiles, nor the light or the spices of the dead, nor the light or the spices which are before an idol.

B. And they do not bless over the light until they make use of its illumination.

The Houses are dropped. We now have a simple statement of what all authorities agree is the rule.

Israelites are not allowed to make use of anything, including spices or light, which has to do with idolatry. The reason one may not use the light of a gentile is not given; the *Gemara* will try to supply an explanation.

It is assumed that the spices have also served an idolatrous purpose—but then the first reference to spices ("of gentiles") duplicates the third ("before an idol"). And one thing the *Gemara* will normally point out is repetitions and duplications in the Mishnah, not to mention internal contradictions of all sorts.

Light used for the corpse is not intended for illumination, but is kindled only for the honor of the corpse. The spices are used as a deodorant, not for a sweet savor. So in this instance the light and spices are not serving their normal purpose. They therefore cannot be used for *Havdalah*.

B gives the rule that one must actually make use of the light. If he has not made use of an object—drunk the wine, smelled the spice—he has no right to say a blessing of thanks for that pleasure. The principles are not different from those of A: (1) Something must be used for its *normal* purpose, and (2) it must *actually* be used, before a blessing is to be said. But then the blessing must be said; one cannot enjoy the benefits of creation without acknowledging the Creator.

What is the meaning of the law before us? Why do the rabbis rule that you cannot recite a blessing over the light or the spices of gentiles in connection with saying the *Havdalah* prayer? Recall what *Havdalah* alleges: God has made a distinction between Israel and the nations. It would contradict the meaning of those very words to say them over the light or spices of the gentiles. But there is a reason: The gentiles are worshipers of idols. To them the qualities intrinsic to light or spices, therefore, may not symbolize or represent, but actually partake of the substance of, the god. Using what may serve the "false worship of idolatry" to the rabbis is an insult to God. Israelites may not do so under any circumstances. For instance, gentiles are supposed always to make an offering of wine before they drink it. It is done by flicking a drop of wine out of the bottle or the cup before using the wine. Gentiles are seen as pious, deeply religious people; they are strict about making such an offering. Then Israelites may under no circumstances make use of wine touched by a gentile, for the pious pagan always will have already devoted it to the god. And this is abnormal. Similarly, you have to use light and spices only in the normal way, for the ordinary purpose—not only not for idolatry, but also not for the honor of the corpse. The light and incense, therefore, have to be freely available for the divine worship, which means, as we now see, they are, first, not contaminated by use in pagan prayer, and second, not rendered unfit by prior use in some extraordinary way or for some unusual purpose. What is natural and freely available—that is to be used in the divine service. These points are important to the Talmud. They will be elaborated, though their reasons will not be spelled out in greater detail.

8:7.A. He who ate and forgot and did not bless [say Grace after meals]—

B. The House of Shammai say, "He should go back to his place and bless."

And the House of Hillel say, "He should bless in the place in which he remembered."

C. Until when does he bless? Until the food has been digested in his intestines.

The Houses have now returned to the text, but in a form very different from before. Instead of extremely abbreviated sayings, lacking a superscription or explanation of the subject matter about which the Houses are supposed to have differed, we have a fully articulated statement of the problem. We further are shifted into an ordinary, everyday circumstance, not only the Sabbath meal, so the frame of reference has changed.

The issue is what a person should do who has eaten a meal and forgotten to say Grace. He is supposed to say a blessing of thanks for every benefit of creation which he enjoys. Obviously, he has to say thank You for the meal. And this should come just as soon as he has eaten it. But he is apt to forget. Should he go back to where he ate? Or may he bless wherever he remembers the blessing? That is the issue before us.

The House of Shammai send the man back where he ate the meal. The House of Hillel rule he may say the blessing wherever he is when he remembers that he forgot it. The *Gemara* will provide theological homilies for both viewpoints.

C is a gloss; once the food is entirely digested, one can no longer make up his failure. But we do not know whence the gloss, or who made it.

8:8.A. Wine came to them after the meal, and there is there only that cup—

B. The House of Shammai say, "He blesses over the wine, and afterward he blesses the food."

And the House of Hillel say, "He blesses the food, and afterward he blesses over the wine."

C. They respond *Amen* after an Israelite who blesses, and they do not respond *Amen* after a Samaritan (Text: *Kuti*) who blesses, until one hears the entire blessing.

Here the answer is clear: Bless the wine, then say Grace, or *vice versa*. The only problem is, What is the question? The meaning of A is obscure. One explanation of the problem is this: The meal is over. There is only one cup (as stated). You may say a blessing for the wine and drink it and then say Grace without the customary further cup of wine, so the Shammaites. The Hillelites require a blessing of wine before the Grace.

C is a separate law. A person should not respond *Amen*—"so may it be done"—until he knows to what he is responding. A Samaritan is here supposed to be unreliable; you have to hear him out before agreeing with his prayer and seconding it.

Who is this Samaritan?

A Samaritan, so casually introduced into our law, clearly is regarded as someone who says blessings—therefore, he must be a kind of an Israelite. The rabbis here refer to a member of a group which took shape in the aftermath of the destruction of the ten northern tribes of Israel by the Assyrians in 722 B.C. The biblical view, which is very hostile to the Samaritans, reports that the Assyrians brought in a new group of people to repopulate the country, after they had deported the northern Israelites. Those new people, plagued by natural disasters, adopted the cult of the land, the worship of Yahweh, not sincerely, but out of "superstition." So they are called "converts on account of lions," for the story is that wild beasts plagued them, and they supposed it was on account of neglect of the god and cult of the land. That is the hostile view. For their part the Samaritans claimed that they were the true "Israel," the followers of Moses and loyal to the Pentateuch, just as much as were the Judeans, the southern tribes clustered around Jerusalem. They worshiped the one God at their sanctuary, Gerizim, instead of at the Judean one in Jerusalem. So before us are two groups, closely related and sharing a single revealed Torah, but differing as to which of the groups is legitimate. These inter-group tensions produce, among the Jews, considerable hostility toward the Samaritans. Yet the rabbis readily concede that when the Samaritans do keep the law, they do so meticulously and lawfully. Now before us is a Samaritan who is saying a prayer just as does a Jew. But before you may reply and say *Amen,* you have to be sure things are done properly.

In this little law we see how the rabbis coped with the existence, within the Jewish community or on its fringes, of dissenting groups (who, to be sure, would have been the rabbis and their followers as the dissenting group on the fringes). They were not prepared to write them off entirely and to declare them utterly beyond the pale of "Israel." But the rabbis also could not amiably admit the legitimacy of the other group's religious deeds and ideas. They believed the Samaritans were very wrong in their view and interpretation of Torah. Tolerance is easy when no one really cares about the differences which have to be tolerated, when religion is a matter of indifference. But how do you cope with difference close at hand, when you think the differences important? The rabbis' response to the problem is not bland acceptance of the difference; that would not be possible if you believe God cares about what you say and do. But the rabbis also do not ignore the good deeds rightly done by the other group, the ways in which Samaritans and Jews worship a single God and revere a single Torah. So they are prepared to declare *Amen* to a blessing properly said. But they add, you have to hear the entire blessing. Again, what is decisive is what you actually do, and if you do the right thing, the rabbi adds his *Amen*.

The Chapter As a Whole

Having examined each element in our chapter, we shall now look at the chapter as a whole, so that we may observe its larger units and how they are put together. I discern four units of tradition: the first, a neat construction of the Houses' disagreements, expressed in the most terse possible language; second, a simple statement of a rule; third, a more sophisticated form of a disagreement between the Houses; and fourth, like the second, a rule in quite separate form from that of the Houses' laws. While parts II and IV do not differ in form, they are sufficiently distinct in substance so that we may not suppose they derive originally from a single rulebook which has been split apart by the insertion of the Houses' disputes. And the materials attributed to the Houses are likewise so different from one another both in form and in substance that they cannot be regarded as originally a unity.

I

8:1.A. These are the things which are between the House of Shammai and the House of Hillel in [regard to] the meal:

B. The House of Shammai say, "One blesses over the day, and afterward one blesses over the wine."

And the House of Hillel say, "One blesses over the wine, and afterward one blesses over the day."

8:2.A. The House of Shammai say, "They wash the lands and afterward mix the cup."

And the House of Hillel say, "They mix the cup and afterward wash the hands."

8:3A. The House of Shammai say, "He dries his hands on the cloth and lays it on the table."

And the House of Hillel say, "On the pillow."

8:4.A. The House of Shammai say, "They clean the house, and afterward they wash the hands."

And the House of Hillel say, "They wash the hands, and afterward they clean the house."

8:5.A. The House of Shammai say, "Light, and food, and spices, and *Havdalah*."

And the House of Hillel say, "'Light, and spices, and food, and *Havdalah*."

B. The House of Shammai say, " 'Who created the light of the fire.' "

And the House of Hillel say, " 'Who creates the lights of the fire."

II

8:6. They do not bless over the light or the spices of gentiles, nor the light or the spices of the dead, nor the light or the spices which are before an idol.

And they do not bless over the light until they make use of its illumination.

III

8:7.A. He who ate and forgot and did not bless [say Grace]—

B. The House of Shammai say, "He should go back to his place and bless."

And the House of Hillel say, "He should bless in the place in which he remembered."

C. Until when does he bless? Until the food has been digested in his intestines.

8:8. A. Wine came to them after the meal, and there is there only that cup—

B. The House of Shammai say, "He blesses the wine, and afterward he blesses the food."

And the House of Hillel say, "He blesses the food, and afterward he blesses the wine."

IV

C. They respond *Amen* after an Israelite who blesses, and they do not respond *Amen* after a Samaritan who blesses, until hearing the entire blessing.

The first unit is introduced by the superscription, 8:1.A, and then continues in the briefest possible language, without further superscriptions, exegeses, debates, or other extraneous materials.

After the superscription serving the whole composite, the first dispute is introduced without an additional superscription to set forth the specific problem. Without it, all we have in effect is *day/wine* vs. *wine/day,* with the same explanatory words in both opinions.

The same form applies in 8:2–5. No general principle, law, or superscription, merely *wash hands, mix cup* vs. *mix cup, wash hands.*

The Hillelite opinion in 8:3 is not a gloss on the foregoing, but rather has been abbreviated. In full form, it would read, *He dries his hands on the napkin and leaves it on the cushion.*

Part II is a separate unit, giving a rule about the light and spices one may not use. It is related to 8:5 in theme, but not in form or expression. The form is a simple statement of fact. The rule is expressed in full detail; no necessary words are omitted, nor does the sense rely upon some foregoing sentence. Complete and fully articulated, the section could have been transmitted all by itself, without reference to any other passage.

Part III introduces a still further dispute about the meal, unrelated to the foregoing. The form is a superscription followed by the opinions of the Houses; each opinion completes the introductory superscription. Without the contrary view of the opposed House, it would have been a simple sentence, not much different from 8:6, thus: "They do not bless the light. . . . He who ate and forgot and did not bless should go back to his place. . . ." What is curious about the formulation of the Houses' opinions is the assumption that all the Houses' viewpoints were preserved in such an antithetical construction.

But is this how the rulings were originally formulated? It seems unlikely that the House of Shammai deliberating on their own, said, "If one forgot to bless, *we say* he should go back, but the House of Hillel say. . . ." More likely, the earliest formulation of an opinion was simple and straightforward, as in 8:6, a plain rule. Only afterward, when an opposed opinion was supplied by another party, could the dispute construction have developed.

And a further requirement for that development must have been a list of items on which the two parties agreed to disagree—and then in diametrically opposite terms: yes or no, but not maybe. So behind the Mishnah before us must lie a considerable corpus of traditions, formulated according to the opinion of an individual authority, or a party, or House. That corpus of opinions only later on was amalgamated with the opinions on the same subject of various other authorities. Then, given the whole range of subjects on which opinions were expressed, a redactional process (which we do not now fully understand) led to the selection, first, of topics for dispute, second, of the particular authorities whose opinions would be allowed to register on those topics, and third, of the actual opinions of the opposed authorities.

We shall review the components of the collection of Houses' opinions:

Shammai			Hillel
		I	
8:1	Day/wine	*Blessing*	Wine/day
		II	
8:2	Hands/cup	*Uncleanness*	Cup/hands
8:3	Table	*Uncleanness*	Cushion
8:4	Sweep/wash	*Uncleanness*	Wash/sweep
		III	
8:5A	Food, spices	*Blessing*	Spices, food
8:5B	*Did* create *light*		*Does* create *lights*
8:7	Forgot: Go back	*Blessing*	Forgot: In the place where where recalled he forgot
8:8	Food/wine	*Blessing*	Wine/food

The subject matter (within "matters pertaining to the meal") is therefore arranged in an orderly and logical way:

> *Before Sabbath-Festival Meals*—Blessing: 8:1
> *During Meals*—Uncleanness: 8:2, 3, 4
> *After Sabbath-Festival Meals*—Blessing: 8:5A, B
> *After Meals* (special case, pertaining to *all*
>   meals): 8:7

And 8:8 is an enigma.

It looks, therefore, as if the collection consists of five separate, anterior elements or collections: 8:2–4, uncleanness rules for meals, a neat and simple collection of laws about saying blessings, consisting of a few words attributed to each House: 8:1; 8:5; 8:7; and 8:8.

But 8:8 looks suspiciously like the reverse of 8:1:

	8:1	8:8
Shammai:		
	Day/Wine (YWM/YYN)	Wine/Food (YYN/MZWN)
Hillel:		
	Wine/Day (YYN/YWM)	Food/Wine (MZWN/YYN)

The superscription of 8:8 thus brings more difficulties than we might have had in its absence.

Memorizing the Mishnah

Since the authorities behind the Mishnah and related literature claimed their traditions were formulated in final form and handed down orally from Sinai and thereafter memorized but not written down, we should not be surprised to observe that the materials before us have been organized so as to facilitate memorization. Mnemonic devices—that is, aids to memorization—are particularly apparent in the Houses' sections of our chapter. To show how these work, I shall give the Hebrew letters. Since Hebrew has no vowels, the consonants will be represented by their equivalents in English; each stands for a syllable. It will quickly become apparent that nearly the same words are used throughout, though in different arrangements, and, of course, the same number of syllables will be assigned to each House's opinion.

8:1–5 can be readily reduced to brief and alliterative mnemonic elements:

8:1:   YWM/YYN vs. YYN/YWM
8:2:   NTL/MZG vs. MZG/NTL
8:3:   SLHN vs. KST
8:4:   KBD/NTL vs. NTL/KBD
8:5:   NR/MZWN/BSMYM/HBDLH vs.
        NR/BSMYM/MZWN/HBDLH
        Thus: MZWN/BSMYM vs. BSMYM/MZWN

The list is constructed of transitive participles, generally given in third-person plural (8:2, 8:4), though I see no principle that explains why one set should be plural, the next singular. Only 8:3 is significantly glossed; there a simple superscription would have allowed the significant difference to be reduced to two substantives. Like parts 8:1 and 8:8, parts 8:2 and 8:4 look suspiciously alike, and it may be that they began as a single saying, only later on developed into two separate arguments. Parts 8:1, 2, 4, and 5 all depend upon word-order, and I see no reason why 8:5 should not have been preserved in fully articulated form right from the outset. In all, it would be difficult to invent a better model of a mnemonic list.

8:7 is another sort mnemonic apparently built out of the same words and mostly the same letters:

HZR MQWM BRK vs. BRK MQWM ZKR

Clearly the word-order is 1, 2, 3, vs. 3, 2, 1. Only the first word of the Shammaite, and the last word of the Hillelite, sayings are different. The difference, surprisingly, is in a single letter, H vs. K. On the whole, therefore, we may suppose the mnemonic pattern has been only lightly reworked with the addition of the dative particles, the personal endings, and the relative pronoun (S) demanded by the Hillelite saying.

Even in the fully articulated form before us, we find obvious balances between the Houses' lemmas. They contain the same number of words throughout, e.g.

8:1: MBRK 'L HYWM W'HR KK MBRK 'L HYNN
MBRK 'L HYYN W'HR KK MBRK 'L HYWM

And these words preserve a fixed order and balance from one House-saying to the next, as is obvious above. So the whole collection is now in mnemonic form. You can easily memorize it.

The Mishnah is not the sole primary component of the Talmud. A second, and equally important collection of traditions, also attributed to first-and second-century masters, is the Tosefta, the supplement to the Mishnah. Indeed, as we shall soon see, the *Gemara,* or commentary to the Mishnah, of both the Babylonian and the Palestinian Talmuds centers more on the analysis of the Tosefta than on the Mishnah. While the Mishnah supplies the form and structure for the Talmud as a whole, for our chapter the Tosefta provides the focus of interest.

CHAPTER

IV

The Tosefta

Tosefta means addition or supplement. The Tosefta is a compilation of traditions and sayings closely related to the Mishnah and deriving from many of the same authorities represented in the Mishnah. The Tosefta is organized like the Mishnah, being divided into the same tractates and mostly the same chapters as well. The relationships between the Tosefta and the Mishnah are extremely complicated. In some tractates the Tosefta tends to follow and to elaborate the main outlines of the Mishnah, with the same agendum of subjects and legal problems as are discussed in the authoritative code. In other tractates the Tosefta stands quite separate and independent of the Mishnah. The elucidation of the relationships between the two documents is still more complicated by the later insertion into the Mishnah of passages originally unique to Tosefta, and the contrary process also took place. A further difficulty is the prevailing assumption that the Mishnah and the Tosefta are unitary texts, compiled at a single point by a single authority, whereas both collections actually are made up of highly discrete units of tradition. They are unitary documents only in the sense in which the Pentateuch—a mosaic of traditions—is a unitary text.

Our interest in the Tosefta is for two reasons. First, the Tosefta contains important materials pertinent to the Mishnah we have just studied. Second, as we shall soon see, the Tosefta constitutes the first stratum and the most important building block of both the Babylonian and the Palestinian *Gemara.* We shall therefore be unable to comprehend the components of the *Gemara* if we do not examine the Tosefta in its own terms. But now it is easy to approach the Tosefta, for it has been edited and elucidated by Saul Lieberman, the great scholar of Talmudic literature. His definitive edition and commentary, which to date have reached the beginning of the fourth order, Damages (*Neziqin*), constitute the authoritative statement both of what is worth knowing about the Tosefta—and that is a great deal—and of what each passage means. In the growth of Talmudic literature, Tosefta forms the connection between the Mishnah, terse, opaque, elliptical, and the *Gemara,* fully articulated, lucid, and elegant. Lieberman's edition and commentary thus permit study of the growth of the Talmudic literature as a whole; he provides the key to the lock of nearly every door.

We shall not be detained by the questions of the date of the Tosefta's compilation and the authorities behind it, because these questions have not been definitively answered, and the answers which have been proposed are based upon primitive methodology and inadequate conceptions of the history of Talmudic literature. When Lieberman expresses his opinion on these questions, it will be time to open further inquiries. Meanwhile, it suffices to view the Tosefta before us as a compilation made at about the same time as, or shortly after, the redaction of the Mishnah. For our chapter, the Tosefta certainly comes before the development of the *Gemara,* for the *Gemara* quotes, depends upon, analyzes, and therefore must follow, the Tosefta in its present form. We shall examine not the complete corresponding chapter of Tosefta, but only those materials pertinent to the Mishnah already studied. Then we shall compare the Mishnah's and the Tosefta's treatments of the same problems.

The Elements of the Tosefta Pertinent to the Mishnah

5:21 (Lieberman, p. 28, ls. 41–2) They answer Amen after a gentile who says a blessing with the divine name. They do not answer Amen after a Samaritan who says a blessing with the divine name until they have heard the entire blessing.

The Mishnah says you answer *Amen* after an Israelite, but not after a Samaritan. The distinction now is between a gentile and a Samaritan. The gentile is not subject to the laws of Moses; he does not have to say blessings or to mention the divine name. You may answer each of his blessings with *Amen,* whether he said the blessing in its proper form or not, for he is thereby blessing the Lord. But a Samaritan is regarded as subject to the commandments concerning blessings and is supposed not to mention the divine name purposelessly. If he has changed the accepted pattern of the blessings, one may not answer *Amen* after him; therefore, a man has to hear the entire blessing, to be certain he will say it properly. What the Samaritan does matters.

5:25 (Lieberman, p. 29, ls. 53–57) A. [The] things which are between the House of Shammai and the House of Hillel in [regard to] the meal:

B. The House of Shammai say, "One blesses over the day, and afterward he blesses over the wine, for the day causes the wine to come, and the day is already sanctified, but the wine has not yet come."

C. And the House of Hillel say, "One blesses over the wine, and afterward he blesses over the day, for the wine causes the Sanctification of the day to be said.

"Another explanation: The blessing over the wine is continual [= always required when wine is used], and the blessing over the day is not continual [but is said only on certain days]."

D. And the law is according to the words of the House of Hillel.

A omits *these are,* with which the Mishnah begins, and is therefore curiously abbreviated.

The Tosefta supplies reasons for the rulings of the Mishnah. B explains the opinion of the House of Shammai. You have to have the wine in order to say the Sanctification of the Sabbath. On an ordinary day, not the Sabbath, the man is not required to have wine before the meal. Therefore, the "day," that is, the Sanctification, supplies the occasion for the wine to be brought. The day is already sanctified, for at sunset one no longer works. The Sabbath Day has already begun. The Evening Prayer for the Sabbath has been said before the meal. So the Sanctification is said first. Then comes the recitation of the blessing over the wine.

The House of Hillel, C, argue that what is essential is the blessing of the wine. Without wine you do not say the Sanctification of the Day at all. Therefore, you bless over the wine first, then the day.

The reasons just adduced recall our earlier observation, that the rabbis take a keen interest in protocol, especially in relationship to prayer. Two blessings are to be said, one for wine, the other for the Sabbath Day. Which comes first? The answer is not a matter of formalism, despite the interest in forms, but of substance. For saying the Sanctification of the Sabbath Day marks the beginning of the holy time. It is not done lightly, but with all due reverence. The course of nature is turning. As the sun sets, you call to mind the Exodus from Egypt, the creation of the world—a great historical event, corresponding to sunset, a decisive event in nature. The one "creates" Israel's sacred history as the other marks creation, the beginning of nature. So the issues are not inconsiderable.

On the other hand, here is the wine in hand. The wine cannot be drunk without a blessing. Humble, ordinary, mundane—the wine is always here. The turning of time is extraordinary and noteworthy. So which takes precedence? The theological issues inherent in the little legal question—the logic-chopping—are not to be ignored. Where is a man to turn his thoughts?

The House of Hillel say the here-and-now comes first. Only then do you turn to the transcendent meaning of the hour. What matters is what is always at hand. Do not neglect the ordinary because of the extraordinary. The profane is always waiting to be sanctified. The House of Shammai take the opposite view. How can you neglect the great moment of sunset at the end of the sixth day of the week and the beginning of the seventh, merely to attend to something which you have in hand only on account of the grand occasion? It stands to reason you cannot and should not. Both Houses have good points. They cannot be resolved. You must in the end choose one over the other.

To return to our text: the House of Hillel are given a second reason for their ruling. The man must always bless wine before he drinks it, on any day of the week. Therefore, the requirement of blessing the wine is continual or perpetual. He first carries out a continuing obligation, then the one which is not continuing, for the former takes precedence under all circumstances.

D then gives the final decision. The law, as is mostly the case, will be observed according to the opinion of the House of Hillel.

5:26 (Lieberman, p. 29–30, ls. 57–61) A. The House of Shammai say, "They wash the hands and afterward mix the cup, lest the liquids which are on the outer surface of the cup be made unclean on account of the hands, and then go back and make the cup unclean."

B. The House of Hillel say, "The outer surfaces of the cup are perpetually unclean.

"Another explanation: The washing of the hands is only [done] near [at the outset of] the meal.

C. "They mix the cup and afterward wash the hands."

As stated above, the hands are presumed to be unclean. But they are in a second degree of uncleanness. They render Heave-offering unfit, and cannot make vessels unclean. But they do make liquids unclean. And the liquids' uncleanness is in the first degree. So then the liquids will render the cup unclean.

The contrary procedure—the Shammaites'—would have one wash his hands first. But then the liquids on the hands may become unclean on account of the still-unwashed cup. They will go and make the hands unclean once again. That is the Hillelites' criticism of the position of the House of Shammai.

The House of Hillel first of all (B) reject the reasoning of the Shammaites. Their view is that the consideration important to the House of Shammai is insufficient to require washing the hands before mixing the cup. No matter what the man does, he may make use of a cup whose outer sides are unclean, for their unclean state will *not* affect the insides. So what difference will it make if one washes his hands before mixing the cup of wine or afterward? If, furthermore, one is concerned about the drops of water on the cup, washing the hands first will do no good. For the liquid dripping on the side of the cup is unclean, and since it is in the first grade of uncleanness, it certainly will make the hands unclean.

Then the House of Hillel give their own reason: It is best to wash the hands right before the beginning of the meal. C then formulates the Hillelite opinion as a general rule.

5:27 (Lieberman, p. 30, ls. 61–65) A. The House of Shammai say, "He dries his hand on the napkin and leaves it on the table, lest the liquids which are in the napkin be made unclean on account of the cushion, and then go and make the hands unclean."

The Shammaites' reason for drying hands on the napkin and then putting the napkin on the table is on account of the liquid in the napkin. If the napkin is put on the cushion, which is presumed unclean, then the liquid in the napkin will be made unclean. It will be touched by the hands, and so make them unclean.

B. And the House of Hillel say, "A doubt in regard to the condition of liquids so far as the hands are concerned is resolved as clean."

The answer of the House of Hillel is a good one. We do not know for sure that the cushion is unclean. It is a matter of doubt. So far as the hands are concerned, we resolve a matter of doubt about the cleanness of liquids in favor of assuming they are clean.

C. "Another explanation: Washing the hands does not pertain to unconsecrated food."

The Hillelites' second reason pulls the rug out from under the Shammaites. They say that if you are eating unconsecrated food, you do not have to wash your hands at all. That is to say, ritually unclean hands do not matter so far as ordinary food is concerned. They will of course make unfit food which derives from the priestly offerings—tithes, Heave-offerings. But they will not affect everyday, nonpriestly food at all. What this means is that the Hillelites have an entirely different picture of the requirements for eating ordinary food in a state of ritual purity.

D. "But he dries his hands on the napkin and leaves it on the cushion, lest the liquids which are in the napkin be made unclean on account of the table, and they go and render the food unclean."

The Hillelites now give instructions about why the napkin is a matter of concern at all. The *table* is presumed unclean. The napkin should not be placed on it, for the liquids in the napkin may be made unclean by the table. They will then go and make the food unclean—in the first degree of uncleanness. In fact, this is a complicated "reason."

We have already reviewed the laws that underlie the rulings of the Houses. The Palestinian *Gemara* will explain that the Hillelites speak of a table which is *not* susceptible to uncleanness; therefore, there is no reason to be concerned about putting the napkin on the table. Then the House of Hillel add that one may place the napkin not only on the table but *also* on the cushion.

The further reason (C) of the Hillelites is that washing the hands, which, when unclean, cannot convey uncleanness *except* to Heave-offering, is not required for eating unconsecrated food at all.

Then D gives the Hillelites' rule for the matter. You put the napkin on the pillow—fully spelled out, "he dries . . . and leaves. . . ."

But this opinion (D) clearly contradicts the presupposition of the Palestinian *Gemara* that the table to begin with cannot receive uncleanness. It can—and therefore the napkin goes down (not *also*) on the pillow. Lieberman therefore concludes that the Palestinian authorities did not have before them the formulation of D at all. D is added, beginning *lest,* according to the interpretation of the (still later) Babylonian *Gemara*. The meaning is that a person does what is comfortable. The custom was to lean on the cushion and to leave the napkin there, not on the table on which the food was laid out, on account of cleanliness. But in point of fact it would be legitimate to put the napkin on the table itself.

5:28 (Lieberman, p. 30, ls. 65–68) A. The House of Shammai say, "They clean the house, on account of the waste of food, and afterward they wash the hands."

B. The House of Hillel say, "If the waiter was a disciple of a sage, he gathers the scraps which contain as much as an olive's bulk."

C. "And they wash the hands and afterward clean the house."

The custom was that, after the meal, but before saying the concluding Grace, the table would be removed and the floor swept. A person does not want to waste the scraps of food. Therefore, you sweep up before washing the hands for the second time, before the Grace after Meals, so that the spilled water will not spoil food which may have dropped to the floor. Then you wash the hands.

The Hillelites say the scraps which are edible (they are pieces as large as an olive) will be picked up by the waiter if he is a disciple of the sages, for he knows what to do. So one washes up, then sweeps.

Let us stand back and look at the law we have just learned. We are not going to be surprised by the problem of the order in which you sweep up and wash the hands at the end of the meal. We are already used to the query, Which comes first? And why? But who is this "disciple of the sages"? Why does he enter the discussion?

The "disciple of the sages" is a student who has attached himself to a rabbi. He does so because he wants to learn "Torah." But what sort of Torah is involved in serving food? The answer is, it indeed *is* a matter of Torah to learn how to eat a meal. That we know from the substance of the law, the detailed discussions of trivial things. But Torah is not learned through the law, but through seeing the law embodied in the gestures and deeds of the living sages. They teach the law by what they do, not alone by what they say. The texts before us do not exhaust the laws they state—they merely hint at them. To apprehend the full weight and meaning of the law, we should need to enter into the household of a master and see just how he does things. We should have to imitate his gestures, not merely reduce them to legal formulae. For studying Torah is through service to the master; through that service one learns to imitate his ways. How, after all, is the master himself supposed within the Torah-myth to have learned what he now teaches if not through service to his master, and his to his, backward to Moses "our rabbi," who received the Torah and learned it from God himself? Imitating the master is imitating Moses' imitation of God.

But this disciple of the sages already knows the law. He is assumed not to be a child, a beginner. He has mastered the rules sufficiently so that he can be relied upon to know what to do with the scraps of food. He is a mature man, worthy of respect and honor. His "service" is not demeaning or degrading; he is not a slave, a major domo. He is an honored man; he brings honor upon himself by his discipleship of the sages. Not everyone is in his place. Only those who are worthy to imitate the master and learn the ways of Moses "our rabbi" may take up the burdens of service.

And, obviously, this Torah is something greater than the histories, laws, and prophecies of Scripture. Scripture says nothing about the conduct of a meal. The revelation of Moses does not include laws about sweeping up the house after a meal. Yet for the rabbis and disciples, how one sweeps the house indeed is a matter of Torah. Nor should Torah be understood only in such a public way, as a matter of communal ritual alone. We have a story about a disciple who hid under the master's bed at night. The disciple heard the master and his wife engaged in sexual intercourse. He was impressed by the enthusiasm of the couple and made a noise. The master looked under the bed and found the disciple. "What are you doing here?" he asked. The disciple answered, "Rabbi, it is a matter of Torah, and I need to learn." This is no exaggeration; rabbinic literature includes stories about how various great authorities engaged in sexual relations, and there are rules about the modesty, the delicacy, but also the vigor and enthusiasm, with which the sexual act is to be performed. People are encouraged to have sexual relations two or three or four times in succession; if they do, they will produce male children, which everyone wants. So "Torah" is not repression, but the liberation of the natural impulses. Law produces freedom, not bondage to the rule. The law gives life and form to the spirit.

Now when I observed that a man is what he does, not what he says, and that "Torah" subsumes all sorts of humble details of life, you probably did not guess the full weight of those words. But now it is clear that "Torah is a way of living" is no abstraction. It is no homily to claim that the rabbis regarded trivialities as part, as the very heart of Torah, God's revealed will. It is not because they were themselves small-minded, or because they had nothing better to do than investigate the reason behind, the logic for, niggling details. It is because to them "life" as an abstraction is nothing, but all the things that, together, add up the way of living—these are everything. Concrete details are not trivial because they are small. They are important because they relate to the whole pattern of conduct and of being, to reason and regulation. If Amos thought that the nation would fall because a shopkeeper cheated a customer, it was not because he claimed the petty thievery led inexorably to the decay af the public interest. He believed God wanted justice, a just society, and he knew these were not abstractions. What do you do to "do justice"? For the rabbis, too, the claims of Torah were important precisely because they extended to the humble things which men actually can control.

I am not going to apologize, therefore, for the "logic-chopping" of the rabbis. That is not what is involved when we wonder, Which comes first, the washing or the sweeping? Nor is it the ultimate issue in what is to follow: In which hand do you hold the cup of wine, in which the sweet oil for the *Havdalah?* If we asked, How do I approach almighty God? What shall I take with me before the throne of his presence?—if we asked such questions, who would call the answers trival? But who could hear and do those answers, if they were *not* trivial? Tell me to come with clean hands and a pure heart, and I shall not know exactly what I am supposed to do next. But tell me to hold the wine in the right hand, the oil in the left—that is something I can do. And, in doing it, I shall know there are rules for guidance, and these rules stand for reverence and awe, for mindfulness and thoughtfulness, in God's presence. You may ask, What difference do these particular rules make? Why not some other ones? To that there is no ready answer, nor should there be. It is Torah, and I need to learn it. For why should I not learn what Moses "our rabbi" has taught my master? The details—sweep, wash, right hand, left hand—these make sense and become vivid only within the rabbinic Torah-myth, and even there, the sense is not spelled out. But the meaning of *having* such details—this I think speaks of something beyond the myth. And the modes of argument about establishing the specifics mean a great deal indeed.

5:29 (Lieberman, p. 30, ls. 68–72) A. The House of Shammai say, "He holds the cup of wine in his right hand and sweet oil in his left hand.

"He blesses over the wine and afterward blesses over the oil."

B. And the House of Hillel say, "He holds the sweet oil in his right hand and the cup of wine in his left hand."

C. He blesses over the oil and smears it on the head of the waiter. If the waiter was a disciple of a sage, he [the diner] smears it on the wall, because it is not praiseworthy for a disciple of a sage to go forth perfumed.

We have come to the end of the banquet. One has to recite the blessing over the wine before saying the final Grace. At the same time, sweet oil has been served to cleanse the hands and remove the odor of food. The House of Shammai say the wine takes precedence—therefore is held in the right hand and blessed first. The House of Hillel say the sweet oil takes precedence. Then, in C, we are told how one gets rid of the excess of oil, so that the hands will not continue to smell of it. For this purpose the waiter serves —or the wall!

But we shall see that the *Gemara* has things reversed, with each House holding the opinion here attributed to the opposite one. And, even more striking, in the Mishnah this is not listed as one of the disputes between the Houses concerning the meal, though it is more pertinent to "the meal" than some items in the Mishnah's list. Lieberman holds that the case before us concerns wine and oil which are brought after the final washing of hands; the case therefore falls *after* the meal, not during it. We therefore have a reference not to the cup of wine to be blessed before reciting the Grace.

The blessing for the oil is, "Blessed are you, Lord our God, who creates sweet oil," or ". . . who put a good scent into sweet oil."

5:30 (Lieberman, pp. 30–31, ls. 72–75) A. R. Judah said, "The House of Shammai and the House of Hillel did not dispute concerning the blessing of the food, that it is first, or concerning the *Havdalah*, that it is at the end.

"Concerning what did they dispute?

"Concerning the light and the spices, for—

"The House of Shammai say, 'Light and afterward spices.'

"And the House of Hillel say, 'Spices and afterward light.' "

5:30 (Lieberman, p. 31, ls. 75–77) B. He who enters his home at the end of the Sabbath blesses the wine, the light, the spices, and then says *Havdalah*.

C. And if he has only one cup [of wine] he leaves it for after the meal and then says all [the liturgies] in order after [reciting the blessing for] it.

A gives us the authority for the Mishnah as we have it: Judah [b. Ilai]. He says the only difference between the Houses is about the middle items, light and spices. Grace comes first, *Havdalah* last. Judah's saying occurs in the Palestinian *Gemara* as "spices and light" for the Shammaites, "light and spices" for the Hillelites. The Babylonian *Gemara* gives Judah's saying as we have it. Therefore, the Tosefta may have been corrected in the Babylonian schools to conform to their tradition of Judah's saying.

Note, however, that the next paragraph follows the Shammaite ruling before us: *light, then spices;* so the anonymous rule is phrased against the Hillelites' opinion; the law—which is decided by attribution to the anonymous party—follows the House of Shammai here. Consistent with its own view, the Palestinian *Ge-*

mara states that the Babylonian master, Rav, held the law is that one says the blessing for the spices, then for the light—the Hillelite position before us.

The man says the blessing for spices whenever he smells them, but light is blessed only at the end of the Sabbath. Therefore, "spices are continual," light is not, for it is blessed only in connection with the Sabbath. Accordingly, the reasoning of the Hillelites in 5:25—wine is perpetual—leads to the same conclusion here: spices, then light.

As it stands, C means that if a person has only one cup of wine, he may eat before *Havdalah,* then bless the cup of wine in connection with *Havdalah.* He says the prayers in the order already given: blessing for the wine, then Grace after Meals, spices, light, *Havdalah.* But C certainly recalls Mishnah 8:8's strange superscription, as we shall see when we compare the Mishnaic and Toseftan materials.

Let us return to Judah's saying. Judah b. Ilai was a master in the circle of Tannaitic authorities assembled in the Galilean town of Usha at the end of the Bar Kokhba War, after A.D. 135. How he knew what the Houses had disputed about and what their opinions were is not our problem. What is important for us is that he alleged the Houses did *not* dispute about certain matters. This must mean someone else said they did.

So Judah knew a version of the dispute something like the following:

The House of Shammai say, "(1) *Havdalah,* (2) light, (3) spices, and (4) food." And the House of Hillel say, "(4) food, (3) spices, (2) light, and (1) *Havdalah.*"

That is, Judah knew a version of the dispute which included disagreements on all items, 1 and 4 as well as 2 and 3. He then said the Houses agreed on those broad issues as are represented in 1 and 4, but differed only on the narrow questions presented by 2 and 3.

This revision is a commonplace trait of the Ushan commentators on traditions of the pre-Bar-Kokhba (A.D. 70–135) generations of authorities. They will tend to narrow the range of disagreements between the Houses or other earlier authorities and to claim that the differences were on ever more refined points of law than those suggested in the original traditions. Whether the alternative tradition was prior to Judah's or was simply an alternative brought up in his own generation is difficult to say. But in other instances of the same phenomenon, it is demonstrably earlier, and so it is likely here that Judah's version also is later than the one which has differences on the order of all four items.

The fact that Judah refers to the Houses' tradition suggests two further points.

First, the fixed form in which the Houses' materials are given— Statement of law, House of Shammai say (not, *said*) . . . , House of Hillel say . . . —that fixed form cannot come later than ca. A.D. 140. In fact, it is very well attested by earlier masters as well, backward nearly to the destruction of the Second Temple, shortly after 70, for we have sayings about disputes between the Houses, such as Judah's, attributed to masters who lived between 70 and 100. These sayings stand outside of a dispute between the Houses and comment on that dispute in full knowledge of what is alleged about the Houses' opinions. Such a saying thus attests to the existence of the form and substance of the dispute between the Houses. It is one important way of tracing the history of laws over the one hundred thirty years of development from the beginnings of the rabbinical movement, after the destruction of the Second Temple in 70, to the completion of the Mishnah and its accompanying Tosefta in ca. 200.

This method of attestations, second, serves to isolate the strata not only of the Mishnah but also of the *Gemara*. It depends upon the assumption that a saying attributed to a master was reliably assigned to him, if not in the exact words before us, then at least in substance. The alternative assumption is that the whole of the literature—Mishnah first, but the *Gemara* afterward—is the work only of the final generation of authorities, the men who actually put the whole thing together. That generation is presumed to have assigned materials to antecedent authorities without regard to the accuracy of such an attribution. The former assumption is much to be preferred, for the literature before us is too complex and full of stylistic and substantive variations to have come from a single group of editors, working entirely out of their own imaginations and in no way relying on antecedent compilations of traditions and commentaries, sayings and stories.

5:31 (Lieberman, p. 31, ls. 81–83, 84–85) A. If a person had a light covered in the folds of his garment or in a lamp, and sees the flame but does not use its light, or uses its light but does not see its flame, he does not bless [that light]. [He blesses only] when he both sees the flame and uses its light.

B. They do not bless over the light of gentiles. One may bless over [the flame of] an Israelite kindled from a gentile, or a gentile who kindled from an Israelite.

The Mishah requires actual use of the light before one may say the blessing for it. Now, in A, the Tosefta introduces the distinction between the illumination of a light and the actual flame. A person must see both the illumination and the actual source of the illumination, the flame. A flame covered in a lantern or seen through a mirror is not available for the blessing. We therefore have three situations: (1) a light in a lantern, which produces heat but not light; (2) a light you can see but not make use of, because of distance; and (3) a light the illumination of which you can use, but which you cannot see.

B rules that a man may not bless a light of a gentile, for the light will not have enjoyed "Sabbath-rest" in the gentile's care.

"Enjoying Sabbath-rest" here means that the light has been used in such a way as to violate the Sabbath. For instance, you are not allowed to kindle a flame on the Sabbath. But this light has been lit on the holy day. So it has not "rested" on the Sabbath.

The Sabbath rules must be kept by the Israelite in such a way that, even indirectly, he does not collaborate in their violation. Using the gentile's flame, even though the Israelite did not participate in lighting it, would be a subterfuge to violate the Sabbath. But you may bless a light kindled by an Israelite from that light. This tradition will be closely examined in the *Gemara*.

5:39 (Lieberman, p. 31, ls. 80–81) In the house of study—
The House of Shammai say, "One [person] blesses for all of them."
And the House of Hillel say, "Each one blesses for himself."

The Babylonian *Gemara*'s version has the opinions reversed. The House of Shammai say each blesses for himself. The House of Hillel say one person does it for all. The bases for the respective positions are given there. The reason each blesses for himself is to avoid a suspension of public study, thus to prevent a waste of time which is to be spent in the study of the Torah. All bless together because it is greater honor to God for a whole congregation to participate in the blessing than for an isolated individual to do so. But we are not told what blessing is being said. The Hebrew reveals a mnemonic pattern:

House of Shammai: 'HD¹ [MBRK] LKWLN² (thus: KL)
House of Hillel: KL² 'HD¹ (W'HD) [MBRK L'SMW]

The key words therefore are 'HD and KL. In the first saying the word-order is 1, 2, and in the second, 2, 1. So, as earlier, differences in word-order will yield the dispute.

The Tosefta and the Mishnah

The relationships between the two compilations of traditions produced in the first- and second-century Palestinian rabbinical academies are complex. Here we shall see two quite different types of relationship.

In the first, covering the laws dealing with the Houses, the Tosefta seems to be a commentary on, and expansion of, the Mishnah. It gives the reasons for the positions taken by the respective Houses.

In the second, covering the anonymous laws, the Tosefta gives rules which are in substance the same as the Mishnah's, but it gives those rules in very different language, generally greatly expanded and more generalized than the Mishnah's very brief statements. Here it looks as though the Tosefta's lengthy sayings have been summarized by the Mishnah's.

The *Gemara* will combine the two sets of traditions and discuss their contents. But it takes for granted that the whole is a seamless fabric of law. It is not going to perceive that the relationships between the traditions and the ways in which they are formulated pose problems for literary analysis. We shall now review the Mishnah and compare the Tosefta's materials pertinent to it. The Tosefta's additions to the Mishnah's language are given in italics.

MISHNAH

M. 8:1.A. These are the things which are between the House of Shammai and the House of Hillel in [regard to] the meal:

B. The House of Shammai say, "One blesses the day, and afterward one blesses over the wine."

And the House of Hillel say, "One blesses the day, and afterward one blesses over the wine."

TOSEFTA

Tos. 5:25. [The] things which are between the House of Shammai and the House of Hillel [as regards] the meal:

The House of Shammai say, "One blesses the day, and afterward one blesses over the wine, *for the day causes the wine to come, and the day is already sanctified, but the wine has not yet come.*"

And the House of Hillel say, "One blesses over the wine, and afterward one blesses the day, *for*

MISHNAH

TOSEFTA

the wine causes the Sanctification of the day to be said.

"Another matter: The blessing of the wine is continual, and the blessing of the day is not continual."

And the law is according to the words of the House of Hillel.

M. 8:2.A. The House of Shammai say, "They wash the hands and afterward mix the cup."

Tos. 5:26. The House of Shammai say, "They wash the hands and afterward mix the cup, lest the liquids which are on the outer surfaces of the cup may be made unclean on account of the hands, and they may go back and make the cup unclean."

And the House of Hillel say, "They mix the cup and afterward wash the hands."

The House of Hillel say, "The outer surfaces of the cup are perpetually unclean.

"Another matter: The washing of the hands is only [done] near [at the outset of] the meal.

"They mix the cup and afterward wash the hands."

8:3.A. The House of Shammai say, "He dries his hands on the cloth and lays it on the table."
And the House of Hillel say, "On the cushion."

5:27. The House of Shammai say, "He dries his hand on the napkin and lays it on the table, lest the liquids which are in the napkin may be made unclean on account of the pillow, and they may go and make the hands unclean."

The House of Hillel say, "A doubt in regard to the condition of liquids so far as the hands are concerned is clean.

"Another matter: Washing the hands does not pertain to uncon-

MISHNAH

TOSEFTA

secrated food. *But he dries his hands on the napkin and leaves it on the cushion, lest the liquids which are in the pillow may be made unclean on account of the table, and they may go and render the food unclean.*"

8:4.A. The House of Shammai say, "They clean the house and afterward wash the hands."

And the House of Hillel say, "They wash the hands and afterward clean the house."

Tos. 5:28. The House of Shammai say, "They clean the house *on account of the waste of food,* and afterward wash the hands."

The House of Hillel say, "*If the waiter was a disciple of a sage, he gathers the scraps which contain as much as an olive's bulk.*

"They wash the hands and afterward clean the house."

8:5.A. The House of Shammai say, "Light, and food, and spices, and *Havdalah.*"

And the House of Hillel say, "Light, and spices, and food, and *Havdalah.*"

5:30. R. Judah said, "*The House of Shammai and the House of Hillel did not dispute concerning the blessing of the food, that it is first, and concerning the Havdalah that it is the end. Concerning what did they dispute? Concerning the light and the spices, for the House of Shammai say, 'Light and afterward spices,' and the House of Hillel say, 'Spices and afterward light.'*"

B. The House of Shammai say, " 'Who created the light of the fire.' "

And the House of Hillel say, " 'Who creates the lights of the fire.' "

[No equivalent.]

The relationships between the Mishnaic and the Toseftan versions of the Houses' disputes are fairly clear. The Tosefta tends to expand the Mishnah's terse laws. In the first instance, Mishnah 8:1/Tosefta 5:25, the expansion takes the form of an addition to the Mishnah. In the second, Mishnah 8:2/Tosefta 5:26, the Tosefta adds a reason to the Shammaite rule, but then provides the Hillelites with an "introduction" to their opinion, which comes only at the end. This tendency is even more pronounced in the next example, 8:3/5:27, in which the Hillelites have a considerable speech, and the Mishnah's elliptical *on the cushion* is set into a complete sentence, which itself is part of a larger explanation. Here we should be hard put to argue that Tosefta has simply expanded Mishnah's Hillelite saying. It has given them a wholly new saying.

The simpler pattern of 8:2/5:26 recurs in 8:4/5:28, where, before the Hillelites' actual opinion, we are told what to do with the oil. But this is irrelevant to the issue addressed by the House of Shammai, and the Shammaites themselves say only what is already in the Mishnah. So this must be classified as an interpolation of entirely new material, not as a gloss of existing sayings.

There is no close correlation between the ruling of Mishnah 8:5A and Judah's saying in Tosefta 5:30. Rather, we have in the Mishnah what is implied by Judah's saying in Tosefta; but Judah's reformulation, naming only items 2 and 3, is not the language of the Mishnah, which gives all four items. There is no Toseftan equivalent to 8:5B, although some pertinent materials do occur.

The construction of the brief formulaic sayings of Mishnah 8:1–5 is to be credited to Judah the Patriarch. He has stressed the simplest possible formulation. The Tosefta constitutes not another version, but a highly glossed copy of the original, with many interpolations. Thus the Hillelite saying supplies reasons for, and only then gives the equivalent of, the Shammaites' primary formula. In 5:26 the Hillelites do not even have such an equivalent. In 5:27 the Hillelites' view is taken for granted, then explained. In 5:28 the waiter-element has no Shammaite counterpart. So Tosefta presupposes and depends upon knowledge of the Mishnah and looks like a commentary on it, with glosses as needed.

MISHNAH

8:8A. Wine came to them after the meal, and there is there only that cup—

B. The House of Shammai say, "He blesses over the wine and afterward he blesses over the food."

And the House of Hillel say, "He blesses over the food and afterward he blesses over the wine."

TOSEFTA

Tos. 5:30 (Lieberman, p. 31, ls. 75–77) A. *He who enters his home at the end of the Sabbath blesses over the wine, the light, the spices, and then says Havdalah.*

B. *And if he has only one cup [of wine], he leaves it for after the meal and then says them all in order after [blessing] it.*

There is no clear relationship between Mishnah 8:8A and Tosefta 5:30B. But Tosefta 5:30B *may* represent a simple, undisputed statement of the position of the House of Shammai in Mishnah 8:8A:

MISHNAH

[If wine came to them after the meal and]
there is there only that cup
House of Shammai say,
"He blesses the wine and then the food."
(House of Hillel say,
"He blesses the food and then the wine.")

TOSEFTA

If he has only one cup [of wine]

[He leaves it for after the meal and then says them all in order, thus:]
Wine, then food.

We see that the net result of the Shammaite position is as is given in Tosefta: The wine is kept for the end of the meal, then blessed in advance of the Grace after Meals, as is normally the case. The Hillelite view then is not pertinent to Tosefta 5:30B.

8:6A. They do not bless the light or the spices of gentiles, nor the light or the spices of the dead, nor the light or the spices which are before an idol.

B. And they do not bless the

Tos. 5:31A. They do not bless the light of gentiles. *An Israelite who kindled [a flame] from a gentile, or a gentile who kindled from an Israelite—one may bless [such a flame].*

MISHNAH
light until they make use of its
illumination.

TOSEFTA
Tos. 5:31B (Lieberman, p. 31,
ls. 81–85) *If a person had a light
covered in the folds of his garment or in a lamp, and he sees
the flame but does not use its
light, or uses its light but does
not see its flame, he does not
bless.* [He blesses only] *when he
both sees the flame and uses its
light.*

Now Mishnah and Tosefta represent separate and independent
statements of substantially the same law. Mishnah 8:6A speaks of
spices, the dead, and idolatry, considerations all absent in Tosefta
5:31A, which speaks only of light and of gentiles. But Tosefta
then introduces a new problem, one which will be important in
the *Gemara:* What of light transferred from a gentile's flame to
one held by an Israelite, or vice versa. The transfer of flame from
a gentile to another gentile is not discussed here; it will occur in
the *Gemara.* Similarly, Mishnah 8:6B states simply that one has
to use the light of the lamp before blessing it. Tosefta 5:31B deals
with various problems which that simple rule is going to raise in
detailed application. While Mishnah 8:6A looks like a considerable elaboration of Tosefta 5:31A, for part B of each rule, the
opposite is the case.

MISHNAH
8:8C. They respond *Amen*
after an Israelite who blesses,
and they do not respond *Amen*
after a Samaritan who blesses,
until one hears the entire blessing.

TOSEFTA
Tos. 5:21 (Lieberman, p. 28,
ls. 41–2) *They answer "Amen"
after a blessing with the divine
name.*

They do not answer *Amen* after a Samaritan who blesses with
the divine name until they hear
the entire blessing.

Here the correlation is close, but curiously different. Mishnah 8:8

speaks of an Israelite and a Samaritan; the Israelite rule is super-fluous. Clearly, if you are going to say *Amen* at all, it is going to be after an Israelite's blessing! Tos. 5:21 introduces the gentile, and that rule is by no means superfluous. Both compilations agree about the Samaritan, but to the Mishnah the problem of the gentile is unknown.

Clearly, both the Mishnah and the Tosefta leave room for elaboration. Simple rules, when applied in practice, raise complicated questions. New conditions of life—for instance, what if you do not have any wine?—will produce still others. Furthermore, as is already obvious, not all of the sayings and rules produced by the authorities in the Mishnah and Tosefta are included in those compilations. Moreover, some rules come down in more than one version. In a few instances the positions of the Houses or other masters are entirely reversed. A still further tendency is pseudepigraphically to create in the names of the early authorities rules and sayings which follow, or might follow, from things they actually did say. These sayings have to be harmonized with those in the Mishnah and the Tosefta; or the position taken by the earlier authorities has to be enlarged to make room for them. This may be done, for instance, by making distinctions among cases so that what seem to be conflicting opinions are shown to refer to differing circumstances. The post-Mishnaic authorities themselves formulated opinions, decided cases to which the former rules did not closely apply, and otherwise participated in the development of pertinent laws. So commentary—the *Gemara*—built in the first instance on the basis of the union of the Mishnah and the Tosefta and the analysis of the correlative traditions of each, is going to proliferate, both as studies continue and as new problems arise.

We turn first to the Babylonian *Gemara,* though it was completed in the seventh century, about a hundred years after the completion of the Palestinian one in the sixth century, because it is the more important of the two, having been edited in a more sophisticated way, and, from the time of its redaction, having been studied far more intensely in medieval and modern times. When one speaks of "the Talmud," he normally means the Babylonian ("Bavli") Talmud, consisting, as we now know, of the Palestinian Mishnah and the *Gemara* produced in the Babylonian rabbinical institutions—courts which served as schools for apprentice lawyers. The Palestinian Talmud ("Yerushalmi," or Jerusalemite), consisting of the Palestinian Mishnah and the *Gemara* produced in the rabbinical institutions of Caesarea, Tiberias, and other centers in Palestine, will follow.

CHAPTER

V

The Babylonian Talmud

THE *Gemara,* the part of the Babylonian Talmud serving as a commentary to the Mishnah, is generally supposed to be the product of approximately three centuries of work, from ca. A.D. 200 to ca. 500. These are conventional dates; we actually do not know either when the study of the Mishnah was reduced to formal commentaries, on the one side, or when the work of Talmudic creativity came to an end, and commentary on the now-completed Talmud began, on the other. Nor do we have a clear picture of the authorities, dates, and method of the final redaction of the Babylonian Talmud; it seems likely to assign the last stages of the work to the sixth and seventh centuries.

Gemara comes from the Aramaic verb to learn or study. *Gemara* is interpreted as the interpretation—"the learning"—or commentary on the Mishnah. What is marked as *Gemara* in the Talmud was in earlier times designated simply *Talmud,* from the Hebrew verb "to study," thus just as with the Aramaic word, "study of the Mishnah," or commentary. We shall use the two words interchangeably, for they are equivalent to each other. A master of the post-Mishnaic age, responsible for the Talmud, is called *Amora* (plural: *Amoraim*), meaning speaker, lecturer, or interpreter.

We have Babylonian Talmud for the larger part of the Mishnah, thirty-seven of the sixty-three tractates. But the whole of the order on Seeds (*Zera'im*), except Blessings (*Berakhot*), and the whole of the order on Purities (*Toharot*), except Menstrual Laws (*Niddah*), lack Talmud, possibly because the agricultural and purity laws had no bearing on Babylonian Jewish life. As a foreign, thus unholy land, Babylonia was not liable to all the agricultural offerings required in Scripture, and of course it was unclean to begin with. But we have a full Talmud for Holy Things (*Qodashim*) while there was no Temple in Babylonia, nor did anyone suppose there ever would be. So that reason for the absence of many tractates is insufficient, yet we have no better one.

The Babylonian *Gemara* began as a commentary on the Mishnah of Judah the Patriarch. The work of commentary and exegesis commenced as soon as the Mishnah and its accompanying, cognate traditions (Tosefta and the like) reached the Babylonian rabbinical academies. The first generation tended to concentrate on providing simple comments and explanations—exegeses—of Mishnaic laws. The next generation of masters was apt to take as its task the identification of the authorities behind the various rulings of the Mishnah, the elucidation of the principles behind their rulings, the discovery of internal contradictions, in detail or in principle, in the Mishnaic corpus. For this purpose the non-Mishnaic traditions bearing Tannaitic authority, such as those found in the Tosefta or redacted outside of both the Mishnah and the Tosefta, called *baraita* (plural: *beraitot*) or "external tradition," were extremely useful. After the turn of the fourth century, the main efforts ceased to focus upon the Mishnah and its exegesis, for much had been accomplished. The center of interest was rather upon the larger principles and generalizations contained within the law. The effort now was to organize and harmonize the fundamental principles of the whole system of the rabbinic law. The work of the fifth, sixth, and seventh centuries is before us: putting together of the whole work of Mishnah-commentary and legal inquiry into well-organized, literarily sophisticated, unitary discussions, and the combination of these many discussions into the final *Gemara*. We shall appreciate the accomplishments of those last generations when we come to the Palestinian Talmud. There we shall see what the Babylonian Talmud would have looked like had the work of the last two centuries been omitted. While the Palestinian Talmud is a compendium of sayings and stories, the Babylonian Talmud transcends mere antiquarianism. It is a work of powerful, vigorous logic and continuous criticism, and that is why it is challenging and interesting, not merely informative.

Some More Essential Facts

The Talmud takes for granted thorough knowledge of the system of ritual purity alluded to above. Let us review some more facts necessary for understanding what is to follow.

First, ritual impurity is acquired by contact with either a primary or a secondary source of uncleanness, called a "father" or a "child," or "offspring" of uncleanness, respectively. In the first category are contact with a corpse, a person suffering a flux, a leper, and the like. Objects made of metal, wood, leather, bone, cloth, or sacking become fathers of uncleanness if they touch a corpse.

Foodstuffs and liquids are susceptible to uncleanness, but will not render other foodstuffs unclean in the same degree of uncleanness which they themselves suffer. Foodstuffs furthermore will not make vessels or utensils unclean. But liquids made unclean by a father of uncleanness will do so if they touch the inner side of the vessel. That is, if they fall into the contained space of an earthenware vessel, they make the whole vessel unclean.

Now there are four degrees of uncleanness in all. Food or liquid which touches a father of uncleanness incurs *first* grade uncleanness. If food touches a person or vessel made unclean by a primary source of uncleanness, it is unclean in the *second* grade uncleanness. Food that touches *second* grade uncleanness incurs *third* grade uncleanness, and food that touches *third* grade uncleanness incurs *fourth* grade uncleanness. But, as we noticed, liquids touching either a primary source of uncleanness (Father) or something unclean in the first or second grade uncleanness (Offspring) are regarded as unclean in the first grade. They *are* able to make something else unclean. If, therefore, the outer side of a vessel is made unclean by a liquid—thus is unclean in the second grade—and another liquid touches the outer side, the other liquid incurs not second, but first grade uncleanness.

As to the hands, they are regarded as perpetually in a second grade uncleanness. But you can cover your hands with a napkin and not wash them to prevent their imparting uncleanness.

Heave-offering—food raised up for priestly use only—unclean in the third grade uncleanness and Holy Things (that is things belonging to the cult) in the fourth grade uncleanness do not make other things unclean—whether liquids or food.

What is the point of these degrees of uncleanness? As we now know, the Pharisees made every effort to eat their ordinary food in a state of ritual purity. Whatever makes food unclean will have to be avoided; food which suffers first or second grade uncleanness therefore is not acceptable. But the difference between grades is important. For first grade uncleanness in common food will covey uncleanness. But while food unclean in the second grade uncleanness will be unacceptable, it will *not* convey uncleanness, that is, third grade uncleanness. But it will render Heave-offering *unfit*.

A further practical consideration affects the priestly offerings. It was the practice to give to the priests the dues the Scriptures had assigned to them. Heave-offering of the crop, among other things, had to be preserved and consumed in a state of ritual purity. As we just saw, it could be made unfit and unclean by a first, and unfit by a second, grade cleanness. If it touches something unclean in the third degree it is made unfit, but itself will not impart fourth grade uncleanness.

Finally, a person had to be concerned for the cleanness of the Temple cult. A Holy Thing suffering first, second, or third grade uncleanness is unclean and conveys uncleanness; if it is unclean in the fourth grade, it is invalid for the cult but does not convey uncleanness. It is thus *much* more susceptible than noncultic things.

For example, common food which suffers second grade uncleanness will render Heave-offering *invalid* (unfit in the third degree). We already know that it makes liquid unclean in the first degree. Likewise, Heave-offering in a third grade uncleanness will make Holy Things invalid and put them into the fourth grade uncleanness. But—a further complication—if common food is prepared in conditions of cleanness which befit Heave-offering, and it then suffers third grade uncleanness, it becomes invalid *like* Heave-offering, in the same condition, at the same degree of suscepti-bility. If it touches a Holy Thing, it does not impart fourth grade uncleanness. On the other hand, if common food is prepared in conditions of cleanness as would be appropriate for Holy Things, its third grade uncleanness is regarded as clean, as is normal with common food. The processes by which things lose their unclean-ness—rites of purification—do not play a role in our chapter of the Talmud.

For our purpose, we have to imagine people eating their meals with the concern for ritual cleanness uppermost in mind. Every aspect of the ritual of the meal—the Grace before Meals (gener-ally said with bread, "Blessed are you, Lord our God, king of the world, who brings forth bread from the earth"), the Grace after Meals "Blessing of Food," the process by which the hands are washed before and after eating, and the like—every aspect is go-ing to be guided by considerations of ritual purity. The food must be preserved from the various sources which may make it unclean. Remember, we are not talking about the acceptability of foods as permitted or prohibited in Scriptures. A cow, properly slaughtered, is *kosher,* that is, fit or acceptable. But its flesh may receive ritual impurity and therefore may become unclean. Bread will be *kosher.* But the Jews whose laws are before us still will not eat it if it is *unclean.*

One last point: There is nothing material, or intrinsic, in ritual purity or impurity. We are not dealing with a belief that some-thing—a demon or devil—really enters into the food and renders it unclean or unfit. Purity and impurity constitute a set of highly complex relationships. But these relationships have nothing to do with the physical world; they are wholly abstract. A great deal depends upon intention and purpose, circumstance and time. For instance, a vessel which is not entirely completed may touch a corpse and yet remain clean. For it is not susceptible to receive uncleanness until it both has been entirely finished, and its owner regards it as completed. A common person is normally regarded as unclean, for he does not observe the various taboos. But during a religious festival, he is regarded as clean. If the outer side of a vessel becomes unclean by a liquid, and food touches the outer side, it remains clean, for a vessel whose outer side alone is unclean does not render food unclean. But if the food is a Holy Thing, it *is* unclean. So you might have two identical substances in different categories—one may be ordinary food or even Heave-offering, the other a Holy Thing; both touch the same outer side of the same vessel. The one is clean, the other unclean! Clearly, everything is relative to everything else.

It remains to observe that while the first- and second-century authorities probably did observe these laws, we have very little evidence of their persistence in later times in the holy land; and in Babylonia everything was, as I said, unclean to begin with. So the theories before us revolve around matters which to begin with were entirely theoretical, a highly intellectual, utterly unworldly enterprise.

The Elements of the Chapter

My translation follows the standard printed text, checked against the manuscript known as *Codex Munich* (95), which dates from 1343, the only manuscript in existence containing the complete text of the Babylonian Talmud. A facsimile edition was printed in Jerusalem in 1971, so the manuscript is now widely available and convenient for everyday use. I further referred to Maurice Simon, *Berakoth, Translated into English with Notes, Glossary,* *and Indices.** As before, we shall first examine the text by units, and afterward see how it has been put together as a whole.

The Talmud is written in two languages, Hebrew and Aramaic. The use of the one rather than the other is by no means accidental. Normally, though not always, the sayings attributed to the Tannaim and statements of normative law will be in Hebrew. The comments and analyses of the Amoraim and stories will be in Aramaic. And the editors' own remarks will be in Aramaic. To signify the differences, which are very important, Hebrew will be in regular type, Aramaic in italics. Boldfaced type is used for citations from the Mishnah, which stand at the head of the major divisions of the chapter. We shall cite the *Gemara* in small sections and comment on each. Then we shall review and comment upon a complete set of arguments or inquiries. Finally, at the end, we shall reread the chapter as a whole and examine its total literary characteristics as a unity.

[51b] *Gemara:* A. *Our rabbis have taught:*
B. The things which are between the House of Shammai and the House of Hillel in [regard to] a meal:

The House of Shammai say, "One blesses over the day and afterward blesses over the wine, for the day causes the wine to come, and the day has already been sanctified, while the wine has not yet come."

And the House of Hillel say, "One blesses over the wine and afterward blesses over the day, for the wine causes the Sanctification to be said.

"Another matter: The blessing over the wine is perpetual, and the blessing over the day is not perpetual. Between that which is perpetual and that which is not perpetual, that which is perpetual takes precedence."

And the law is in accordance with the words of the House of Hillel.

* London, 1948: Soncino Press.

The *Gemara* opens with a simple citation of the Tosefta we have already studied. It then proceeds to analyze the passage.

C. What is the purpose of "another matter"?

The first peculiarity is simply the second "reason" assigned to the Hillelites. Why should we require *two* reasons for their position, while we have only one for the Shammaites?

If you should say that there [in regard to the opinion of the House of Shammai] *two* [reasons are given], *and here* [in regard to the opinion of the House of Hillel] *one, here too* [in respect to the House of Hillel], *there are two* [reasons, the second being]: "The blessing of the wine is perpetual and the blessing of the day is not perpetual. That which is perpetual takes precedence over that which is not perpetual."

The *Gemara* reads into the Shammaite saying two separate reasons, and so explains that in order to balance those two reasons, the Hillelites likewise are given two.

D. "And the law is in accord with the opinion of the House of Hillel."

The statement of the final decision is cited from Tosefta, but this poses a new problem. For the law normally will follow the Hillelites. Why say so?

This is obvious [that the law is in accord with the House of Hillel], *for the echo has gone forth* [and pronounced from heaven the decision that the law follows the opinion of the House of Hillel.]

Now the question is spelled out. In rabbinic lore, it was believed that a few years after the destruction of the Temple in 70, a heavenly echo had announced that the law follows the House of Hillel.

E. *If you like, I can argue that* [this was stated] before the echo.

F. *And if you like, I can argue that* it was after the echo, and [the passage is formulated in accord with the] opinion of [52a] R. Joshua, who stated, "They do not pay attention to an echo [from heaven]."

Two answers are given. The first is that the final decision was formulated before the echo had been heard, the second, that it came afterward but accords with the view of those who nonetheless deny supernatural intervention into the formulation of the law, for instance, Joshua b. Hananiah, who lived at that time and was alleged to have rejected the testimony of supernatural signs.

Let us review the whole pericope.

The Talmud opens with a citation (A) of the Tosefta's parallel to the Mishnah. Our chapter consistently supplements the Mishnah with the Tosefta, primarily in order to analyze the latter. The Tosefta is cited with the introduction of A, a fixed formula which indicates that a Tannaitic source is quoted. Other such formulae include *We have learned,* the formula for introducing a citation to the Mishnah, *It has been taught,* introducing a teaching attributed to the authority of Tannaim, though not necessarily to a specific Mishnaic teacher. These Aramaic formulae function like footnotes, providing information on the source of, or type of authority behind, materials cited in the text.

B simply cites the Tosefta we have already examined. Then C undertakes the analysis of the passage. The explanation and elucidation are ignored; it is assumed that these are clear. What C wants to know is why the House of Hillel give two reasons for their opinion. The "two reasons" of the Shammaites are (1) the wine is brought on account of the Sabbath, and (2) it is already the Sabbath, yet the wine is still lacking. The Hillelites' reason then is cited without comment.

D continues the analysis of the Toseftan passage. The statement that the law follows the House of Hillel is regarded as obvious, since normally that is so. The presupposition of the Talmud is that nothing will be stated which is obvious; redundancy, it goes without saying, will not occur. But the Talmud also objects to the inclusion of well-known facts. This is regarded as bad style. The reference to the "echo which has gone forth" alludes to a story about the House of Shammai's and the House of Hillel's debating for three years, until Heaven intervened with the divine announcement, delivered by an echo, that both Houses possess the words of the living God, but the law follows the House of Hillel. Supernatural intervention into legal matters is commonplace. The Talmud was created in a world which took for granted that Heaven cared about, therefore influenced or interfered in, the affairs of men, particularly the affairs of the people of Israel, and especially those of the rabbis, who were believed to study Torah on earth exactly as it was studied by Moses "our rabbi" in the Heavenly Academy.

E provides a simple, "historical" answer: D was included before the echo had delivered its message. F then gives a somewhat more substantial response: Some rabbis opposed accepting supernatural signs of the determination of the law by Heaven. Chief among these is Joshua b. Hananiah (ca. A.D. 90), who, when presented by Eliezer b. Hyrcanus with supernatural evidence in behalf of the latter's position, proclaimed, "It—the Torah—is not in heaven" (Deuteronomy 30:12). D thus is credited to Joshua, who would not accept the heavenly decision and therefore had to provide earthly counsel based on reason.

The foregoing issue, about whether supernatural intervention may determine a moot point of law, raises a very large question. It is, What are the limits of Talmudic supernaturalism? Where does the force of reason and logic end, and the power of Heaven begin? On the one side is the view of Joshua. God has given the Torah to man. It now is in man's hands to do with as he finds reasonable. Reason becomes the way of continuing, of elaborating revelation. The Torah lays forth the principles of rational inquiry. Once set forth, these will work their own way. The processes of thought no longer are subject to the modulation of revelation—for they themselves continue the process of revelation. If you want to know what God now wants, you turn not to prayer or to the expectation of miraculously imparted inspiration or insight. You turn rather to the laws already revealed, laws of substance and laws of reason, and you think further according to rational principles about these laws. On the other side is the view of Eliezer. God not only revealed the Torah in times past. He continues to reveal, he himself. You cannot close off the possibility of divine participation in the arguments of men, of rabbis. If you do, you say God is no longer interested. He has wound up the watch; now let it run on. That is not so. God so loved Israel that he gave to them his Torah. He continues to love Israel—that is shown by his punishing them for their transgressions, a sign he will reward them for their regeneration and repentance. So he may, too, continue to give them Torah, instruction. The arguments of rabbis on earth are heard and joined by God and the angels in heaven. What prevents the heavenly party from intervening in the affairs of the earthly one? It is not easy to resolve this question, for within it are fundamental issues facing religious people.

It remains to observe that Hebrew is consistently used in the formulation of the normative law, and Aramaic is equally consistently used for the discussion and analysis of the law. The Palestinian Talmud's pattern is similar. This pattern is repeated throughout our chapter. I shall point to its significance in the last chapter.

A. *And is it the reasoning of the House of Shammai that the blessing of the day is more important?*

When you examine the position of the House of Shammai,

which rule that you bless the day and then the wine, it appears that they regard the day as more important than the wine, so it takes precedence.

But has a Tanna not taught: "He who enters his house at the close of the Sabbath blesses over the wine and the light and the spices and afterward he says *Havdalah*. And if he has only one cup, he leaves it for after the food and then says the other blessings in order after it." [*Havdalah* is the blessing of the day, yet comes last!]

We presently assume that the House of Shammai stand behind the cited tradition. Then the tradition contradicts their position that the day takes precedence.

B. *But lo, on what account* [do you say] *this is the view of the House of Shammai? Perhaps it is the House of Hillel[*'s opinion]?

The obvious solution is to assign the cited tradition to the House of Hillel. But this solution is forthwith challenged.

C. *Let* [such a thought] *not enter your mind, for a Tanna teaches:* "Light and afterward spices." *And of whom have you heard who holds this opinion? The House of Shammai, as a Tanna has taught:*
R. Judah said, "The House of Shammai and the House of Hillel did not differ concerning the [blessing of the] food, that it is at first, and *Havdalah*, that is at the end.
"Concerning what did they dispute? Concerning the light and the spices.
"For the House of Shammai say, 'Light and afterward spices.'
"And the House of Hillel say, 'Spices and afterward light.'"

The House of Shammai are shown to stand behind the foregoing tradition. Judah's verson, quoted in Tosefta, is that the Houses agree that *Havdalah* comes at the end. The Shammaites say the right order is light, then spices. So they *must* stand behind the tradition which contradicts the view that the day takes precedence—and thus are shown not consistent!

D. *And on what account* [do you suppose that] *it is the House of Shammai as* [interpreted by] *R. Judah? Perhaps it is* [a teaching in accord with] *the House of Hillel* [as interpreted by] *R. Meir?*

The solution to this problem is that Judah's version of the House of Shammai's position is not the only one. We have another, which is Meir's and the opposite—The House of Shammai will say light comes after the spices. So the originally cited tradition does not belong to the Shammaites at all.

E. *Do not let such a thing enter your mind, for lo, a Tanna teaches here in our Mishnah: The House of Shammai say,* "Light and food and spices and *Havdalah.*"
And the House of Hillel say, "Light and spices, food and *Havdalah.*"
But there, *in the baraita, lo he has taught:* "If he has only one cup, he leaves it for after the food and then says the other blessings in order after it."
From this it is to be inferred that it is the House of Shammai's teaching, according to the [interpretation] *of R. Judah.*

We may now demonstrate that that original tradition, in A, *has* to belong to the House of Shammai. But no matter how you solve that problem, you still have the House of Shammai's ruling that the wine takes precedence over the day, and this contradicts their ruling that the day takes precedence over the wine.

F. *In any event there is a problem* [for the House of Shammai now give precedence to reciting a blessing for the wine over blessing the day].

We shall now solve the problem by distinguishing between the two contradictory rulings. One deals with the advent of the Sabbath, the other with the end of the Sabbath. These should not be regarded as comparable, for they have different traits. The difference will be spelled out.

The House of Shammai suppose that the coming of the [holy] day is more important than its leaving. As to the coming of the [holy] day, the earlier one may bring it in, the better. As to the leaving of the festival day, the later one may take leave of it, the better, so that it should not seem to us as a burden.

One central interest of criticism is the examination of the whole of a given philosophy, to see that the parts are harmonious with one another. The Talmud's criticism of antecedent traditions therefore compares the suppositions of a master in one ruling with those evident in his rulings on other matters. A review of the pericope shows how this criticism takes shape. In A the conclusion is reached from the House of Shammai's statement that the Sabbath Day takes precedence over the wine; the blessing of the day— Sanctification—is more important. A contrary viewpoint, assumed to be held by the House of Shammai, is immediately cited (as we surmised in examining the Tosefta, above), to the effect that the blessing of the Day—*Havdalah*—comes last, not first.

The best answer is that it is not the opinion of the House of Shammai at all. B states exactly that. But C then rejects this response. Judah's tradition on the pertinent dispute between the Houses is that all parties agree *Havdalah* comes at the end. The tradition is cited in full. To this, D replies that Judah's tradition is not the only one concerning the opinions of the Houses on this question. His contemporary, Meir, had a different tradition, which

assigned the cited passage to the House of Hillel. But, more decisive still, E points out that the Mishnah before us is consistent
with Judah's picture of the opinion of the House of Shammai,
which places *Havdalah* at the end.

F then points out the question is still a very real one; however
you assign the authority for the tradition, the House of Shammai
is still represented as giving precedence to the wine over the day.
The solution has to be to distinguish between the beginning of the
Sabbath, when the Sanctification will take precedence, and the end
of the Sabbath, when wine comes first. The distinction then is
drawn between the start of the Sabbath, which one wants to move
up if one can, and the end of the Sabbath, when one wants to de-
lay matters, so that the Sabbath may be extended, rather than
concluded in unseemly haste.

The upshot is that the position of the House of Shammai no
longer will consistently favor first blessing the day. Circumstances
change, and the Shammaites' opinion will change accordingly. So
the introductory question is now answered in the negative. The
argument, however, is so constructed as, first, to take account of
all possible conditions according to the authorities behind them;
second, to examine the reliability of the foregoing distinctions; and
finally, to provide a new basis for argument, this time distinguishing among the situations represented by superficially contradictory
laws.

A. *And do the House of Shammai hold the opinion that
Grace requires a cup [of wine]? And lo, we have learned:* [If]
wine came to them after the food, and there is there only that
cup, the House of Shammai say, "He blesses over the wine
and afterward blesses over the food." [So Grace is said without the cup.]

In the tradition we cited above, we saw that the House of Shammai say if the man has only one cup of wine, he holds it until
after he eats, then says the blessing of the food with that cup. This

seems to suggest that one must have wine for saying the blessing of food after meals. The position of the House of Shammai will now be investigated on the question of whether one must have and drink a cup of wine in connection with the Grace after Meals.

B. *Does this not mean that he blesses it and drinks* [it]? *No. He blesses it and leaves it.*
C. But has not a master said, "He that blesses must [also] taste [it]."
He does taste it.

Now we ask, Does the aforecited tradition not mean that the man says the blessing for the wine, then drinks the wine in connection with the Grace after Meals? The answer is that the man does *not* have to drink the wine on the occasion of the Grace after Meals. But this is immediately challenged. A person has, after all, to make use of the thing he has blessed. So we suppose the man does taste the wine.

D. And has not a master said, "Tasting it is spoiling it."
He tastes it with his hand [finger].

If we agree the man does taste the wine, then he is supposed to have spoiled it, so it cannot be used again.

E. And has not a master said, "The cup of blessing requires a [fixed] measure." *And lo, he diminishes it from its fixed measure.*
[We speak of a situation in which] *he has more than the fixed measure.*

If we say the man merely tastes the wine with his finger, then we still have a problem, because he is supposed to have a full measure of wine, and here he no longer has a full measure. The solution is that we posit the man has more than enough wine.

F. *But lo, has it not been taught:* "If there is there only *that* cup" . . . [so he has no more].

G. *There is not enough for two, but more than enough for one.*

The solution that the man has more than enough wine is contrary to the original case, which specifies he has only a single cup, in full, but fixed measure. So we posit he has a bit more than a single cup.

H. *And has not Hiyya taught:* The House of Shammai say, "He blesses over the wine and drinks it, and afterward he says Grace."

I. Then we have two Tannas' [traditions] in respect to the opinion of the House of Shammai.

The foregoing solutions are not possible. We have a tradition from Hiyya that explicitly states the man must bless the wine and say Grace. The only way out is to suppose we have two contradictory traditions in the name of the House of Shammai. Now let us reconsider the entire argument.

The position of the House of Shammai is further investigated, a curious inquiry, considering that the practical law follows the House of Hillel. The issue is whether the Shammaites require that one have a cup of wine before saying Grace after Meals. The thrust of the argument is to show that this is *not* the opinion of the House of Shammai.

A cites the primary datum, Mishnah 8:8. B then makes the point explicit. The Mishnah seems to specify that the man says the blessing, drinks the wine, and *then* says the Grace. But this is rejected: The blessing is said for the wine, then the wine is left over. C objects that this procedure is contrary to law. This is answered: He does taste the wine, but does not finish the whole cup. D objects to this procedure too. But, it is explained, the tasting is with a finger. E still again objects to the new theory of what is to be done, for the wine has to fill the cup. But the cup is more than full. F points out this contradicts the original statement. To this G replies there is more than one cup, less than two. Then H provides a definitive statement: The House of Shammai explicitly rule one *does* drink the wine, which means the Grace after Meals does *not* require a cup of wine in addition. The only possible solution is given in I: We have contradictory opinions attributed to the House of Shammai.

Clearly, the construction is "artificial." The series of questions is asked in full awareness of the consequent replies. A simple contruction would have given A, then H-I. But, as we see, the Talmud normally prefers to lay out and explore all possible routes through an inquiry. The simple and definitive answer is the least likely to come at the outset. Rather, the argument will move from point to point, back and forth, before it is allowed to close with a simple solution.

The House of Shammai say [They wash the hands and afterward mix the cup] . . .

A. *Our rabbis have taught:*

The House of Shammai say, "They wash the hands and afterward mix the cup, for if you say they mix the cup first, [against this view is] a [precautionary] decree to prevent the liquids on the outer sides of the cup, which are unclean by reason of his hands' [touching them], from going back and making the cup unclean."

The Tosefta pertinent to the Mishnah is simply cited.

B. *But will not the hands make the cup itself unclean* [without reference to the liquids]?

Now the problem is raised: Whether or not there are liquids, why will the *hands* themselves not make the cup unclean? The question is asked as if we did not know the following answer. But as a matter of fact, what follows is established law:

The hands are in the second degree of uncleanness, and the [object unclean in] the second degree of uncleanness cannot [then] render [another object unclean] in the third [degree] in respect to profane foods [but only to Heave-offering]. But [this happens] only by means of liquids [unclean in the first degree].

The answer simply reviews the well-known law. Something unclean in the second degree of uncleanness cannot make another object unclean so far as ordinary food is concerned. This is done only by means of liquids, which are always unclean in the first degree and therefore render food unclean.

C. And the House of Hillel say, "They mix the cup and afterward wash the hands, for if you say they wash the hands first, [against this view is] a [precautionary] decree lest the liquids which are [already] on the hands become unclean on account of the cup and go and render the hands unclean."

We turn to the opinion of the House of Hillel, first of all citing the Tosefta.

D. *But will not the cup* [itself] *make the hands unclean?*
A vessel cannot render a man unclean.

The question addressed to the House of Shammai is repeated to the House of Hillel, which also have to answer it. The answer is simply that a man is *not* made unclean by a vessel, but only by something unclean from a primary source ["Father"] of uncleanness.

E. *But will they* [the hands] *not render the liquids which are in it* [the cup] *unclean?*

Here we are dealing with a vessel the outer part of which has been made unclean by liquid. The inner part is clean but the outer part is unclean. *Thus we have learned:*

[If] a vessel is made unclean on the outside by liquid, the outside is unclean, [52b] but its inside and its rim, handle, and haft are clean. If, however, the inside is unclean, the whole [cup] is unclean.

Now comes the problem of the liquid, just as with the Shammaites. Will not the liquid in the cup be made unclean? The answer is that we distinguish among the parts of a cup. The outer part is regarded as separate from the inner part. If the outer part is unclean, the inner part remains clean. But if the inner part is unclean, however, the whole is regarded as unclean. And this is an established tradition.

E. *What, then, do they* [the Houses] *dispute?*

If so, what can the issue possibly be, on which the Houses are supposed to differ? What we originally supposed to be under discusion is obviously not at issue at all.

The House of Shammai hold that it is prohibited to make use of a vessel whose outer parts are unclean by liquids, as a decree on account of the drippings. [There thus is] *no* [reason] *to decree* lest the liquids on the hands be made unclean by the cup.

The House of Shammai say we take precautions about a vessel whose outer part is unclean by liquids. Since we do take such a precaution, we do not have to worry that the liquid on the hands is going to be affected by the cup, for the cup to begin with is *not* going to be unclean.

And the House of Hillel reckon that it is permitted to make use of a vessel whose outer part is made unclean by liquids, *for drippings are unusual. But there is reason to take care lest* the liquids which are on the hands may be made unclean by the cup.

The Hillelites say you may make use of a cup which is wet and unclean on the outside. Drippings are not commonplace. But you do have to worry about the liquid on the hands, which may be made unclean by the cup. The difference, therefore, concerns the sort of precautions one takes in respect to the cup. This is a far cry from our original supposition. It strongly suggests the later authorities were not entirely clear about what had originally bothered the Houses and led to their contradictory rulings.

G. Another matter: [So that] immediately upon the washing of the hands [may come] the meal [itself].

We return to the Tosefta and cite its second reason for the Hillelite position.

What is the reason for this additional explanation?
This is what the House of Hillel said to the House of Shammai: "According to your reasoning, in saying that it is prohibited to make use of a cup whose outer parts are unclean, we decree on account of the drippings. But even so, [our opinion] is better, for immediately upon the washing of the hands [should come] the meal."

Now we explain why the second reason is given. No matter what you say, the Hillelite ruling is better, for it is appropriate that one start the meal immediately after washing hands.

To review the entire argument: Once again, the Talmud focuses upon the Tosefta, ignoring the simpler formulation of the law by the Mishnah. B and D are matched: The same question is directed toward each House. Each is assumed to have good, logical reasons for its opinion. The House of Shammai say a person washes the hands to keep the liquid on the outside of the cup from being made unclean by them. If touched by the unclean hands, the liquid would then go and make the cup itself unclean. But why should the hands themselves not make the cup unclean? B asks. This question feigns ignorance of the well-known law, immediately following, about the hands' degree of uncleanness. Obviously, the person who raised the question knew the answer, which was a commonplace, so asking the question represents a rhetorical and pedagogical device. The question is asked so that the information may be imparted in a pertinent way. The hands cannot make the cup unclean. But they can make liquid unclean, and in a first degree of uncleanness at that, so liquid will affect the cup.

The Hillelites then have to explain why the cup cannot make the hands unclean. The vessel is no different from the hands. Now in E a further, obvious question is raised: Will not the unclean liquid on the outside of the cup make the liquid *in* the cup unclean?

But the answer is equally obvious: No, the liquid on the outside has no affect on the liquid inside. (E is greatly augmented in the Palestinian version.)

Having elucidated the pertinent laws through questions and answers, the Talmud has now to explain the issue between the Houses. It is shown to be considerably less obvious than we had originally supposed. The House of Shammai say that, whatever the law may be, you should not use a cup the outer part of which is unclean by liquids lest the liquids drip. Since such a cup will not be used, however, then you do not have to worry about the cup's making the hands unclean. The House of Hillel say such a vessel may be used; therefore, you have to take care lest the liquid on the hands be made unclean by the cup.

G then explains why the House of Hillel are given a second reason: We take account of your view, but ours is better overall, because the meal should follow immediately upon the washing of the hands.

The House of Shammai say, "After wiping his hand with
the napkin . . ."

A. *Our rabbis have taught:*

The House of Shammai say, "He wipes his hands with the
napkin and lays it on the table, for if you say, 'on the cushion,'
[that view is wrong, for it is a precautionary] decree lest the
liquids which are on the napkin become unclean on account
of the cushion and go back and render the hands unclean."

Again we begin simply by citing the Tosefta pertinent to the
Mishnah. We then analyze it according to the positions of each
House, just as we did above.

B. *And will not the cushion* [itself] *render the napkin unclean?*

A vessel cannot make a vessel unclean.

The first, obvious question is: Why should we *not* worry about
the cushion? Will it not make the napkin unclean? The obvious
answer is that it cannot.

And will not the cushion [itself] *make the man unclean?*

A vessel cannot make a man unclean.

The second, still obvious, question is, Will the cushion not make
the man unclean? And the answer is equally obvious—it really
is the same as the one in regard to the cushion. The principle is no
different.

C. And the House of Hillel say, " 'On the cushion,' for if
you say, 'on the table,' [that opinion is wrong, for it is a] decree lest the liquids become unclean on account of the table
and go and render the food unclean."

We turn to the opinion of the House of Hillel, as elaborated by the Tosefta.

But will not the table render the food which is on it unclean?

We here deal with a table which is unclean in the second degree, and something unclean in the second degree does not render something unclean in the third degree in respect to unconsecrated food, except by means of liquids [which are always unclean in the first degree].

If we do not worry about the cushion, why should we not worry about the table? Will the table not make the food unclean? So why the concern about the cushion, which is a minor matter, if the table on which the food is set itself will make the food unclean! The answer is that the table is unclean in the second degree (like the hands) and does not make the food unclean. Only a wet table will do that, and we take for granted our table is dry.

D. *What* [principle] *do they dispute?*

The House of Shammai reckon that it is prohibited to make use of a table unclean in the second degree, as a decree on account of those who eat Heave-offering [which is rendered unfit by an object unclean in the second degree].

Once again, we have to discover the principle on which the Houses disagree. It is the status of the *table*. The House of Shammai say you cannot use a table unclean in the second degree. The reason is that, while ordinary food will not be affected by such a table, Heave-offering, which is a priestly gift, *is* going to be made unfit by it. We worry therefore about the priests who may be eating Heave-offering. Their food will be made unfit by the table unclean in the second degree.

And the House of Hillel reckon that it is permitted to make use of a table unclean in the second degree, for those who eat Heave-offering [the priests] are careful.

The Hillelites are more practical here. They say that people who eat Heave-offering are used to taking precautions to preserve its fitness against second degree uncleanness. Ordinary folk may make use of a table unclean in the second degree, and priests are not going to stumble thereby.

E. Another matter: There is no Scriptural requirement to wash the hands before eating unconsecrated food.

Again we have a second reason. This one is important, however, for it reviews the principles on which the reasons just now given actually are based. Hands are unclean in the second degree. They will not make ordinary food unclean, therefore unfit. So a man really does not have to wash his hands before eating unconsecrated, that is, ordinary, food.

What is the purpose of "another explanation"?
This is what the House of Hillel said to the House of Shammai: If you ask what is the difference in respect to food, concerning which we take care, and in respect to the hands, concerning which we do not take care—even in this regard [our opinion] is preferable, for there is no Scriptural requirement concerning the washing of the hands before eating unconsecrated food.
It is better that the hands should be made unclean, for there is no Scriptural basis for [washing] them, and let not the food be made unclean, concerning which there is a Scriptural basis [for concern about its uncleanness].

Why do the Hillelites need this other reason? The food has to be protected; the hands do not form an equally serious consideration. Therefore, we take care to protect the food, but we are not so concerned about the hands.

Notice the highly formal pattern according to which the several arguments we have reviewed are constructed. It is astonishingly consistent. We are now well aware that our chapter of the Talmud is constructed according to a simple but rigid pattern. First, the Tosefta will be cited, then the opinions of each House will be tested against certain obvious considerations; third, the underlying principle at issue will be spelled out, and that issue will be remote from the original terms of the argument; fourth, the second reason of the House of Hillel will be turned into a full argument against the House of Shammai, thus shown not irrelevant or tacked on, but central to the issue.

A–C thus are not much different from what has already been examined. D then brings the issue of the sort of table one may use, parallel to the foregoing, in which the condition of the cup is debated. Finally, in E, the House of Hillel is made to claim a distinction between the food and the hands. But, be that as it may, the Hillelites say their position is better, for what Scripture requires has to be done.

At this point we probably could construct our own Talmud, at least in the model of the present form. The rhetorical and critical principles are sufficiently clear so that, given other materials such as those before us, we might apply them on our own within the established pattern.

The House of Shammai say, They clean the house and afterward wash the hands . . .

A. *Our rabbis have taught:*

The House of Shammai say, "They clean the house and afterward wash the hands, for if you say, 'They wash the hands first,' it turns out that you spoil the food."

Once again we investigate the reasons behind the rulings of the two Houses. We begin with the Shammaites. They say you should sweep up first so that you will not moisten, therefore ruin, the crumbs of food.

B. *But the House of Shammai do not reckon that one washes the hands first.*
What is the reason?
On account of the crumbs.

The reason is now spelled out, as if it were not already clear. You do not first wash your hands, so that water will not spill onto the remaining food.

C. And the House of Hillel say, "If the servant is a disciple of a sage, he takes the crumbs which are as large as an olive [in bulk] and leaves the crumbs which are not so much as an olive [in bulk]."

The opinion of the House of Hillel now is cited, and its pertinence to the opinion of the House of Shammai is taken for granted. The Hillelites say there is not going to be food left over to be spoiled by the water. In that case, the two Houses are in agreement.

D. (*This view supports the opinion of R. Yohanan, for R. Yohanan said, "Crumbs which are not an olive in bulk may be deliberately destroyed."*)

This is the first interpolation from a later authority we have seen. Yohanan's saying is cited, because it is relevant to what has been said, but it does not fit into the established construction. It breaks what has been until now a perfect structure. Yohanan lived two centuries after the Houses, ca. A.D. 250, in the land of Israel.

E. *In what do they differ?*
The House of Hillel reckon that it is prohibited to employ

a servant who is an ignorant man, *and the House of Shammai reckon that* it is permitted to employ a servant who is an ignorant man.

The issue between the Houses is now made explicit. They differ not about spoiling food, but about the conditions of the meal. An ignorant man will not know he should collect the crumbs of a certain size. The Hillelites say you will not have such a servant to begin with, so you do not have to worry about the crumbs. The Shammaites say you may. All of this looks to be much after the fact.

F. *R. Yosé bar Hanina said in the name of R. Huna, "In our entire chapter the law is in accord with the House of Hillel, excepting this matter, in which the law is in accord with the House of Shammai."*

And R. Oshaia taught the matter contrariwise. And in this matter too the law is in accord with the House of Hillel.

Apart from D, which is an obvious interpolation, and F, which provides a general ruling on the final decision of the law, the construction before us is consistent with the foregoing. B explains the position of the House of Shammai, E draws the obvious conclusion that the Houses differ about exactly what their original sayings make clear is their disagreement.

The House of Shammai say, Light and food . . .

We cite a new Mishnaic paragraph. Instead of analyzing it, we shall first review a repertoire of pertinent stories. But the stories lead to the sort of inquiry we have just now completed. The form is different, but the point of analysis is not: Just what traditions belong to the respective Houses, and what are the reasons behind the traditions, or how are they accurately to be assigned? The story concerns two fourth-century masters and how they said the *Havdalah* blessings.

A. R. Huna bar Judah happened by the house of Rava. He *saw that Rava blessed the spices first.*

He said to him, "Since the House of Shammai and the House of Hillel did not dispute concerning the light, [it should come first].

"For it was taught: The House of Shammai say, 'Light, and food, spices, and Havdalah,' and the House of Hillel say, 'Light, and spices, and food, and Havdalah.' "

Rava answered him, "This is the opinion [= version] of R. Meir, but R. Judah says, 'The House of Shammai and the House of Hillel did not differ concerning the food, that it comes first, and concerning the Havdalah, that it is at the end.

" 'Concerning what did they differ?'

" 'Concerning the light and the spices.'

"For the House of Shammai say, 'The light and afterward for the spices.'

"And the House of Hillel say, 'The spices and afterward the light.' "

B. And R. Yohanan said, "The people were accustomed to act in accord with the House of Hillel as presented by R. Judah."

The Mishnah and Tosefta now fade into the background. The law is taken for granted, and its practical application comes to the fore. The story, concerning fourth-century Babylonian Amoraim, shows, however, that accurate traditions were earnestly sought out. Rava is able to show Huna that he has acted in accord with a sound version of the Houses' opinions. B is an independent saying, substantiating the action of Rava by pointing out that the ordinary folk likewise did as Judah said the House of Hillel had ruled.

The search for, and analysis of, accurate versions of what is attributed to the earlier authorities is a primary trait of the Talmudic argument. We discern no vested interests in a given version; if it can be shown that there are several views of what an earlier master had taught, then all have to be taken into account. The critical and rational spirit of Talmudic inquiry is revealed in many different ways; this is one of the most characteristic.

The House of Shammai say, "Who created . . ."

Once again, we begin with a citation of the Mishnah. Then the fourth-century authorities will try to explain the difference between the Houses.

A. Rava said, *"Concerning the word 'bara' [created], everyone agrees that 'bara' implies [the past tense]. They differ concerning 'boré' [creates]. The House of Shammai reckon that 'boré' means 'Who will create in the future.' And the House of Hillel reckon that 'boré' also means what was created [in the past]."*

Rava claims that the issue is the meaning of the present-tense form of the verb *boré,* who creates. The Shammaites say *boré* refers to creation in the future. The House of Hillel say that the participle *boré* may refer also to creation in the past.

B. *R. Joseph objected, " 'Who forms light and creates darkness' [Isaiah 45:7], 'Creates mountains and forms the wind' [Amos 4:13], 'Who creates the heavens and spreads them out' " [Isaiah 47:5].*

Joseph rejects the Shammaite position out of hand. We have numerous examples of the use of the form *boré* to refer to what was done in the long-distant past. The Shammaites cannot have held otherwise, for they are presumed to be as well informed as the Hillelites.

"But," R. Joseph said, "Concerning 'bara' and 'boré' everyone agrees that [the words] refer to the past. They differ as to
whether one should say 'light' or 'lights.'

"The House of Shammai reckon there is one light in the
fire.

"And the House of Hillel reckon that there are many lights
in the fire."

Joseph provides a better interpretation of the difference between the Houses. They are supposed to have agreed on the meaning of the verb "to create." That is no problem. The issue is
whether one speaks of *light* or *lights*. And that devolves upon the
nature of fire. Then the editor of the *Gemara* supplies a Tannaitic
tradition in support of Joseph's interpretation of the dispute. The
curious thing, of course, is that the Houses *do* differ about *creates*
vs. *created* [*boré/bara*], as much as about *light/lights,* but no one
is able to explain that difference!

C. We have a Tannaitic teaching along the same lines:
The House of Hillel say to the House of Shammai, "There
are many illuminations in the light."

To review the whole: Rava explains the issue between the
Houses. The House of Shammai prefer the past tense, *who created,* for the blessing is on account of the fire which has already
been created in the past. The present participle, e.g., *boré,* may
imply the present or the future tense. The House of Shammai
therefore reject the present participial form of the verb "create,"
for, as stated, the blessing is for fire already created. The House
of Hillel reject this view—so Rava. In B, Joseph proves the difference cannot be as Rava suggests, for Scripture contains present
participles referring to the very acts of creation which, everyone
knows, took place in the long-distant past. That is the reason Joseph quotes the several Scriptures before us. These constitute solid
grammatical evidence.

The Houses therefore cannot be thought to have differed on that issue, for the House of Shammai know Scriptures. The difference between the Houses, rather, is about whether one says *light* or *lights*. The House of Shammai prefer the singular, the House of Hillel, the plural, for the reasons given. C then gives us a formulation, attributed to a Tannaitic authority, of the same issue; it looks like a fragment of a larger debate between the Houses. But we have no further evidence of the rest of the debate. And Joseph does not account for the obvious fact that the Houses *do* differ about *created* vs. *create;* since he cannot find a rational basis for the difference, he simply prefers to ignore the evidence that there was one. Bad form indeed!

A blessing is not said . . .

The Mishnah is cited in abbreviated form. The rule is that you may not say a blessing either over the light or over the spices of gentiles.

A. *Certainly,* [in the case of] *the light* [of idolators, one should not say a blessing] *because it did not rest on the Sabbath. But what is the reason that for spices* [one may not say the blessing]?

We take for granted that there is a good reason for not blessing the light of the gentiles. But why should you not bless over their spices? Rav will provide the answer.

R. Judah said in the name of Rav, "*We here deal with a banquet held by idolators,* because the run-of-the-mill banquet held by idolators is for the sake of idolatry."

Rav's reason is that whenever spices are used, it is going to be for idolatrous purposes.

B. *But since it has been taught at the end of the clause,*

"Or over the light or spices of idolatry," *we must infer that
the beginning of the clause does not deal with idolatry.*

Rav's reason is challenged. The Mishnah already includes a
reference to the spices used for idolatrous purposes. So the first
reference must be to something other than spices used for gentile
worship, for the Mishnah does not repeat itself.

C. R. *Hanina from Sura said,* "[The master explains] *what
is the reason:* What is the reason that they do not bless the
light or spices of idolators? Because the run-of-the-mill banquet held by idolators is for the sake of idolatry."

Hanina's explanation is not a bad one. The Mishnah will sometimes give a rule, then spell it out. In effect Hanina says the Mishnah sometimes will repeat itself—just like modern writers—for the
purpose of making clear the meaning only implied in what is said
just once. Repetition is not always for the sake of introducing a
new point; it sometimes serves pedagogical purposes.

To review the whole: The simple rule given in the Mishnah is
examined. The reason taken for granted in respect to the gentile's
light in fact has not yet been adduced; it will come later on. The
issue of spices is raised, and this permits Rav's comment on the
Mishnah to be stated: The idolators' spice normally serves their
cult. The language of Rav's saying is curious. It begins in Aramaic—
"we deal here"—but then the substantive rule—"because . . ."—
is given in concise, Mishnaic Hebrew, again as though cited from
some already-known formula. B then challenges Rav's interpretation of the Mishnah by analyzing the language of the Mishnah itself, a fair test. Since the latter part of the rule explicitly refers
to idolatry, it may be assumed that the former part does *not* deal
with idolatry, contrary to Rav's assertion. Hanina in C explains
the Mishnah's language in another way. The first clause is expanded by the second, which provides the reason. But this seems
forced.

Our rabbis have taught:

A. One may bless a light which has rested on the Sabbath, but one may not bless a light which has not rested on the Sabbath.

B. *And what is the meaning of* "which has not rested on the Sabbath"?

We earlier alluded to the light "which has not rested on the Sabbath." What can this possibly mean?

[53a] *Shall we say* it has not rested on the Sabbath on account of the work [which has been done with it, including] even work which is permitted?

The obvious answer is posited. Work has been done by this light. But what sort of work? Some things, after all, may be done on the Sabbath.

C. *And has it not been taught:* They do bless light [kindled on the Sabbath for] a woman in confinement or a sick person.

We continue to belabor the obvious. There is work you may do by a light on the Sabbath—for example, tending to the needs of sick people.

D. R. Nahman bar Isaac said, "*What is the meaning of* 'which enjoyed Sabbath-rest'? Which enjoyed Sabbath rest on account of work the doing of which is a transgression [on the Sabbath]."

Nahman b. Isaac now says what was clear at the outset. The light has been used for prohibited work.

E. *We have learned likewise in a baraita:*
They may bless a lamp which has been burning throughout the day to the conclusion of the Sabbath.

At the end we cite a *baraita,* that is, a tradition attributed to the second-century masters, the Tannaim, which reinforces our conclusion.

Let us review the argument as a whole. The Talmud introduces materials pertinent to the theme of the Mishnah, but not directly alluded to in the Mishnah's own laws. The first item has to do with the Sabbath-rest of flame; this will recur in the next pericope. A gives the rule, then B begins the analysis. Obviously, the question of what one might possibly mean by a flame's "resting on the Sabbath" has to be answered. But the analysis is obtuse: Do we mean to exclude even light which has served a permissible purpose? Obviously not. C then explains the question: There are things you may do with the light on the Sabbath. Nahman b. Isaac, in D, then says what everyone knows to begin with, and the *baraita,* E, is cited to show that his interpretation has excellent precedent. Here again the artifice of the editor accounts for what must otherwise appear to be a foolish inquiry into obvious things. The editor wishes to make a simple distinction about blessing light which has not rested on the Sabbath. So instead of citing E, he raises in B the possible alternatives and in C-D dismisses them, one by one.

Our rabbis have taught:
A. They bless [a light] kindled by a gentile from an Israelite, or by an Israelite from a gentile, but they do not bless [a light] kindled by a gentile from a gentile.

We now begin the analysis of a new teaching, one which specifies which light may, and which may not, be blessed.

B. *What is the reason one does not do so* [from a light kindled by] *a gentile from a gentile?*
Because it did not enjoy Sabbath-rest.

First we have a repetition of what we already know. You cannot bless a light of a gentile because it did not "enjoy Sabbath-rest."

C. *If so, lo, [a light kindled by] an Israelite from a gentile also has not enjoyed Sabbath-rest.*

We challenge that reason, which cannot be sufficient, for an Israelite may kindle from a gentile. So the Israelite's light has its beginning in a flame which did not "enjoy Sabbath-rest"!

D. *And if you say this prohibited [light] has vanished, and the one [in hand] is another and was born in the hand of the Israelite, [how will you deal] with this teaching?*
He who brings out a flame to the public way [on the Sabbath] is liable [for violating the Sabbath rule against carrying from private to public property].
Now why should he be liable? What he raised up he did not put down, and what he put down he did not raise up.

One solution is to posit that the light of the gentile has vanished, and in the Israelite's hand is a new light. But that solution is impossible. For the law explicitly takes for granted the "unity" of a flame. You cannot take something out from private property to the public road on the Sabbath. If you take out a flame, you are liable for punishment. But if the flame you put down is different, you should not be liable, as is clearly explained.

E. *But [we must conclude] that the prohibited [flame] is present, but when he blesses, it is over the additional [flame], which is permitted, that he blesses.*

The best solution is that in addition to the original flame there is additional flame, which has begun after the prohibited flame, and that is the part which one is allowed to bless.

F. *If so, a gentile['s flame kindled] from a gentile['s flame] also* [should be permitted].

That is a good solution, it is now argued, but it should likewise apply to a gentile's flame kindled from a gentile's flame. That too is a new flame, or there is an additional part which is not prohibited. That is the point of F.

That is true, but [it is prohibited by] decree, on account of the first gentile and the first flame [of light kindled on the Sabbath by the gentile].

We explicitly agree that the same principle applies, but we take extra precautions in regard to the gentile's flame.

We shall see how the argument is put together as a whole. The earlier discussion assumes greater importance. It has prepared the way for the substantive analysis before us. A provides the important rule about not blessing a light kindled by a gentile from a gentile's light. B gives the reason, which we already knew from the antecedent pericope. But this reason is flawed, for the light kindled by an Israelite from a gentile is in the same category as one kindled by a gentile from a gentile; neither one has rested on the Sabbath. D then presses the question home. The obvious answer is that the light is changing, therefore the Israelite may use the gentile's light, since it is not the same one that has been improperly used on the Sabbath.

But that answer is impossible, for we have a teaching which explicitly rejects the distinction between the original light and the one now in hand. On the Sabbath a person is not supposed to move something from the private to the public domain. We are explicitly informed that that rule applies to a flame. But if the flame changes in character, then why should a person be prohibited from moving it? What he takes up in the private domain is not the same flame as he puts down in the public domain. E then draws the necessary inference, the prohibited flame (which has "worked," not rested, on the Sabbath) indeed is present. But *together* with it is additional flame, produced by the original. It is that part of the flame which one may bless.

F is absolutely necessary. If so, we cannot distinguish between an Israelite's kindling from a gentile's flame, and a gentile's doing so. G provides the answer. Logically, one cannot. But the gentile's flame is prohibited because of its illicit origin. On this Rashi comments, "If you permit a flame in the case of a gentile who kindled from a gentile after dark, one will end up blessing a light in the case of a gentile who kindled while it was still the Sabbath day; and it is that very light itself, to which no further light has been added, that one might then bless right after dark."

Once again, let us stand back from the materials before us and ask about their place within the larger Talmudic interpretation and construction of reality. The first thing we notice is that the Jews take for granted they may make some decisions in respect to gentiles. They may decide whether or not to make use of light kindled by gentiles or reflected from their homes. Now to the gentiles it can hardly have mattered whether or not Jews say blessings over their candles, or sniff their incense, or sip their wine. Being people of good will, they will not have objected to the Jews' doing so. But what difference can it make to them if the Jews do not? To the Jews that decision is represented as a matter of some weight, as if it truly matters.

That representation revises the realities of power confronting Israel. It imparts to the Jews' decisions in respect to the gentiles an importance quite incommensurate with either the character of those decisions or the worldly power of the Jews who made them. And lending importance to what one does—whether known or not—with the gentile's flame is part of a much larger tendency of the rabbis. That tendency was to interpret what the people did in terms of a much larger, grander scale of transcendent values than might be implied by the significance of the actions themselves.

The Jews did not have much say about their own fate. The power available within the Jewish community was derivative, episodic, and inconsequential. It derived from the wishes of men and from forces eternal to Jewry. What Jews did, did not make a great deal of difference in the larger world in which they found themselves. All they could really control, in the end, was their private affairs. So the rabbis made the issues of those humble lives into matters of enormous cosmic consequence. The placing of a napkin expressed a grand, invisible concern for the unseen relationships of purity and impurity. And placing the napkin in the correct way assured that the man would be clean, just like a priest in the holy Temple. It expressed the view that here is not an ordinary man, eating his piece of bread and drinking his beer in a little hovel in the hot and dusty Babylonian plains. Here is a priest. The hovel is the Temple. The table is the altar. God is being worshiped and served. What incongruity between the reality and the interpretation of reality!

By this point in our consideration of the details of the laws and how they were decided, it is easy to forget the larger context in which they are set to make sense. But the trivialities are commensurate, as I said, to the power in the hands of the Jews, to the sorts of things they actually could decide and control. What the rabbis accomplished was to impart to these trivialities so great an importance that ordinary folk could conceive themselves significant beyond their perceived weakness. If the Jews could not determine the natural course of history, the rabbis would teach them about their power in the supernatural structure of reality. That is the importance of the messianic claim made in behalf of keeping the "Torah of Moses our rabbi" by the rabbis themselves.

So said one of them, "If Israel obeys the will of their Father in Heaven, then no nation or race can rule over them." "When Israel casts words of Torah to the ground, the heathen are able to decree and carry out their decrees." "When the haughty people will disappear within Israel, then the haughty gendarmes will disappear among the Iranians." These words are not idle homilies. They provide the key to understanding why such stress was laid upon the legal and social reformation of Israel. It is through the concrete achievement of the teachings of the Torah, here and now, that the rabbis intended to bring redemption. Defining the will of God in terms of deeds people actually could do, expressing "Torah" in matters of the household and the hearth—these were ways to make concrete, therefore open to attainment, the large and weighty promises of the prophets. If all you can do is decide what food you will eat and how you will consume it, or whether or not you will recite a blessing over a candle lit by a gentile, then you are fortunate indeed to believe your decision bears consequence even for the cosmic order of being. True, you may be deluded. But the ultimate test of the rabbis' convictions is yet to come.

Our rabbis have taught:

A. [If] one was walking outside of the village and saw a light, if the majority [of the inhabitants of the village] are gentiles, he does not bless it. If the majority are Israelites, he blesses it.

B. *Lo, the statement is self-contradictory. You have said,* "If the majority are gentiles, he does not bless it." *Then if they are evenly divided, he may bless it.*

But then it teaches, "If the majority are Israelites, he may bless." *Then if they are evenly divided, he may not bless it.*

C. *Strictly speaking, even if they are evenly divided, he may bless. But since in the opening clause* [the language is], "The majority are gentiles," *in the concluding clause,* [the same language is used:] "The majority are Israelites."

The *baraita,* or Tannaitic tradition, A, is subjected to the sort of quibble for which the Talmud is (unjustly) famous. What is the rule if the inhabitants were evenly divided? The implication of the first half of the rule is that one may bless the light; of the second, one may not. C then reduces the quibble; it is a matter of the language used in the tradition. The formulation will be consistent, even though it may produce an (immaterial) measure of obscurity. The Palestinian Talmud explicitly rejects this tradition and says if only one Jew is present, the light may be blessed.

Our rabbis have taught:

A. [If] a man was walking outside of a village and saw a child with a torch in his hand, he makes inquiries about him. If he is an Israelite, he may bless [the light]. If he is a gentile, he may not bless.

B. *Why do we speak of a child? Even an adult also* [would be subject to the same rule].

C. *Rav Judah said in the name of Rav, "In this case we are dealing with* [a time] *near sunset. As to a gentile, it will be perfectly clear that he certainly is a gentile* [for an Israelite would not use the light immediately after sunset]. *If it is a child, I might say it is an Israelite child who happened to take up* [the torch]."

The analysis of the language of the *baraita* is consequential. The specification of "child" seems strange. Rav provides an answer (more persuasive then than now): It will be obvious whether an adult is gentile or Jewish, for, if he has a light right after sunset, he assuredly is not a Jew. But a child might not be so scrupulous.

Our rabbis have taught:

A. [If] one was walking outside of a village and saw a light, if it was as thick as the opening of a furnace, he may bless it, and if not, he may not bless it.

The decisive principle is that you must bless a flame only if it is used for the purpose of light. But if a light does not serve for illumination, but for some other, extraneous purpose, it cannot serve for the blessing in *Havdalah*. We shall now consider a whole series of contradictory opinions, and each is going to be resolved in the same way. If you say one may bless such-and-such a light, it is because it is used for illumination. If you say one may not, it is because the light is not used for illumination, but for some other purpose.

B. *One Tanna* [authority] [says], "They may bless the light of a furnace," *and another Tanna* [says], "They may not bless it."

C. *There is no difficulty. The first speaks at the beginning* [of the fire], *the other at the end.*

Here is the first such effort. The furnace may be blessed at the outset, for the fire is large and does not serve only to heat up the coals. At the end the flame is kept burning only to keep the oven hot, in no sense for illumination.

D. *One authority says,* "They may bless the light of an oven or a stove," *and another authority says,* "They may not bless it."

There is no problem. The former speaks of the beginning, the latter of the end.

One authority says, "They may bless the light of the synagogue and the school house," *and another authority says,* "They may not bless it."

There is no problem. The former speaks [of a case in which] *an important man is present, the latter* [of a case in which] *an important man is not present.*

Now we have a synagogue. If an important man is present, the light is kindled in his honor, not for illumination. Where the light is not for illumination, it may not be blessed.

F. *And if you want, I shall explain both teachings as apply-*
ing to a case in which an important man *is present. There*
still is no difficulty. The former [teaching speaks of a case in
which] *there is a beadle* [who eats in the synagogue], *the latter*
in which there is none.

We begin to make things still more complicated. What is decisive is not the important person's presence, but the beadle. Perhaps the light comes from the fire kindled by the beadle to warm
his food. Then it may not be blessed.

The last case involves moonlight. If there is moonlight, then the
light is not kindled for illumination.

And if you want, I shall explain both teachings as applying
to a case in which a beadle is present. There still is no diffi-
culty. The former teaching [speaks of a case in which] *there*
is moonlight, the latter in which there is no moonlight.

We shall review the argument as a whole: A takes for granted
a person may bless the light of a furnace. B informs us some say
he may not do so, and C resolves the contradiction. The authorities do not really differ from one another. At the outset the furnace, presumed to be for the burning of lime, is lit to burn the
lime, therefore it may not be used. Afterward it is kept lit for the
purpose of light, so it may be used. D and E follow the same pattern. The oven is lit for cooking; the light may not be blessed. It
is kept lit for the light; now the illumination is acceptable for the
blessing. In E the problem again is the purpose for which the light
is kindled. If an important person—this is a technical term, referring to a distinguished Talmudic authority—is present, the light
is kindled in *his* honor, not for light, and may not be blessed.
Otherwise, it may be blessed. The principle here is the same as
applies to not blessing light or spices prepared for the dead.

F then is an elegant spinning out of the possibilities of the synagogue. If an important man is present, it may still be permitted to

bless the light; if there is a beadle, it is permitted, for he eats in the synagogue and may have kindled the flame for light to eat by. Or both traditions speak of a case in which there is a beadle *and* an important man; if there is moonlight, the lights in the synagogue are for the important man, not the beadle's meal, and it is prohibited. This sort of thing can produce an infinite number of further qualifications; it is an open-ended progression. But when I spoke of the Talmud as a continuing conversation, this is not what I meant.

Our rabbis have taught:

A. [If] they were sitting in the school house, and light was brought before them—

The House of Shammai say, "Each one blesses for himself."

And the House of Hillel say, "One blesses for all of them, as it is said, 'In the multitude of people is the King's glory'" [Proverbs 14:28].

B. *Certainly* [we can understand the position of the House of Hillel because] *the House of Hillel explain their reason.*

But what is the reason of the House of Shammai?

They reckon [it as they do] *on account of* [avoiding] *interruption in* [Torah-study] *in the school house.*

C. *We have a further Tannaitic tradition to the same effect:*

The members of the house of Rabban Gamaliel did not say [the blessing], "Good health" [after a sneeze] in the school house on account of the interruption [of study] in the school house.

The "reason" of the House of Hillel is a gloss; the Shammaite saying has not been glossed, so the Talmud asks for their reason. A *baraita* tells us that the same consideration was important to Gamaliel, toward the end of the first century. By now it is commonplace to expect that after an Amoraic discussion of a Tannaitic tradition, a further Tannaitic saying will be adduced in evidence of the correctness of the Amoraic interpretation. Here again we conclude that if the Tannaitic saying was known at the outset, the pericope has been constructed so as to give full expression to the Amoraic analysis before the decisive evidence is adduced.

They say a benediction neither on the light nor on the spices of the dead . . .
A. *What is the reason?*
The light is made for the honor [of the deceased], *the spices to remove the bad smell.*

The principle, already established, that you bless light only if it is used for its normal purpose as illumination, is extended to spices. The light is not for illumination, but for the honor of the corpse. The spices are not for the pleasure of their scent, but as a deodorant.

B. Rav Judah in the name of Rav said, "[Light made for] whoever [is of such importance that] they take out [a light] before him both by day and by night is not blessed. [And light made for] whoever [is not important, so that] they take out [a light] before him only by night, is blessed."

Rav gives the same principle as was applied in the earlier discussion. But he applies that principle to the light kindled in honor of the corpse. Much depends upon the importance of the corpse. Rav explains the several distinctions.

C. R. Huna said, "They do not bless spices of the privy and oil made to remove the grease."

Huna's is an independent saying, which applies the same principle to other cases. But then we challenge the entire principle: Do we say things must be used only for their primary purpose? But we have a contrary rule.

D. *Does this saying imply that wherever [spice] is not used for smell, they do not bless over it? It may be objected:*

He who enters the stall of a spice dealer and smells the odor, even though he sat there all day long, blesses only one time. He who enters and goes out repeatedly blesses each time.

And lo, here is a case in which it is not used for the scent, and still he blesses.

We have a rule which seems to contradict the established principle. How can a law for a specific case contradict the general principle governing the determination of all laws? The solution is simple: The case is not exceptional at all.

E. *Yes, but it also is used for the odor—so that people will smell and come and purchase it.*

The Mishnah is supplied with a rational basis. As is already obvious, the issue will be whether the spice or light is prepared for its normal use, in which case it may be blessed, or for some extrinsic purpose, in which case it may not be blessed. The material to be blessed thus must be used in a normal way. A explains that the light and spices are in abnormal usage. B brings us back to the problem reviewed above, concerning blessing light of a furnace, oven, stove, or synagogue; the principle has not changed, and the applications here are not original. Rav in B simply says what was already clear in the Mishnah as interpreted in A.

C introduces new materials, which illustrate the same principle. Then D raises the fundamental challenge to all of the foregoing, though it responds directly to C. If spice is not used for its odor, are we not to bless it? The objection draws on a rule which takes for granted, in both of its cases, that one does bless the odor of the spice in a spice-dealer's stall. And, it is made explicit, that is not used for the scent. It is for sale. E says the odor is not secondary, for in order for people to buy the spice, they want to smell it.

Our rabbis have taught:

A. If one was walking outside of a village and smelled a scent, if most of the inhabitants are idolators, he does not bless it. If most are Israelites, he blesses it.

R. Yosé says, "Even if most are Israelites, he *still* may not bless, because Israelite women use incense for witchcraft."

B. *But do they "all" burn incense for witchcraft!*

A small part is for witchcraft, and a small part is also for finishing garments, which yields a larger part not used for scent, and wherever the majority [of the incense] is not used for scent, one does not bless it.

C. R. Hiyya bar Abba said in the name of R. Yohanan, "He who walks on the eve of the Sabbath in Tiberias and at the end of the Sabbath in Sepphoris and smells an odor does not bless it, because it is presumed to have been made only to perfume garments."

D. *Our rabbis taught:* If one was walking in the gentiles' market and was pleased to scent the spices, he is a sinner.

The rules in A are further elaborations of the foregoing principle. It is taken for granted that the scent is from incense used for idolatry. Yosé adds that Israelite women also make illicit use of spices. B then asks (incredulously) whether it is alleged that *all* Israelite women practice witchcraft. The answer is that some goes for that purpose, some for finishing garments, leaving only a minor part of the spices to be used for scent alone. The use of spices for cleaning garments is then illustrated by C. D is tacked on, but it is a continuation of A.

We notice that the rabbis are not unaware of the religious practices of the ordinary folk, just as they take account of the Samaritans' views. On the contrary, the pages of the Talmud reveal an endless conflict between the rabbis and other Jews. Here we find the laconic observation, not accompanied by cries of wrath or woe, that Jewish women practice witchcraft. What is meant by "witchcraft" is of no consequence to us. What is striking is that the rabbis' formulation of the law is going to take account of the unpleasant or distasteful doings of other Jews. They are not attempting to create laws for angels, beings without the impulse to do evil, without the pressures and needs of fleshly, frail mortals. They legislate so as to form a perfect society, a people made in the model of the Torah. But they do so in full awareness that the people to be perfected and regenerated are flesh and blood, unreliable, impetuous, credulous, doubting, human. And so too are the rabbis themselves.

That is what makes the effort noble: the capacity to face up to people's ornery or slovenly ways, yet to want to make them something more and better. And what makes the hope real and plausible is the means chosen for the task, the instrument of law and lawful ordering of the behavior and beliefs of the folk. What finally gives the rabbis their optimistic willingness to struggle with people who are assumed to practice witchcraft is their faith in three things: God, who made the people what they are, the Torah, which has the power to change and reshape them, and the Jews themselves, who come from worthy fathers and mothers, people who could make a golden calf, but who also could say, "We shall do and obey."

[53b] **They bless the light once it has been used . . .**

A. Rav Judah said in the name of Rav, "Not that he has actually used it, but if anyone stood near enough so that he might use the light, even at some distance, [he may say the blessing]."

B. So too R. Ashi said, "We have learned this teaching even [concerning] those at some distance."

Rav and Ashi both interpret the original rule about using the light. It is not that you have actually to make use of the light. But you have to be *able* to use it. We shall now have an objection, based on a Toseftan tradition:

C. *It was objected* [on the basis of the following teaching]: If one had a light hidden in the folds of his cloak or in a lamp, or saw the flame but did not make use of its light, or made use of the light but did not [actually] see the flame, he may not say the blessing. [He may say the blessing only when] he [both] sees the flame and uses its light.

Rav's and Ashi's principle thus contradicts the rule that you have got both to see the flame and to use the light. We shall apply that rule to show the contradiction to Rav's and Ashi's interpretation of the Mishnah.

Certainly one finds cases in which one may use the light and not see the flame. *This may be when the light is in a corner.*
But where do you find a case in which one may see the flame and not make use of its light. *Is it not when he is at a distance?*

If you examine the cases to which the Toseftan tradition may refer, you come to one which has to stand against the principle of Rav and Ashi. A person may both use the light and not see the flame. But when can you see the flame but not use it? Surely that is when you are at a distance. And so Ashi and Rav are wrong, for the case implied by the Tosefta contradicts their interpretation of the Mishnah. But no, we have a way out of that dilemma:

D. *No, it is when the flame keeps on flickering.*

Rav's comment on the Mishnah is important: The law is not to be interpreted literally to mean that the light has *actually* been used. It merely must be *possible* to use it, whether one actually does so or not.

The objection of C is serious. The several cases listed in the Tosefta's tradition seem to include one involving light at some distance. D replies that the cases involve not distance but the quality of the light iself. This satisfactorily takes care of the potential challenge to Rav's interpretation.

C–D are a good example of the Talmud's testing its interpretation of the Mishnah against potentially contradictory cases or rules. The authority of Rav, the first great Babylonian Talmudic authority, along with Samuel, and founder of the study of the Mishnah in Babylonia, is insufficient against contrary evidence or reason. Reason, not authority, consensus, or appeal to piety, is decisive.

A. *Our rabbis have taught:*
They may say a blessing over glowing coals, but not over dying coals ['*omemot*].

B. *What is meant by* glowing coals?
R. Hisda said, "If one puts a chip into them and it kindles on its own, [these are] all [glowing coals]."

C. *It was asked: Is the word* '*omemot* ['*alef*] *or* '*omemot* ['*ayin*]?
Come and hear, for R. Hisda b. Abdimi said, "The cedars in the garden of God could not darken ['*amamuhu*] it" [Ezekiel 31:8].

The elucidation of the *baraita* poses no difficulties. The word for glowing coals is '*omemot,* spelled with an '*alef,* one of two Hebrew letters not sounded in Babylonia (called "silent" letters). C then asks for the spelling of the word: with an '*alef,* or with an '*ayin?* Evidence is drawn from Scripture. But the Mishnah uses an '*alef*—it has not been corrected to conform to the result of the *Gemara's* discussion!

A. And Rava said, "He must make actual use of it."

B. *And how* [near must one be]?

Ulla said, "So that he may make out the difference between an *issar* and a *pundion* [two small coins]."

Hezekiah said, "So that he may make out the difference between a *meluzma* [a weight] of Tiberias and one of Sepphoris."

C. *Rav Judah would say the blessing* [for the light of the] *house of Adda the waiter* [which was nearby].

Rava would say the blessing [for the light of the] *house of Guria bar Hama.*

Abbaye would say the blessing [for the light of the] *house of Bar Abbuha.*

D. R. Judah said in the name of Rav, "They do not go looking for the light in the way they go looking for [means to carry out other] commandments."

R. Zira said, "At the outset, I used to go looking [for light]. Now that I have heard this teaching of R. Judah in the name of Rav, I too will not go searching, but if one comes my way, I shall say the blessing over it."

Rava's opinion, A, brings us back to the interpretation of the Mishnah: People bless the light once it has been used. Rav has been quoted by Rav Judah, a master in the generation preceding Rava, that you do not have to make actual use of the fire. Rava says you must really use it. Then how near must you be? The question in effect pertains to the opinions of both Rav and Rava. B provides two answers, then C gives three examples of the actual practice of important masters. The assumption is that the practice of a rabbi is as adequate evidence of what to do as the theoretical statement of a law. The rabbi is a living commentary on the Torah.

D contains a further ruling of Rav Judah in Rav's name: You do not have to take the trouble to find the fire. Then Zira's saying is given to make clear that once an authority has given his opinion, others may take advantage of its leniency. But you must take

the trouble of finding the means of carrying out other commandments.

He who ate [and did not say Grace] . . .

We cite the Mishnah once again. If a person forgot to say
Grace, and so goes away from the place where he ate, does he
have to go back to recite the Grace? Or may he say it wherever
he remembers? The Hillelites take the latter, lenient position, the
Shammaites the former, strict one.

A. *R. Zevid, and some say, R. Dimi bar Abba, said, "The
dispute* [between the Houses] *applies to a case of forgetfulness, but in a case in which a person deliberately* [omitted
Grace], *all agree that he should return to his place and say the
blessing."*

Zevid now tries to clarify what is at issue. He says the Houses
differ concerning a person who forgot to say Grace. But if a person deliberately omitted the prayer, he is required to go back to
where he ate.

This is perfectly obvious. It is [explicitly] *taught, "And he
forgot."*

The *Gemara* points out that Zevid's interpretation is not necessary. The Mishnah has already stated what he claims is "his" interpretation. So we have to explain what Zevid's interpretation
was meant to imply.

B. *What might you have said? That is the rule even where
it was intentional, but the reason that the Tanna taught, "And
he forgot,"* is to tell you how far the House of Shammai was
willing to go [in requiring the man to go back to where he
ate. They did so even if a man accidentally forgot]. *Thus we*

are *taught* [the contrary. Even if one forgot, unintentionally, he must go back].

Zevid's effort at defining the issue between the Houses proves hopeless. What he says is at issue is explicitly stated in the Mishnah itself. B then tries to straighten things out.

A. *It was taught:*

The *baraita* now provides a dialogue between the Houses, supplementing their simple disagreement about the rule. This is a kind of debate. Each side makes clear the advantage of its own viewpoint and the disadvantage of that of the opposition.

The House of Hillel said to the House of Shammai, "According to your opinion, someone who ate on the top of the Temple Mount and forgot and went down without saying Grace should go back to the top of the Mount and say the blessing."

The House of Shammai said to the House of Hillel, "According to your opinion, someone who forgot a purse on the top of the Temple Mount would not go back and retrieve it.

"For his own sake, he [assuredly] will go back. For the sake of Heaven [should he] not all the more so [go back]?"

After the debate the editor provides a couple of stories to make the point that people who are strict with themselves are rewarded, but those who are slovenly in the performance of their religious duties are punished supernaturally.

B. *There were these two disciples. One did it* [forgot Grace] *accidentally, and, following the rule of the House of Shammai,* [went back to bless], *and found a purse of gold. And one did it deliberately* [omitted Grace], *and following the rule of the House of Hillel* [did not go back to say it], *and a lion ate him.*

C. *Rabbah b. b. Hanna was traveling in a caravan. He ate and was sated but* [forgot and] *did not say Grace.*

He said, "What shall I do? If I tell the men [of the caravan with me] *that it is to bless* [that I go back], *they will say to me, 'Bless here. Wherever you say the blessing, you are saying the blessing to the Merciful* [God].' *It is better that I tell them I have forgotten a golden dove."*

So he said to them, "Wait for me, for I have forgotten a golden dove."

He went back and blessed and found a golden dove.

Ordinary folk are presumed to be uninterested in the Houses' rules. Now the Talmud will explain a detail in the foregoing story about Rabbah. The dove is an important symbol in his story. Why?

D. *And why was a dove so important?*

Because the community of Israel is compared to a dove, as it is written, "The wings of the dove are covered with silver, and her pinions with the shimmer of gold" [Psalm 58:14]. *Just as the dove is saved only by her wings, so Israel is saved only by the commandments.*

To review: The little debate between the Houses, A, leaves the Shammaites with the last word, therefore in the winning position. Each side takes the position of the other to its logical extreme. But the Hillelites can only point up the Shammaites' severity, while the Shammaites produce a theological absurdity out of the Hillelite position. B then tells a story showing that true piety is rewarded. In this case the disciple who did not say the prayer accidentally, not intentionally, nonetheless followed the Shammaite rule and was rewarded. The disciple who deliberately neglected the Grace and said it in some other place was eaten by a lion. The story of the good disciple is then topped by Rabbah b. b. Hanna, who went to some trouble to return to the place in which he had eaten, though he cannot be thought to have deliberately moved on to say Grace in some other place. He was appropriately rewarded. Then the key detail in that story is explained.

Until when can he say the Grace? Until the food is digested in his bowels . . .

A. How long does it take to digest the food?

R. Yohanan said, "As long as one is no longer hungry."

Resh Laqish said, "As long as one [still] is thirsty on account of his meal."

B. *R. Yemar bar Shelamia said to Mar Zutra—and some say, Rav Yemar bar Shizbi said to Mar Zutra—"Did Resh Laqish really say this? And did not R. Ammi say in the name of Resh Laqish, 'How long does it take to digest a meal? The time it takes to go four miles.'"*

There is no problem: Here [we speak of] a big meal, there [we speak of] a small meal.

A comments on the Mishnah, B then analyzes A in terms of other sayings of the master represented therein. Resh Laqish has two explanations for the Mishnah, and these have to be distinguished, therefore harmonized. It takes a walk of four miles to digest the big meal, and the end of thirst marks the digestion of a small one.

If wine came to them . . .

Once more we return to the Mishnah. The citation is abbreviated. You will want to reread the entire paragraph of the Mishnah. We are going to analyze only the part about saying *Amen* after an Israelite, but not after a gentile or Samaritan.

A. *This implies that in the case of an Israelite['s saying Grace], even though one has not heard the entire blessing, he responds [Amen].*

But if he has not heard [the whole Grace], *how can he have performed his duty by doing so* [assuming he has eaten also?

For he has to hear the entire Grace to carry out his obligation
to say Grace].

What good does it do to respond *Amen* if a person has not
heard the whole Grace? That does not relieve you of the obligation to say Grace. Hiyya will now explain that we have made a
false assumption. The man did *not* eat with the party. He came
later. He should still say *Amen.*

B. Hiyya bar Rav said, "[We speak of a case] in which he
did not eat with them."

So too did R. Nahman say in the name of Rabbah bar Abbuha, "[We speak of a case] in which he did not eat with
them."

We introduce a new question: Is it better to say Grace in behalf of the whole assembly, or simply to answer *Amen?* We have
two examples of rabbis' advice to their sons to try to have the
honor of saying Grace in behalf of the whole company, rather
than simply answering *Amen.*

C. *Rav said to Hiyya his son, "My son, seize* [the cup] *and
bless."*

So did R. Huna say to Rabbah his son, "Seize and bless."

D. *This implies that he who says the blessing is better than
he who answers "Amen." But has it not been taught:*

R. Yosi says, "The one who answers Amen is greater than
the one who says the blessing."

R. Nehorai said to him, "By heaven! It is so. You should
know it, for behold, common soldiers go down and open the
battle, but the heroes go down and win it."

E. *It is a matter of dispute between Tannaim, as it has
been taught:*

Both the one who says the blessing and the one who answers Amen are implied [in the Scripture (Nehemiah 9:5)].

But the one who says the blessing is more quickly [answered] than he who answers Amen.

A thus assumes that the Israelite has eaten. He therefore responds Amen to Grace in order to carry out his obligation to say Grace. The question follows, How may he do so, for he has to hear the entire prayer? The Mishnah states one may say Amen even having heard only part of it. B gives the obvious answer. The man did not eat at all. A could have been replaced by, "And this speaks of a case in which he did not eat." Further discussion would have been unnecessary, but then the reason for the gloss would have been left unarticulated. So for the sake of a clear statement of the operative considerations, the question had to be fully stated.

C is unrelated to the foregoing. A cup of wine is brought in preparation for the Grace after Meals. Rav and Huna advise their sons to make every effort to take the cup, so as to recite Grace for the rest of the assembled group. D then asks the obvious question: Is the reason for this advice that it is better to say the prayer than to respond to it? But the contrary is stated. E settles the matter, as we by now have come to expect. Some people hold one opinion, some people hold the other.

The reference in E is to Nehemiah 9:5, "Stand up and bless the Lord your God from everlasting to everlasting. Blessed be thy glorious name which is exalted above all blessing and praise." The first part is understood to have been stated by the one who says the blessing, the last by the one who answers Amen. Both therefore are equally represented in the blessing.

The larger issue in E is whether it is better to perform a religious action or to stand by and let someone else do it for you. The rabbis, for their part, claim no special role in the liturgical life. A prayer or a blessing said by a rabbi is not more pleasing to God than one said by an ordinary person. The rabbi has no special religious duties not incumbent upon everybody else. He also has no privileges or rights which others do not enjoy. He sees himself as a Jew like any other. And he wants the other to be like him. So he is not willing to claim that someone—even a rabbi—has a priestly function which pleases God especially, or that someone else—a "layman"—who stands by and forms part of the larger community, is less important to God. The priesthood of all Israel, which is expressed in the rules about cleanness at the table, also forms the basis for the rule before us. Everyone is as good as everyone else. No special sanctity is imputed to the one who prays in behalf of the community. Anyone may do so, if he knows the way. To be sure, the rabbis will teach the right way. But after learning Torah properly, the disciple also is a rabbi.

A. Samuel asked Rav, "Should one answer *Amen* after [the blessings of] children in the school house?"

He said to him, "They answer *Amen* after everyone except children in the school house, since they are [saying blessings solely] for the sake of learning."

B. *And this applies when it is not the time for them to say the "Haftarah," but in the time to say "Haftarah," they do respond* ["Amen."]

Since the subject of saying *Amen* is introduced, a further issue is raised and settled, then the rule is further analyzed in B. The point is that in the school the blessings are said only as an exercise and do not require *Amen*. But the blessings for Scriptural readings by children—as in reading in the prophets' writings, the *Haftarah*—are responded to.

Our rabbis have taught:

A. "The absence of oil holds up the blessing [Grace]," the words of Rabbi Zilai.

R. Zivai says, "It does not hold it up."

R. Aha says, "[The absence of] good oil holds it up."

We have three possible opinions on whether you have to have oil with which to clean the hands before one says Grace. Zilai says you have to have oil. Zivai says you do not have to have oil. Aha says you have to have good oil—the most extreme position. Now we shall have a parallel opinion, that you have to clean the hands, but there is no reference to the question of oil.

R. Zuhamai says, "Just as a dirty person [*mezuham*] is unfit for the Temple service, so dirty hands are unfit for the blessing."

B. R. Nahman b. Isaac said, "I know neither Zilai nor Zivai nor Zuhamai. But I know a teaching which R. Judah said in the name of Rav, and some say it was taught as a baraita:

Nahman rejects the foregoing rulings, but instead is going to cite an exegesis of Leviticus 11:44, which proves that you *do* have to have oil before blessing the food after the meal. The exegesis explicitly says one must first wash, then put oil on his hands, and finally say Grace. This means that, according to Nahman, the position of Zilai, Aha, and Zuhamai is correct, because a tradition bearing the authority of the Tannaim has shown that rule derives from Scripture itself—the highest authority of all.

" 'And be you holy' [Leviticus 11:44]—this refers to washing the hands before the meal.
" 'And you shall be holy'—this refers to the washing after the meal.
" 'For holy'—this refers to the oil.
" 'Am I the Lord your God'—this refers to the blessing [Grace]."

The teachings about oil are in the names of authorities unknown to Nahman, and at least one of them, Zuhamai, seems to be a play on the word "dirty," so the whole tradition may be spurious. Rav's exegesis, however, introduces the same requirement: One must have oil before saying the Grace after Meals.

The exegesis of the Scripture, B, involves the allegorical interpretation of each of its parts in terms of some other system of values or religious practices. The elements of "sanctification" ("You shall be holy") are taken to mean, or are applied to, the rite of eating a meal—a fitting conclusion to the chapter.

The Chapter As a Whole

Having examined the Babylonian Talmud's individual units of tradition, we shall review the chapter as a whole. The natural divisions are set by the Mishnah's paragraphs. The whole *Gemara* now will be clearly seen as an extended well-organized commentary on the Mishnah and on some elements of its accompanying Tosefta. Very little occurs, the theme of which could not have been predicted on the basis of the two earlier documents. The neatly ordered chapter splits naturally into four divisions, first, the discussion of some, though not all, of the disputes between the Houses, then, in the next three, the elucidation of the other parts of the Mishnah and related Tosefta.

I
THE HOUSES' DISPUTES

[51b] Gemara: *Our rabbis have taught:*

The things which are between the House of Shammai and the House of Hillel in [regard to] a meal:

The House of Shammai say, "One blesses over the day and afterward blesses over the wine, for the day causes the wine to come, and the day has already been sanctified, while the wine has not yet come."

And the House of Hillel say, "He blesses over the wine and afterward blesses over the day, for the wine causes the Sanctification to be said.

"Another matter: The blessing over the wine is perpetual, and the blessing over the day is not perpetual. Between that which is perpetual and that which is not perpetual, that which is perpetual takes precedence."

And the law is in accordance with the words of the House of Hillel.

What is the purpose of "another matter"?

If you should say that there [in regard to the opinion of the House of Shammai] *two* [reasons are given] *and here* [in regard to the opinion of the House of Hillel] *one, here too* [in respect to the House of Hillel], *there are two* [reasons, the second being]: "The blessing of the wine is perpetual and the blessing of the day is not perpetual. That which is perpetual takes precedence over that which is not perpetual."

And the law is in accord with the opinion of the House of Hillel.

This is obvious [that the law is in accord with the House of Hillel], *for the echo has gone forth* [and pronounced from heaven the decision that the law follows the opinion of the House of Hillel.]

If you like, I can argue that [this was stated] *before the echo.*

And if you like, I can argue that it was after the echo, and [the passage is formulated in accord with the] opinion of [52a] R. Joshua, who stated, "They do not pay attention to an echo [from heaven]."

And is it the reasoning of the House of Shammai that the blessing of the day is more important?

But has a Tanna not taught: "He who enters his house at the close of the Sabbath blesses over the wine and the light and the spices and afterward he says *Havdalah*. And if he has only one cup, he leaves it for after the food and then says the other blessings in order after it." [*Havdalah* is the blessing of the day, yet comes last!]

But lo, on what account [do you say] *this is the view of the House of Shammai? Perhaps it is the House of Hillel*['s opinion]?

Let [such a thought] not enter your mind, for a Tanna teaches: "Light and afterward spices." And of whom have you heard who holds this opinion? The House of Shammai, as a Tanna has taught:

R. Judah said, "The House of Shammai and the House of Hillel did not differ concerning the [blessing of the] food, that it is at first, and the *Havdalah*, that it is at the end.

"Concerning what did they dispute? Concerning the light and the spices.

"For the House of Shammai say, 'Light and afterward spices.'

"And the House of Hillel say, 'Spices and afterward the light.' "

And on what account [do you suppose that] *it is the House of Shammai as* [interpreted by] *R. Judah? Perhaps it is* [a teaching in accord with] *the House of Hillel* [as interpreted by] *R. Meir?*

Do not let such a thing enter your mind, for lo, a Tanna teaches here in our Mishnah: The House of Shammai say, "Light and food and spices and *Havdalah*."

And the House of Hillel say, "Light and spices, food and *Havdalah*."

But there, in the "baraita," lo he has taught: "If he has only one cup, he leaves it for after the food and then says the other blessings in order after it."

From this it is to be inferred that it is the House of Shammai's teaching, according to the [interpretation] of R. Judah.

In any event there is a problem [for the House of Shammai now give precedence to reciting a blessing for the wine over blessing the day].

The House of Shammai suppose that the coming of the [holy] day is more important than its leaving. As to the coming of the [holy] day, the earlier one may bring it in, the better. As to the leaving of the festival day, the later one may take leave of it, the better, so that it should not seem to us as a burden.

And do the House of Shammai hold the opinion that Grace requires a cup [of wine]? And lo, we have learned: [If] wine came to them after the food, and there is there only that cup, the House of Shammai say, "He blesses over the wine and afterward blesses over the food." [So Grace is said without the cup.]

Does this not mean that he blesses it and drinks [it]?

No. He blesses it and leaves it.

But has not a master said, "He that blesses must [also] taste [it]."

He does taste it.

And has not a master said, "Tasting it is spoiling it."

He tastes it with his hand [finger].

And has not a master said, "The cup of blessing requires a [fixed] measure." And lo, he diminishes it from its fixed measure.

[We speak of a situation in which] he has more than the fixed measure.

But lo, has it not been taught: If there is there only that cup . . . [so he has no more].

There is not enough for two, but more than enough for one.

And has not R. Hiyya taught: The House of Shammai say, "He blesses over the wine and drinks it, and afterward he says Grace."

Then we have two Tannas' [traditions] in respect to the opinion of the House of Shammai.

The House of Shammai say [They wash the hands and afterward mix the cup] . . .

Our rabbis have taught:

The House of Shammai say, "They wash the hands and afterward mix the cup, for if you say they mix the cup first, [against this view is] a [precautionary] decree to prevent the liquids on the outer sides of the cup, which are unclean by reason of his hands' [touching them], from going back and making the cup unclean."

But will not the hands make the cup itself unclean [without reference to the liquids]?

The hands are in the second degree of uncleanness, and the [object unclean in] the second degree of uncleanness cannot [then] render [another object unclean] in the third [degree] in respect to profane foods, [but only to Heave-offering]. But [this happens] only by means of liquids [unclean in the first degree].

And the House of Hillel say, "They mix the cup and afterward wash the hands, for if you say they wash the hands first, [against this view is] a [precautionary] decree lest the liquids which are [already] on the hands become unclean on account of the cup and go and render the hands unclean."

But will not the cup [itself] *make the hands unclean?*

A vessel cannot render a man unclean.

But will they [the hands] *not render the liquids which are in it* [the cup] *unclean?*

Here we are dealing with a vessel the outer part of which has been made unclean by liquid. The inner part is clean but the outer part is unclean. *Thus we have learned:*

[If] a vessel is made unclean on the outside by liquid, the outside is unclean, [52b] but its inside and its rim, handle, and haft are clean. If, however, the inside is unclean, the whole [cup] is unclean.

What, then, do they [the Houses] *dispute?*

The House of Shammai hold that it is prohibited to make use of a vessel whose outer parts are unclean by liquids, as a decree on account of the drippings. [There is] *no* [reason] *to* decree lest the liquids on the hands be made unclean by the cup.

And the House of Hillel reckon that it is permitted to make use of a vessel whose outer part is made unclean by liquids, *for drippings are unusual. But there is reason to take care lest* the liquids which are on the hands may be made unclean by the cup.

Another matter: [So that] immediately upon the washing of the hands [may come] the meal [itself].

What is the reason for this additional explanation?

This is what the House of Hillel said to the House of Shammai: "According to your reasoning, in saying that it is prohibited to make use of a cup whose outer parts are unclean, we decree on account of the drippings. But even so, [our opinion] is better, for immediately upon the washing of the hands [should come] the meal."

The House of Shammai say, "After wiping his hand with the napkin . . ."

Our rabbis have taught:

The House of Shammai say, "He wipes his hands with the napkin and lays it on the table, for if you say, 'on the cushion,' [that view is wrong, for it is a precautionary] decree lest the liquids which are on the napkin become unclean on account of the cushion and go back and render the hands unclean."

And will not the cushion [itself] render the napkin unclean?

A vessel cannot make a vessel unclean.

And will not the cushion [itself] make the man unclean?

A vessel cannot make a man unclean.

And the House of Hillel say, " 'On the cushion,' for if you say, 'on the table,' [that opinion is wrong, for it is a] decree lest the liquids become unclean on account of the table and go and render the food unclean."

But will not the table render the food which is on it unclean?

We here deal with a table which is unclean in the second degree, and something unclean in the second degree does not render something unclean in the third degree in respect to unconsecrated food, except by means of liquids [which are always unclean in the first degree].

What [principle] *do they dispute?*

The House of Shammai reckon that it is prohibited to make use of a table unclean in the second degree, as a decree on account of those who eat Heave-offering [which is rendered unfit by an object unclean in the second degree].

And the House of Hillel reckon that it is permitted to make use of a table unclean in the second degree, for those who eat Heave-offering [the priests] are careful.

Another matter: There is no Scriptural requirement to wash the hands before eating unconsecrated food.

What is the purpose of "another explanation"?

This is what the House of Hillel said to the House of Shammai: If you ask what is the difference in respect to food, concerning which we take care, and in respect to the hands, concerning which we do not take care—even in this regard [our opinion] *is preferable for* there is no Scriptural requirement concerning the washing of the hands before eating unconsecrated food.

It is better that the hands should be made unclean, *for there is no Scriptural basis for* [washing] *them,* and let not the food be made unclean, *concerning which there is a Scriptural basis* [for concern about its uncleanness].

The House of Shammai say, They clean the house and afterward wash the hands . . .

Our rabbis have taught:

The House of Shammai say, "They clean the house and afterward wash the hands, for if you say, 'They wash the hands first,' it turns out that you spoil the food."

But the House of Shammai do not reckon that one washes the hands first.

What is the reason?

On account of the crumbs.

And the House of Hillel say, "If the servant is a disciple of a sage, he takes the crumbs which are as large as an olive [in bulk] and leaves the crumbs which are not so much as an olive [in bulk]."

(*This view supports the opinion of R. Yohanan, for R. Yo-hanan said, "Crumbs which are not an olive in bulk may be deliberately destroyed."*)

In what do they differ?

The House of Hillel reckon that it is prohibited to employ a servant who is an ignorant man, and the House of Shammai reckon that it is permitted to employ a servant who is an ignorant man.

R. Yosi bar Hanina said in the name of R. Huna, "In our entire chapter the law is in accord with the House of Hillel, excepting this matter, in which the law is in accord with the House of Shammai."

And R. Oshaia taught the matter contrariwise. And in this matter too the law is in accord with the House of Hillel.

The House of Shammai say, Light and food . . .

R. Huna bar Judah happened by the house of Rava. He saw that Rava blessed the spices first.

He said to him, "Since the House of Shammai and the House of Hillel did not dispute concerning the light, [it should come first].

"For it was taught: The House of Shammai say, 'Light, and food, spices, and Havdalah,' and the House of Hillel say, 'Light, and spices, and food, and Havdalah.'

Rava answered him, "This is the opinion [= version] of R. Meir, but R. Judah says, 'The House of Shammai and the House of Hillel did not differ concerning the food, that it comes first, and concerning the Havdalah, that it is at the end.

" 'Concerning what did they differ?'

" 'Concerning the light and the spices.'

"For the House of Shammai say, 'The light and afterward the spices.'

"And the House of Hillel say, 'The spices and afterward the light.' "

And R. Yohanan said, "The people were accustomed to act in accord with the House of Hillel as presented by R. Judah.

The House of Shammai say, "Who created . . ."

Rava said, "Concerning the word 'bara' [created] everyone agrees that 'bara' implies [the past tense]. They differ concerning 'boré [creates]. The House of Shammai reckon that 'boré' means, 'Who will create in the future.' And the House of Hillel reckon that 'boré' also means what was created [in the past]."

R. Joseph objected, " 'Who forms light and creates darkness' [Isaiah 45:7], 'Creates mountains and forms the wind' [Amos 4:13], 'Who creates the heavens and spreads them out' " [Isaiah 47:5].

"But," R. Joseph said, "Concerning 'bara' and 'boré' everyone agrees that [the words] refer to the past. They differ as to whether one should say 'light' or 'lights.'

"The House of Shammai reckon there is one light in the fire.

"And the House of Hillel reckon that there are many lights in the fire."

We have a Tannaitic teaching along the same lines:

The House of Hillel said to the House of Shammai, "There are many illuminations in the light."

The Talmud to this point is constructed of a series of inquiries which follow a single pattern. The structure is tight, and the argument orderly and logical. The whole set of elements is put together with little artifice; the Mishnah is cited, then the same inquiry recurs, time and again. Only the very last item—"Who created"—breaks the orderly sequence. And this element is ignored in Tosefta.

The second and third divisions of the chapter are thematically well-integrated, though the same forms are not so consistently followed as earlier. The theme now is the light and the spices. After the Mishnah is analyzed, a series of *beraitot,* Tannaitic traditions mostly found in Tosefta, are introduced and analyzed, one by one.

II
THE LIGHT AND THE SPICES

A blessing is not said . . .

Certainly, [in the case of] *the light* [of idolators, one should not say a blessing] *because it did not rest on the Sabbath. But what is the reason that for spices* [one may not say the blessing]?

R. Judah said in the name of Rav, "*We here deal with a banquet held by idolators,* because the run-of-the-mill banquet held by idolators is for the sake of idolatry."

But since it has been taught at the end of the clause, "Or over the light or spices of idolatry," we must infer that the beginning of the clause does not deal with idolatry.

R. Hanina from Sura said, "[The master explains] *what is the reason:* What is the reason that they do not bless the light or spices of idolators? Because the run-of-the-mill banquet held by idolators is for the sake of idolatry."

Our rabbis have taught:
One may bless a light which has rested on the Sabbath, but one may not bless a light which has not rested on the Sabbath.

And what is the meaning of "which has not rested on the Sabbath"?

[53a] *Shall we say* it has not rested on the Sabbath on account of the work [which has been done with it, including] even work which is permitted?

And has it not been taught: They do bless the light [kindled on the Sabbath for] a woman in confinement or a sick person.

R. Nahman bar Isaac said, "*What is the meaning of* 'which enjoyed Sabbath-rest'? Which enjoyed Sabbath rest on account of work, the doing of which is a transgression [on the Sabbath]."

We have learned likewise in a baraita:
They may bless a lamp which has been burning throughout the day to the conclusion of the Sabbath.

Our rabbis have taught:
They bless [a light] kindled by a gentile from an Israelite, or by an Israelite from a gentile, but they do not bless [a light] kindled by a gentile from a gentile.

What is the reason one does not do so [from a light kindled by] *a gentile from a gentile?*

Because it did not enjoy Sabbath-rest.

If so, lo, [a light kindled by] *an Israelite from a gentile also has not enjoyed Sabbath-rest.*

And if you say this prohibited [light] *has vanished, and the one* [in hand] *is another and was born in the hand of the Israelite,* [how will you deal] *with this teaching?*

He who brings out a flame to the public way [on the Sabbath] is liable [for violating the Sabbath rule against carrying from private to public property].

Now why should he be liable? What he raised up he did not put down, and what he put down he did not raise up.

But [we must conclude] *that the prohibited* [flame] *is present, but when he blesses, it is over the additional* [flame], *which is permitted, that he blesses.*

If so, a gentile['s flame kindled] *from a gentile*['s flame] *also* [should be permitted].

That is true, but [it is prohibited by] *decree, on account of the first gentile and the first flame* [of light kindled on the Sabbath by the gentile].

Our rabbis have taught:
[If] one was walking outside of the village and saw a light, if the majority [of the inhabitants of the village] are gentiles, he does not bless it. If the majority are Israelites, he blesses it.

Lo, the statement is self-contradictory. You have said, "If the majority are gentiles, he does not bless it." Then if they were evenly divided, he may bless it.

But then it teaches, "If the majority are Israelites, he may bless." Then if they are evenly divided, he may not bless it.

Strictly speaking, even if they are evenly divided, he may bless. But since in the opening clause [the language is], "The majority are gentiles," in the concluding clause, [the same language is used:] "A majority are Israelites."

Our rabbis have taught:
[If] a man was walking outside of a village and saw a child with a torch in his hand, he makes inquiries about him. If he is an Israelite, he may bless [the light]. If he is a gentile, he may not bless.

Why do we speak of a child? Even an adult also [would be subject to the same rule].

Rav Judah said in the name of Rav, "In this case we are dealing with [a time] near sunset. As to a gentile, it will be perfectly clear that he certainly is a gentile [for an Israelite would not use the light immediately after sunset]. If it is a child, I might say it is an Israelite child who happened to take up [the torch]."

Our rabbis have taught:
[If] one was walking outside of a village and saw a light, if it was as thick as the opening of a furnace, he may bless it, and if not, he may not bless it.

One Tanna [authority] [says], "They may bless the light of a furnace," and another Tanna [says], "They may not bless it."

There is no difficulty. The first speaks at the beginning [of the fire], the other at the end.

One authority says, "They may bless the light of an oven or a stove," and another authority says, "They may not bless it."

There is no problem. The former speaks of the beginning, the latter of the end.

One authority says, "They may bless the light of the synagogue and the school house," and another authority says, "They may not bless it."

There is no problem. The former speaks [of a case in which] an important man is present, the latter [of a case in which] an important man is not present.

And if you want, I shall explain both teachings as applying to a case in which an important man is present. There still is no difficulty. The former [teaching speaks of a case in which] there is a beadle [who eats in the synagogue], the latter in which there is none.

And if you want, I shall explain both teachings as applying to a case in which a beadle is present. There still is no difficulty. The former teaching [speaks of a case in which] there is moonlight, the latter in which there is no moonlight.

Our rabbis have taught:

[If] they were sitting in the school house, and light was brought before them—

The House of Shammai say, "Each one blesses for himself."

And the House of Hillel say, "One blesses for all of them, as it is said, 'In the multitude of people is the King's glory' " [Proverbs 14:28].

Certainly [we can understand the position of the House of Hillel because] the House of Hillel explain their reason.

But what is the reason of the House of Shammai?

They reckon [it as they do] on account of [avoiding] interruption in [Torah study] in the school house.

We have a further Tannaitic tradition to the same effect:

The members of the house of Rabban Gamaliel did not say [the blessing] "Good health" [after a sneeze] in the school house on account of the interruption [of study] in the school house.

They say a benediction neither on the light nor on the spices of the dead . . .

What is the reason?

The light is made for the honor [of the deceased], *the spices to remove the bad smell.*

Rav Judah in the name of Rav said, ["Light made for] whoever [is of such importance that] they take out [a light] before him both by day and by night is not blessed. [And light made for] whoever [is not important, so that] they take out [a light] before him only by night, is blessed."

R. Huna said, "They do not bless spices of the privy and oil made to remove the grease."

Does this saying imply that wherever [spice] *is not used for smell, they do not bless over it? It may be objected:*

He who enters the stall of a spice dealer and smells the odor, even though he sat there all day long, blesses only one time. He who enters and goes out repeatedly blesses each time.

And lo, here is a case in which it is not used for the scent, and still he blesses.

Yes, but it also is used for the odor—so that people will smell and come and purchase it.

Our rabbis have taught:

If one was walking outside of a village and smelled a scent, if most of the inhabitants are idolators, he does not bless it. If most are Israelites, he blesses it.

R. Yosi says, "Even if most are Israelites, he *still* may not bless, because Israelite women use incense for witchcraft."

But do they "all" burn incense for witchcraft!

A small part is for witchcraft, and a small part is also for finishing garments, which yields a larger part not used for scent, and wherever the majority [of the incense] *is not used for scent, one does not bless it.*

R. Hiyya bar Abba said in the name of R. Yohanan, "He

who walks on the eve of the Sabbath in Tiberias and at the end of the Sabbath in Sepphoris and smells an odor does not bless it, because it is presumed to have been made only to perfume garments."

Our rabbis taught: If one was walking in the gentiles' market and was pleased to scent the spices, he is a sinner.

III
USING THE LIGHT

[53b] **They bless the light once it has been used . . .**

Rav Judah said in the name of Rav, "Not that he has actually used it, but if anyone stood near enough so that he might use the light, even at some distance, [he may say the blessing]."

So too R. Ashi said, "We have learned this teaching even [concerning] those at some distance."

It was objected [on the basis of the following teaching]: If one had a light hidden in the folds of his cloak or in a lamp, or saw the flame but did not make use of its light, or made use of the light but did not [actually] see the flame, he may not say the blessing. [He may say the blessing only when] he [both] sees the flame and uses its light.

Certainly one finds cases in which one may use the light and not see the flame. This may be when the light is in a corner.

But where do you find a case in which one may see the flame and not make use of its light? Is it not when he is at a distance?

No, it is when the flame keeps on flickering.

Our rabbis have taught:

They may say a blessing over glowing coals, but not over dying coals ('omemot).

What is meant by glowing coals?

R. Hisda said, "If one puts a chip into them and it kindles on its own, [these are] all [glowing coals]."

*It was asked: Is the word 'omemot [*alef*] or 'omemot [*'ayin*]?*

Come and hear, for R. Hisda b. Abdimi said, " 'The cedars in the garden of God could not darken [*'amamuhu*] it' " [Ezekiel 31:8].

And Rava said, "He must make actual use of it."

And how [near must one be]?

Ulla said, "So that he may make out the difference between an issar and a pundion [two small coins]."

Hezekiah said, "So that he may make out the difference between a meluzma [a weight] of Tiberias and one of Sepphoris."

Rav Judah would say the blessing [for the light of the] house of Adda the waiter [which was nearby].

Rava would say the blessing [for the light of the] house of Guria bar Hama.

Abbaye would say the blessing [for the light of the] house of Bar Abbuha.

R. Judah said in the name of Rav, "They do not go looking for the light in the way they go looking for [means to carry out other] commandments."

R. Zira said, "At the outset, I used to go looking [for light]. Now that I have heard this teaching of R. Judah in the name of Rav, I too will not go searching, but if one comes my way, I shall say the blessing over it."

The first problem of part II concerns the light and spices of gentiles. The sequence begins with Rav's interpretation of the Mishnah's referent. Then we have a series of *beraitot,* introduced by *Our rabbis have taught.* Each is analyzed in sequence. The point of analysis is, What is the reason for the rule? When a reason is adduced, the next question is, Is the reason logical and harmonious with other laws? Finally, where possible, a further Tannaitic teaching is introduced in support of the accepted interpretation. The sequence, after the discussion of the light and spices of idolatry, is as follows: (1) a light which has not rested on the Sabbath; then (2) a light kindled by an Israelite (or a gentile) from a light which has not rested on the Sabbath; then (3) further examples of the light of gentiles—(4) the light of a village, (5) a child carrying a torch.

Since light is under discussion, a new problem occurs: Does one bless light seen from a distance? The first issue is light from a furnace, then from a synagogue. Once the school house is introduced, light brought to the school house is naturally going to be discussed; here the issue is drawn from the life of study.

We then turn to the Mishnah on the light and spices of the dead. The issue is whether these are used for their normal purpose, in which case they may be blessed. Once that principle is laid down, further examples are analyzed, beginning with incense smelled from afar.

The unit concludes with an analysis of a new Mishnah, this one on using the light. Rav Judah in Rav's name says one does not have actually to use the light. There follows a brief interpolation, then comes Rava's opinion, pertinent to the Mishnah, that one does have to make actual use of the light. Afterward we define the distance one may stand from a light and still be able to make use of it. Finally comes another interpolation, this in the name of the first master, Rav Judah in the name of Rav.

IV
FORGETTING GRACE. AMEN.

He who ate [and did not say Grace] . . .

R. Zevid, and some say, R. Dimi bar Abba, said, "The dispute [between the Houses] applies to a case of forgetfulness, but in a case in which a person deliberately [omitted Grace], all agree that he should return to his place and say the blessing."

This is perfectly obvious. It is [explicitly] taught, "And he forgot."

What might you have said? This is the rule even where it

was intentional, but the reason that the Tanna taught, "And he forgot," is to tell you how far the House of Shammai was willing to go [in requiring the man to go back to where he ate. They did so even if a man accidentally forgot]. *Thus we are taught* [the contrary. Even if one forgot, unintentionally, he must go back].

It was taught:
The House of Hillel said to the House of Shammai, "According to your opinion, someone who ate on the top of the Temple Mount and forgot and went down without saying Grace should go back to the top of the Mount and say the blessing."

The House of Shammai said to the House of Hillel, "According to your opinion, someone who forgot a purse on the top of the Temple Mount would not go back and retrieve it.

"For his own sake, he [assuredly] will go back. For the sake of Heaven [should he] not all the more so [go back]?"

There were these two disciples. One did it [forgot Grace] *accidentally, and, following the rule of the House of Shammai,* [went back to bless], *and found a purse of gold. And one did it deliberately* [omitted Grace], *and following the rule of the House of Hillel* [did not go back to say it], *and a lion ate him.*

Rabbah b. b. Hanna was traveling in a caravan. He ate and was sated but [forgot and] *did not say Grace.*

He said, "How shall I do? If I tell the men [of the caravan with me] *that it is to bless* [that I go back], *they will say to me, 'Bless here. Wherever you say the blessing, you are saying the blessing to the Merciful* [God].' *It is better that I tell them I have forgotten a golden dove."*

So he said to them, "Wait for me, for I have forgotten a golden dove."

He went back and blessed and found a golden dove.

And why was a dove so important?

Because the community of Israel is compared to a dove, as

it is written, "The wings of the dove are covered with silver, and her pinions with the shimmer of gold" [Psalm 58:14]. Just as the dove is saved only by her wings, so Israel is saved only by the commandments.

Until when can he say the Grace? Until the food is digested in his bowels . . .

How long does it take to digest the food?

R. Yohanan said, "As long as one is no longer hungry."

Resh Laqish said, "As long as one [still] is thirsty on account of his meal."

R. Yemar bar Shelamia said to Mar Zutra—and some say, Rav Yemar bar Shizbi said to Mar Zutra—"Did Resh Laqish really say this? And did not R. Ammi say in the name of Resh Laqish, 'How long does it take to digest a meal? The time it takes to go four miles.'"

There is no problem: Here [we speak of] a big meal, there [we speak of] a small meal.

If wine came to them . . .

This implies that in the case of an Israelite['s saying Grace], even though one has not heard the entire blessing, he responds [Amen].

But if he has not heard [the whole Grace], *how can he have performed his duty by doing so* [assuming he has eaten also? For he has to hear the entire Grace to carry out his obligation to say Grace.]

Hiyya bar Rav said, "[We speak of a case] in which he did not eat with them."

So too did R. Nahman say in the name of Rabbah bar Abbuha, "[We speak of a case] in which he did not eat with them."

Rav said to Hiyya his son, "My son, seize [the cup] and bless."

So did R. Huna say to Rabbah his son, "Seize and bless."

This implies that he who says the blessing is better than he who answers "Amen." But has it not been taught:

R. Yosé says, "The one who answers Amen is greater than the one who says the blessing."

R. Nehorai said to him, "By heaven! It is so. You should know it, for behold, common soldiers go down and open the battle, but the heroes go down and win it."

It is a matter of dispute between Tannaim, as it has been taught:

Both the one who says the blessing and the one who answers Amen are implied [in the Scripture (Nehemiah 9:5)]. But the one who says the blessing is more quickly [answered] than he who answers Amen.

Samuel asked Rav, "Should one answer [Amen] after [the blessings of] children in the school house?"

He said to him, "They answer Amen after everyone except children in the school house, since they are [saying blessings solely] for the sake of learning."

And this applies when it is not the time for them to say the "Haftarah," but in the time to say "Haftarah," they do respond ["Amen"].

Our rabbis have taught:

"The absence of oil holds up the blessing [Grace]," the words of Rabbi Zilai.

R. Zivai says, "It does not hold it up."

R. Aha says, "[The absence of] good oil holds it up."

R. Zuhamai says, "Just as a dirty person [mezuham] is unfit for the Temple service, so dirty hands are unfit for the blessing."

R. Nahman b. Bar Isaac said, "I know neither Zilai nor Zivai nor Zuhamai. But I know a teaching which R. Judah said in the name of Rav, and some say it was taught as a 'baraita':

" 'And be you holy' [Leviticus 11:44]—this refers to washing the hands before the meal.

" 'And you shall be holy'—this refers to the washing after the meal.

" 'For holy'—this refers to the oil.

" 'Am I the Lord your God'—this refers to the blessing [Grace]."

The final unit is introduced by the analysis of the Houses' differences about what to do if one has forgotten to say Grace after Meals. After Zevid's abortive gloss, we have discrete materials—the fragment of a debate, then stories illustrative of the principles of the debate, but all in favor of the stand of the House of Shammai. The Mishnaic teaching about digesting the food is then explained. Finally, the question of responding *Amen* raised in the Mishnah is worked out, but only in one detail, an Israelite's saying *Amen* at the end of Grace. The little story about answering *Amen* after school children treats a problem related in theme, but not in principle. Finally, a further addition, about oil in connection with the Grace after Meals, permits the conclusion of the chapter on an exalted note.

We see that the chapter is tightly organized according to the themes of the Mishnah to which it is a commentary. It contains remarkably little extraneous material; almost everything in the chapter is pertinent to the themes of the Mishnah. Most materials are relevant not only in substance, but in detail. The editors had to work with discrete materials—the Mishnah, the Tosefta in its several elements, opinions of Amoraim from Rav, in the early third century, to Ashi, in the fifth, not to mention teachings of Tannaim from the first and second centuries, stories about rabbis, Scriptural exegeses, parables, legends. Considering the hodgepodge of materials handed on for five centuries, beginning with a barely intelligible mnemonic list possibly dating to pre-70 times, we can hardly fail to be astonished at the neat, orderly, thematically logical, and pedagogically illuminating arrangement accomplished by the editors. They have not only brought good order to chaos. They have done so in such a way that the critical interest of the reader is maintained, his powers to participate in the argument enhanced.

For what is *Talmudic* about the chapter before us, Talmudic and not merely encyclopedic and antiquarian, is the persistence of the spirit of criticism in four modes: (1) abstract, rational criticism of each tradition in sequence and of the answers hazarded to the several questions; (2) historical criticism of sources and their (un)harmonious relationship; (3) philological and literary criticism of the meanings of words and phrases; and (4) practical criticism of what people actually do in order to carry out their religious obligations.

It goes without saying that these four modes of criticism are peculiarly contemporary. Careful, skeptical examination of answers posed to problems is utterly commonplace to modern men and women. Historical criticism of sources, which does not gullibly accept whatever is alleged as fact, is the beginning of historical study. Philological study of the origins and meanings of words, literary criticism of the style of expression—these are familiar. Finally, we take for granted that it is normal to examine people's actions against some large principle of behavior. These are traits of inquiry which are both Talmudic and routinely modern.

What makes them different from modern modes of thought? It is the remarkable claim that in the give and take of argument, in the processes of criticism, you do something transcendent, more than this-worldly. I cannot overemphasize how remarkable is the combination of rational criticism and supernatural value attached to that criticism. You simply cannot understand the Talmud and take seriously its claim upon modern men and women without confronting the other-worldly context in which this so completely secular thinking goes forward. The claim is that in seeking reason and order, you serve God. But what are we to make of that claim? Does lucid thinking bring heavenly illumination? How can people suggest so?

Perhaps the best answer may be sought in your own experience. Whence comes insight? Having put everything together in a logical and orderly way, we sometimes find ourselves immobilized. We know something, but we do not know what it means, what it suggests beyond itself. We sometimes catch an unexpected insight and come in some mysterious way to a comprehension of a whole which exceeds the sum of its parts. And we cannot explain how we have seen what, in a single instant, stuns us by its ineluctable rightness, fittingness—by the unearned insight, the inexplicable understanding. For the rabbis that stunning moment of rational insight comes with *siyyata dishamaya,* the help of Heaven. The charisma imparted by the rabbinic imagination to the brilliant man is not different in substance from the moral authority and spiritual dignity imparted by contemporary intellectuals to the great minds of the age. The profound honor to be paid to the intellectual paragons—the explorers of the unknown, the men and women of courage to doubt the accepted truths of the hour—is not much different from the deference shown by the disciple to the rabbi. So the religious experience of the rabbi and the secular experience of the intellectual differ not in quality. They gravely differ in the ways by which we explain and account for that experience. Still, in reflecting upon the commonalities of experience, we are enabled to enter into the curious mode of religiosity discovered within the Talmud. That accounts for our capacity to follow the primary question of the Talmud: Why are things as you claim? Perhaps they are just the opposite.

The persistent issue is, What is the reason for the ruling? Once reasons are adduced, they may be criticized and replaced. Changing situations may produce new reasons and end the pertinence of old ones. Just as the argument moves from point to point, so it remains open-ended. Not only new data, but also new intelligence and ideas may be introduced to change the course of the legal discussion. Thus the editors of the Talmud have turned materials of merely historical interest and authority into a living and vigorous discussion of wholly contemporary concern, vivid so long as the living choose to engage their minds with the ideas and the reasoning of the long-dead.

It must have taken considerable courage to criticize an authoritative law code, the Mishnah, and its accompanying supplement, the Tosefta. It would have been pious merely to accept those laws and digest them for future generations to memorize and copy. Judah the Patriarch, called "our holy rabbi," and those whose traditions he organized and handed on were very ancient authorities. Two or three centuries later the prestige of the Mishnah, regarded, as we saw, as the "Oral Torah" revealed by Moses at Sinai, was considerable. To ask for reasons, to criticize those reasons, to seek contradictions, to add to the law, to revise or even reject what the ancients had said—these were acts of men who had no equivalent claim either to firsthand knowledge of the Oral Torah or to the sanctity and prestige of the Tannaim. Yet that is exactly what the Amoraim did. And they did so in such a way as to revise everything that had gone before, to place upon the whole heritage of the past the indelible and distinct, unmistakable stamp of their own minds.

The reason is that the Amoraim did not confuse respect with servility. They carefully nurtured the disciples' critical and creative faculties. Gibbon said (probably unfairly) of the Byzantine schools, "Not a single composition of history, philosophy, or literature has been saved from oblivion by the intrinsic beauties of style, or sentiment, or original fancy, or even of successful imitation." By contrast, the Babylonian Talmud is the product not of servility to the past or of dogmatism in the present, but of an exceptionally critical, autonomous rationalism and an utterly independent spirit. The Amoraim gave to pedantry a cool welcome. Clearly, to them mere learning was insufficient. Not what one knew, but what he could do with what he knew was decisive. The authority and approbation of the elders were set aside by the critical accomplishments of the newest generation. In the fullest sense, the Amoraim were not traditionalists. They took the laws and traditions of the early generations into their care, respectfully learning them, reverently handing them on. But these they thoroughly digested and made their own. Their minds were filled with the learning of the ancients. But their rational wisdom and unrelenting criticism were wholly their own.

CHAPTER
VI

The Palestinian Talmud

THE PALESTINIAN TALMUD—composed of the Mishnah and the *Gemara* produced in the third-, fourth-, and early fifth-century Palestinian academies, chiefly at Tiberias, Caesarea, and Sepphoris—in general did not enjoy the benefit of the sophisticated editing and critical development evident in the Babylonian one. It contains full Gemara for the first Order, Seeds (*Zeraʻim*), because the agricultural laws were applied to the Holy Land long after the destruction of the Temple, and for tractate *Sheqalim* (the *Sheqel* offering for the Temple), both of which are absent in the Babylonian Talmud. But it lacks Talmud for the whole fifth and sixth Orders, Holy Things (*Qodashim*) and Purities (*Toharot*), and is slight for the fourth, Damages (*Neziqin*). Only the beginning of the tractate, in Purities, in Menstrual Women (*Niddah*), is available. Allusions in medieval commentaries to the Palestinian Talmud suggest that *Gemara* for other tractates then was available. The process of disappearance continued even into early modern times; we have a fourteenth-century reference to a Palestinian *Gemara* for *Avot* (The Fathers), and a sixteenth-century one to *Gemara* for *Makkot,* chapter three, while we now have it only for the first two chapters. In all, we have *Gemara* for thirty-nine tractates, but for each tractate it is considerably briefer than the Babylonian equivalent; in quantity, the Babylonian Talmud is three times larger than the Palestinian.

As it happens, the Palestinian *Gemara* for our chapter is no less interesting than the Babylonian: some of the early discussions, indeed, are better balanced and more elegant than anything we have seen until now.

The Palestinian Talmud is divided according to the divisions of the Mishnah. The several sections, therefore, are numbered not by page but by Mishnah. As before, the Mishnah is in boldfaced type; Aramaic is in italics.

8:1. . . . **The House of Shammai say, "One blesses the day and afterward one blesses over the wine."**
And the House of Hillel say, "One blesses over the wine and afterward one blesses the day."
A. *What is the reason of the House of Shammai?*
The Sanctification of the day causes the wine to be brought, and the man is already liable for the Sanctification of the day before the wine comes.
What is the reason of the House of Hillel?
The wine causes the Sanctification of the day to be said.
Another matter: Wine is perpetual, and the Sanctification is not perpetual. [What is always required takes precedence over what is required only occasionally.]

The *Gemara* first cites the available Toseftan explanations for the positions of the two Houses. All that is added is the introduction, "What is the reason . . ."

B. R. Yosé said, "[It follows] from the opinions of them both that with respect to wine and *Havdalah*, wine comes first."

Now Yosé begins the analysis of the two opinions. He wants to prove that both Houses agree the wine takes precedence over *Havdalah*. That is, you bless the wine, then you say the *Havdalah* prayer.

"*Is it not the reason of the House of Shammai* that the Sanctification of the day causes the wine to be brought, and here, since *Havdalah* does not cause wine to be brought, the wine takes precedence?"

Since the Shammaites hold that the reason wine comes after the Sanctification is that the Sanctification is the cause, then, when the prayer is *not* the reason for saying a blessing over wine, as in the case of *Havdalah,* the wine will normally take precedence over the prayer.

"*Is it not the reason of the House of Hillel that* the wine is perpetual and the Sanctification is not perpetual, and since the wine is perpetual, and the *Havdalah* is not perpetual, the wine comes first?"

Similarly, since the Hillelites say what is perpetual takes precedence over what is episodic, they will agree the wine takes precedence over *Havdalah*. So both Houses will agree on this point.

C. R. Mana said, "From the opinions of both of them [it follows] that with respect to wine and *Havdalah*, *Havdalah* comes first."

Now Mana wants to turn things upside down. The opinions of both Houses are such that they will agree *Havdalah* takes precedence over wine—the opposite of Yosé's claim!

"*Is not the reason of the House of Shammai that* one is already obligated [to say] the Sanctification of the day before the wine comes, and here, since he is already obligated for *Havdalah* before the wine comes, *Havdalah* comes first?"

The Shammaites' principle is that a person carries out the obligation which already applies—the Sanctification—before the obligation which does not *yet* apply. The reason the Sanctification comes before the wine is that, as soon as the sun sets, you are obligated to say the Sanctification. But the wine only comes later.

"*Is it not the reason of the House of Hillel that* the wine causes the Sanctification of the Day to be said, and here, since the wine does not cause the *Havdalah* to be said, *Havdalah* comes first?"

The Hillelites are going to agree with Mana's proposition, for they say wine comes first when it is the pretext for some other prayer. But the wine is not the pretext for saying *Havdalah*.

D. R. Zeira said, "From the opinions of both of them [it follows] that they say *Havdalah* without wine, but they say the Sanctification only with wine."

Zeira draws from the foregoing the necessary consequence: You may say *Havdalah* without wine. But you may say the Sanctification only in connection with wine. The House of Hillel make this point clear: Wine is not the pretext for saying *Havdalah*. Therefore, *Havdalah* may be said without wine. The House of Shammai say that the Sanctification of the day supplies the pretext for reciting the blessing over the wine. The *Havdalah* does not. So they will agree also. Zeira's point seems well-founded.

E. *This is the opinion of R. Zeira, for R. Zeira said, "They may say Havdalah over beer, but they go from place to place* [in search of wine] *for the Sanctification."*

Now Zeira's rule is applied. You must go in search of wine for Sanctification. But *Havdalah* may be said over beer.

Let us now review the argument as a whole.

Once again, we first observe that the Talmud's interest is to find the reasons for the laws. These will be elucidated, then criticized according to logic, finally tested against the evidence supplied by related rules. Like the Babylonian *Gemara,* the Palestinian one draws heavily upon the Tosefta. Its inquiry into the Tosefta, however, tends to be more thorough and systematic than the one we have seen in the Babylonian version. The opinions of both sides are examined; questions addressed to the one will be brought to the other. Thus a perfect balance is maintained throughout. Then new issues will be raised and worked out.

A sets the stage for what is to follow, rapidly reviewing the reasons given in the Tosefta for the opinions of the respective Houses. Then B, C, and D draw conflicting inferences from the foregoing in respect to *Havdalah.*

Yosé's view, B, is that both Houses agree that the wine comes before the *Havdalah* prayer. The Houses' principles are reviewed. As to the Shammaites: Which one supplies the pretext for the other? *Havdalah* does not require wine, therefore the wine will take precedence. As to the Hillelites: Which is "perpetual"? The wine. The wine therefore is going to precede *Havdalah.* So both Houses will agree that the order is wine, *Havdalah.*

Mana, in C, takes the opposite view. If the reason of the House of Shammai is that the obligation to say the Sanctification is already present, then *Havdalah,* the obligation of which *likewise* is already present, will come first. If the reason of the House of Hillel is that wine comes first on the evening of the Sabbath because the Sanctification may not be said without it, then at the end of the Sabbath, *Havdalah* will come first, for it *may* be said without wine. The dispute is made possible, therefore, because both Houses give two reasons for their opinions. Yosé concentrates on one of the reasons of each of the Houses, Mana on the other.

Zeira, D, then concludes that in the opinion of both Houses,

Havdalah may be said without wine, but Sanctification may not.
E then provides an abstract formulation of Zeira's view.

A. R. Yosé b. Rabbi said, "They are accustomed there [in
Babylonia], where there is no wine, for the prayer-leader to go
before the ark and say one blessing which is a summary of the
seven, and complete it with, 'Who sanctifies Israel and the
Sabbath Day.' "

The next analysis begins with the simple observation that in
Babylonia the custom is to say the Sanctification as part of the
synagogue prayers on the eve of the Sabbath. But matters are
quickly made complicated, for this is one of the two most difficult
discussions of the whole Palestinian Talmud before us. (The other
is 8:2B.)

B. And this poses a difficulty for the opinion of the House
of Shammai: How should one act on the evenings of the Sabbath?
He who was sitting and eating on the evening of the Sabbath, and it grew dark and became Sabbath evening, and there
was there only that one cup—[The House of Shammai say,
"Wine, then food," and the House of Hillel say, "Food, then
wine," so Mishnah 8:8].

Now we review the Mishnah and the Shammaite position in
connection with the Sanctification of the day on the evening of
the Sabbath.

Do you say he should leave it for the end of the meal and
say all of them [the blessings] on it?

What is the proper order of blessing? We have said "food"
takes precedence over wine, that is, the blessing of food, and so
does Grace over the blessing of the day. We have also agreed the

wine takes precedence over the food. So should the order be food, then wine, then day? But we also have said the wine takes precedence over the "food"! So the Talmud points out.

What do you prefer?
Should he [first] bless the day? The food takes precedence.
Should he bless the food? The wine takes precedence.
Should he bless the wine? The food takes precedence.

Now comes the effort at spelling out the answer. We first allude to Mishnah 8:8, which says wine is blessed, then put aside, and Grace is said; then the wine is drunk.

C. *We may infer* [it] *from this:*
If wine came to them after the meal, and there is there only that cup—

R. Ba will explain that there is a distinction to be made between the end of the Sabbath and the beginning. You bless the wine first, so that you will not forget it. But now, at the end of the Sabbath, when there are several blessings to be said over the same cup of wine, you will not likely forget the wine.

[R.] Ba said, "Because it [the wine's] is a brief blessing, [he says it first, for] perhaps he may forget and drink [the wine]. But here, since he says them all over the cup, he will not forget [to say a blessing over the wine in the cup]."

Now we spell out just what the man is to do: food, day, wine.

D. What, then, should he do according to the opinion of the House of Shammai?
Let him bless the food first, then bless the day, and then bless the wine.

Now we turn matters around. We pointed out that the problem confronts the House of Shammai on the evening of the Sabbath. But it also faces the House of Hillel at the end of the Sabbath, on Saturday night.

E. *And this poses difficulty for the opinion of the House of Hillel: How should one act at the end of the Sabbath?*
If he was sitting and eating on the Sabbath and it grew dark and the Sabbath came to an end, and there is there only that cup—

What order should the blessings follow? When should he say a blessing over the cup of wine?

Do you say he should leave it [the wine] *for after the meal and say them all on it?*
What do you prefer?
Should he bless the wine? The food comes first.
Should he bless the food? The light comes first.
Should he bless the light? *Havdalah* comes first.

We have agreed the food comes before the wine. But the light comes before the food. And the Hillelites are supposed to hold that the *Havdalah* comes before the light. The solution derives from Judah's version of the Houses' dispute. All agree the *Havdalah* comes at the end.

F. *We may infer* [it] *from this:* R. Judah said, "The House of Shammai and the House of Hillel did not differ concerning the blessing of the food, that it comes first, nor concerning *Havdalah*, that it comes at the end.
"Concerning what did they differ?
"Concerning the light and the spices, for:
"The House of Shammai say, 'The spices and afterward the light.'

"And the House of Hillel say, 'The light and afterward the spices.' "

[G. R. Ba and R. Judah in the name of Rav (said), "The law is according to him who says, 'Spices and afterward light.' "]

Now we have the instructions: Food, then wine, then light.

H. What should he do according to the opinion of the House of Hillel?

Let him bless the food, afterward bless the wine, and afterward bless the light.

Let us review this whole, elegant construction.

Yosé's observation, A, concerns Babylonia, where viticulture was impossible, because the climate was unsatisfactory. Since the Babylonian Jews could not get cheap wine—beer was used instead—the Sanctification of the Sabbath was done publicly, in the synagogue service, thus saving the private person from considerable expense. The Sabbath evening service included a sevenfold blessing, ending, "Blessed are you . . . who sanctifies Israel and the Sabbath Day." This is regarded as adequate substitution for the Sanctification of the day with a cup of wine.

This practice has to be measured against the opinions of the Houses. The Shammaites have to deal with an anomaly posed by the advent of the Sabbath, the Hillelites with one at the end.

The pericope before us presents a neat balance. B, C, and D are exactly paralleled by E, F, and H. G is an interpolation into an otherwise completed structure, but is essential to the structure, as well as to F.

The introductions, the Aramaic parts of B and E, allude to Mishnah 8:8. A man is eating and has only one cup of wine. On the eve of the Sabbath, what should he do? He needs the cup for the Sanctification of the Sabbath, but also for the Grace after Meals. No matter how you arrange matters, there is a problem according to the Shammaites' opinion. Do you tell the man to leave the wine for after the meal and to say all the blessings in order over it? That is what the Mishnah says he should do. Then he is to say the Sanctification and the Grace after Meals. If that is your instruction, then what will be the proper order of the blessings? Should he say the Sanctification? But the food takes precedence, for he already is obligated, having eaten, to say the Grace after Meals. That is, after all, in accord with the fundamental reasoning of the Shammaites. Then should he bless the food first? The wine takes precedence over the food, as the Mishnah has already ruled in the name of the House of Shammai: "He blesses the wine, then the food." Then do you tell the man to bless the wine first? But this is also impossible, for the House of Shammai say that the Sanctification takes precedence over the wine! We are at an impasse.

C provides the solution. First, Mishnah 8:8 is again cited, this time as the source of the solution. Then Ba explains the opinion of the House of Shammai in the afore-cited Mishnah. He removes the difficulty altogether. The reason of the House of Shammai in the situation addressed by Mishnah 8:8 is simply that the blessing of the wine is brief; therefore, it should be said first, lest it be forgotten. But here we are dealing with substantial blessings—Sanctification, Grace after Meals—so it is unlikely the man will forget the wine. Then D provides exact instructions: The Grace after Meals will take precedence, then the Sanctification, then the wine, thus preserving for the last two items the order originally prescribed the Shammaites.

E addresses the same problem to the House of Hillel. Now the situation concerns the end of the Sabbath, Saturday night, and *Havdalah,* rather than the beginning, Friday evening, and the Sanctification of the Sabbath Day. Mishnah 8:8 poses no problem to the Hillelites. They say one blesses the food, then the wine, then the day—consistent with their ruling in Mishnah 8:1. If a man was sitting and eating toward sunset on the Sabbath, and it grew dark, he now has to say *Havdalah.* But if he has only one cup, what should he do? If he says *Havdalah,* he will have no wine for the Grace after Meals.

Now, if you rule that he should leave the cup for after the meal and say all the blessings in order over it, you do have a problem. Should he first bless the wine? But food takes precedence in the rule of Mishnah 8:8. Should he first bless the food? But the light takes precedence, for the House of Hillel and the House of Shammai both agree that the order is light at first; they differ on spices and food. Then should he bless the light first? But if he does, the *Havdalah* will come before the Grace after Meals.

F then goes back over the presupposition of this analysis. Judah [b. Ilai, a second-century Tanna] has told us all parties agree food comes first, *Havdalah* at the end; the issue between the Houses is about the blessings which go along with *Havdalah*—light, spices. But these are kept together. If one blesses the light before the food, then the others will follow in sequence, and *Havdalah* will have to come first. But Judah b. Ilai also holds that the food comes first, and *Havdalah* comes at the end. Then what should the man do? He should bless the food, then the wine—as stated in Mishnah 8:8—and only then come the light and the subsequent blessings of *Havdalah.*

What is striking in this construction? First, the careful analysis of the opinions of each party shows a concern for reason, not for politics. We stand, after all, perhaps two or three hundred years after the decision that the law will normally follow the opinion of the House of Hillel in preference to that of the House of Shammai. So it might be natural to dismiss the latter and analyze only the former. The rabbis do no such thing, for they suppose each side has its reason, and under analysis this may produce new insight. The inquiry into theory is no game or puzzle. It is a most serious effort to extend the established rules to new cases, without regard to whether the rules are normative, as with the Hillelites, or merely a matter of discarded theory, as with the Shammaites.

Second, we continue to be confronted with the rabbis' efforts to discover the right order in which to say prayers, the proper way and form. The ideas of the House of Shammai are going to reveal something new in respect to a novel problem on the eve of the Sabbath, those of the House of Hillel to one on the end of the Sabbath. So these ideas are going to be tested against that new problem and worked out. We cannot suppose that for many hundreds of years, this "new" problem had never occurred in actual fact. It is unlikely that one day in the year A.D. 349, a man came home and wondered, Now which shall I bless first in this "new" situation? The contrary is the case. What probably happened is that for many centuries, no one wondered at all. Either things were established according to a rule long taken for granted, or, more likely, people simply did not give heed to the way they did things at all. The editors who construct the argument before us also raise to the level of conscious analysis what formerly cannot have been given any mind. That is the larger meaning of this inquiry into the opinions of the first-century authorities—people who themselves clearly did not pay attention to the issue to begin with. Asking the question, more than supplying the answer, yields the view that in an unexamined action is something worth asking about—so the action may no longer be left out of mind, outside of rational inquiry. We return to our text.

A. As to [the beginning of the] festival day which coincides with the end of the Sabbath—

The Sabbath comes to an end on Saturday night. But a festival day immediately follows on Saturday night and Sunday. What is the order of blessings?

R. Yohanan said, "[The order of prayer is] wine, Sanctification, light, *Havdalah*."

Yohanan inserts the Sanctification of the festival day after the blessing over the wine, but before *Havdalah*. Then Hanin in Rav's name will agree and add two further blessings.

Hanin bar Ba said in the name of Rav, "Wine, Sanctification, light, *Havdalah*, *Sukkah*, and season."

R. Hanina said, "Wine, light, *Havdalah*, Sanctification."

And did not Samuel rule according to this teaching of R. Hanina.

B. R. Aha said in the name of R. Joshua b. Levi, "When a king goes out and the governor comes in, they accompany the king and afterward bring in the governor."

C. Levi said, "Wine, *Havdalah*, light, Sanctification."

It stands to reason that Levi gave a summary of both of them. [That is, *Havdalah* is before Sanctification, as R. Hanina says, and then light and *Havdalah* are kept together, as R. Yohanan says.]

At the end of the Sabbath, as we already know, a person has to bless wine, food, light, spices, and say *Havdalah*. What does he do when a festival day, requiring a prayer of Sanctification as does the Sabbath, begins at the end of the Sabbath? (The several answers omit reference to the Grace after Meals.)

Yohanan says the man blesses the wine first, as the Hillelites say, then come the Sanctification, finally light, and *Havdalah*. To this list Hanin adds the blessings necessary for *Sukkot,* the festival of Tabernacles. He is in the tabernacle and has to say a blessing as he takes up residence there, ". . . who has sanctified us by his commandments and commanded us to dwell in the *Sukkah*." Then he says the blessing for the festival season, "Blessed are you, Lord our God, who sanctifies Israel and the seasons."

B then explains the view of those who place *Havdalah* first. You bid farewell to the Sabbath—the king, before bringing in the festival—the governor. The former is more important than the latter.

A. R. Zeira asked before R. Yosé, "How shall we do it in practice?"

He said to him, "According to Rav, and according to R. Yohanan."

And so too did the rule come out in practice—according to Rav and according to R. Yohanan.

B. *And when R. Abbahu went south, he would act in accord with R. Hanina, but when he went down to Tiberias, he would act in accord with R. Yohanan, for one does not differ from a man['s ruling] in his own place [out of courtesy].*

C. *According to the opinion of R. Hanina this poses no problem.*

But it poses a problem to the opinion of R. Yohanan: In the rest of the days of the year does he not bless the light, lest it go out [because of a draft, and he lose the opportunity to say the blessing]? And here too he should bless the light before it goes out!

What did R. Yohanan do in this connection? [How did he explain this difficulty?]

Since he has wine [in hand], his light will not go out [for it is protected].

Then let him bless the light at the end?

So as not to upset the order [of prayer; lit.: time] of the coming Sabbaths, [he does not do so].

The normative rule for actual practice is given by Yosé: wine, Sanctification, light, *Havdalah,* plus *Sukkah* and the blessing of the festival season. B explains that the great fourth-century authority, Abbahu, who lived in Caesarea, would follow the rule of Hanina when he went to Hanina's locale, and of Yohanan when he went to his. That is, in Tiberias the order was (1) wine, (2) Sanctification, (3) light, and (4) *Havdalah;* in the south, meaning Lydda, it was (1) wine, (3) light, (4) *Havdalah,* and (2) Sanctification. Thus the rabbi paid due respect to his peers.

C continues to analyze the foregoing rulings. The opinion of

Hanina poses no problems. After the wine, you bless the light right away; since you already see the light, you are obligated to bless it. And all will agree that the wine comes first.

But Yohanan's view does pose a problem, for he inserts Sanctification (2) between wine (1) and light (3), even though the man sees the light and therefore should bless it right away. On the rest of the days of the year, does he not bless the light right away, so that it not go out and he lose the opportunity to say the blessing? And if now he does not bless the light forthwith, lest it go out and he lose the occasion to say the blessing, he conducts himself contrary to normal usage. So why does Yohanan split up the wine (1) from the light (3)?

Yohanan's solution ("What did . . . do . . .") to the problem is this: Since the man has a cup of wine in his hand and has blessed it but not drunk it, he carefully guards it until he completes the entire order of blessings. He similarly is going to watch out that the light not go out until he says the appropriate blessing. If so, why not leave the light for last? So long as he has not drunk the wine, which he will do only at the end, obviously he likewise will continue to watch out that the light not go out. The answer is, since at the end of all Sabbaths he blesses the light before *Havdalah,* here too he should not change the order on account of all those Sabbaths coming later in the year. C is expressed in extremely apocopated language, but the thrust of the argument is clear. Both opinions have been fully examined and each is shown to be based upon sound reason.

8:2. **The House of Shammai say, They wash the hands and afterward mix the cup. And the House of Hillel say, They mix the cup first and afterward wash the hands.**

As before, we shall first go over the reasons given for the Houses' opinions by the Tosefta.

A. *What is the reason of the House of Shammai?*
So that the liquids which are on the outer side of the cup

may not be made unclean by his hands and go and make the cup unclean.

What is the reason of the House of Hillel? The outer side of the cup is always unclean [so there is no reason to protect it from the hands' uncleanness].

Another matter: One should wash the hands immediately before saying the blessing.

There is nothing new in these citations. But now comes a new problem. We shall try to show that the first-century Houses' opinions are consistent in principle with opinions assigned to later, second-century masters on a different subject entirely. The point is that in both cases the moot principles are the same.

B. *R. Biban in the name of R. Yohanan* [said], *"The opinion of the House of Shammai is in accord with R. Yosé and that of the House of Hillel with R. Meir, as we have learned there* [Mishnah Kelim 25:7–8]:

"[In all vessels an outer part and an inner part are distinguished, and also a part by which they are held.]"

The case involves a utensil, which has three elements, an inner part, an outer part, and a handle. These are regarded as separate from one another. If one part is unclean, the others are not necessarily unclean.

"R. Meir says, 'For the hands they are unclean and clean.'
"R. Yosé said, 'This applies only to clean hands alone.' "

Meir says that if your hands are unclean and you touch the outer side of the vessel, you do not make the handle unclean. If your hands are clean, and you touch one part which is clean, another part which is unclean has no effect on your hands. The hands still are clean.

Yosé says this distinction among the elements of the cup applies *only* if the hands are clean. How does this have anything to do with the Houses' opinions? I shall give the answer in the extended commentary below.

Firsts let us complete the discussion. The next question is whether you have to go to a lot of trouble to find water to wash your hands.

C. R. Yosé in the name of Rabbi Shabbetai, and R. Hiyya in the name of R. Simeon b. Laqish [said], "For *Hallah* [Dough-offering] and for washing the hands, a man goes four miles [to find water]."

Abbahu says you do *not* have to go to trouble to find water to clean the hands so as to touch the outer sides of a vessel.

R. Abbahu in the name of R. Yosé b. R. Hanina [said], "This is what he said, 'Before him [one must proceed to find water.] But for the outer sides they do not trouble him to backtrack.' "

Now we ask about people who have the job of guarding a field. We have to take account of their obligation to the employer. They should not be asked to leave their job without good reason. Are they expected to go looking for water to wash the hands so as to preserve the cleanness of both the inside and the outside of a cup?

D. Regarding those who guard gardens and orchards, *what do you do for them* as to the insides and the outer sides [of a cup]?

The answer derives from a different, but related law. A woman is allowed to do her religious duty of separating the dough-offering even without clothes on. You do not make her go to the trouble of getting a cloak. Yet that is a simple act. Obviously, if you do not bother her to do a very easy thing, you are not going to put a guardian of a field to a great deal more trouble in the same connection.

Let us infer the answer from this [Mishnah Hallah 2:3]:
The woman sits and cuts off her dough-offering [*Hallah*] while she is naked, because she can cover herself up, but a man cannot.
Now does not a woman sit in the house, yet you say they do not bother her? So too here they do not bother him.

Let us review the entire construction. We shall want to know, in particular, the relationship between the opinions of Meir and Yosé, on the one hand, and of the Houses of Shammai and Hillel on the other. For it is not yet obvious to us that the two disputes have anything to do with each other.

A is already familiar from the Babylonian Talmud. It is nothing more than the Tosefta's reason.

In B Yohanan tries to show that the position of the first-century Houses is taken up by later masters—mid-second-century authorities—who reason in a similar way on a parallel issue.

Mishnah Kelim 25:7 states that utensils are regarded as divided among an outer part, an inner part, and a handle. If one part becomes unclean, the others do not automatically become unclean. That is the meaning of the "division."

Meir then says this rule applies to unclean and clean hands. That is, if one touched the outer part with unclean hands, he does not make the handle unclean. If, reciprocally, clean hands touched a part, and the other part was unclean, the hands thereby are not made unclean. That is the meaning of "[This ruling applies] to unclean and clean hands." Therefore, according to Meir, the utensil is not regarded as wholly unclean if part of it is unclean.

Yosé says the distinction among parts of the cup is made only in the case of clean hands. They will not be made unclean if they touch the outer side, which is clean, even though the handle is unclean. But unclean hands do not follow this rule.

Both Yosé and the House of Shammai therefore hold that the outer part may be clean, even while the inner part is unclean. If the outer part is unclean, the handle may still be clean. So Yosé says the outer side of the cup is *not* always unclean. And this is contrary to the Hillelites' claim. If the hands were clean and liquid was dripping on them, and the outside of the cup was unclean, one may nonetheless hold the cup with the handle and not fear lest his hand may be unclean by the unclean outer part of the cup. We do not suppose, according to the Hillelites, that the liquid on the hands will be made unclean by the outer part of the cup and then go and make the hands unclean.

The House of Hillel therefore do not take account of the possibility important to the House of Shammai. Yosé, by contrast, says this rule applies only to clean hands. That is, if the hands are clean, and the outer part of the cup is unclean, we do not have to worry about uncleanness. But if the hands are unclean, we have to take precautions lest the liquid touch the unclean outer part of the cup and go and make the whole cup unclean.

The parallels therefore are clear. Yosé and the House of Shammai are concerned about unclean hands' not touching the liquid on the outer part of the cup, which then will go and make the cup unclean.

And the House of Hillel and Meir do not take account of that possibility *even* in the case of unclean hands' touching the liquid on the *outside* of the cup and making the whole cup unclean.

In C we have the rule that in order to prepare the dough for *Hallah*—the dough-offering—in a state of cleanness, or to wash hands, one has to take trouble to find water. This rule is then qualified: If one has the water in front of him, he has to go to get it, but he is not put to the trouble of walking back.

D asks whether watchmen have to take the trouble to leave their posts and go looking for water—forward or backward. The solution is found in the allusion to Mishnah Hallah 2:3. A woman is not required to get up and dress when she prepares the bread-offering. Then the authorities certainly will not bother the guards to leave their posts to go look for water. That is, if the law is lenient where only a slight inconvenience is involved, it certainly will be lenient where a major inconvenience is at hand.

To this point in the Palestinian Talmud we have seen arguments as intricate and well-constructed as any in the Babylonian one. In the first unit we found a careful analysis of the reasoning of each House, followed by an effort to draw further conclusions based on the respective Houses' principles. The pericope is well-balanced, fair to both sides, characterized by close and careful reasoning. No assertion is allowed to pass without criticism and testing. If the Palestinian Talmud exhibits stylistic differences from the Babylonian one, these are primarily in the mode of expression. The former seems more terse, less fully spelled out. But there is no qualitative difference in the rational process. The second unit, about the difficulty in finding wine, is certainly the most sophisticated pericope of our chapter in either Talmud. Here we introduce a practical problem and ask for concrete instructions. But the way of defining those instructions leads directly into the theoretical analysis and testing of the fundamental reasoning of each House. The evidence of established law is adduced, then applied in each case. The third and fourth units focus upon the actual procedures of major authorities; but these are more than mere stories or case reports, for each involves reconsideration of basic principles.

The discussion of Mishnah 8:2 brings us into a still more intricate problem: how to establish the continuity of legal opinion from the Houses, in the first century, to the masters of post-Bar Kokhba times ca. A.D. 150? For the Talmud, much is clear in a mere allusion to a law; the commentaries make lucid for us what already was obvious then. C and D introduce a further rule, about not going to a great deal of trouble to find water.

Had the Palestinian *Gemara* ended here, you would reasonably conclude that it in no way is inferior to the Babylonian one in its capacities for logical and sophisticated inquiry into legal principles and cases. And that would have been a quite false conclusion. For the Palestinian Talmud characteristically lacks the sustained, dialectical effort to establish continuities and harmonies, to make sense of simple sayings and cases in terms of larger principles, in all to employ the faculties of rational criticism in the analysis of each and every story and rule.

The exercise of practical reason, such as we have seen in the Palestinian *Gemara* to this point, hereinafter tends not to be consistently carried through and universally applied. We have just seen what *might* have been accomplished. We shall now observe how little was actually achieved in applying reason to practical law. For, from this point onward, our chapter of the Palestinian Talmud consists of little more than a compendium of sayings and stories pertinent to the Mishnah. It is solely of historical and antiquarian interest. But it exhibits few of the aesthetically satisfying and intellectually engaging traits of the other Talmud. Had the Babylonian Talmud looked like what is to follow, it probably would not have earned for itself the central place in the intellectual life of the Jewish people which it in fact enjoyed for fifteen centuries, and which it will continue to enjoy wherever people gather to devote intellect to the service of the religious life. It would have provided only important information for lawyers in the traditional court system and for historians and philologians interested in the Near East of late antiquity. It would, in other words, have functioned not much differently from the Palestinian Talmud.

A. *It has been taught:*
Washing before the meal is a matter of choice, but afterward it is a matter of obligation.

But in respect to the first washing, he washes and interrupts, and in the case of the second washing, he washes and does not interrupt.

We have two rules. First, a man is obligated to wash the hands after the meal, before reciting the Grace after meals. Beforehand, he may or may not do so. Second, he "washes and interrupts" in the first washing, not in the second. This now has to be explained.

B. What is the meaning of, "He 'washes and interrupts'?"
R. Jacob b. Aha said, "He washes and then repeats the washing."

Jacob b. Aha's reason seems obvious. Washing and interrupting means you have to wash a second time if you have not completed the action in the first place. But this is going to pose a problem. If you are *required* to repeat the washing, then how can you say it is a matter of choice?

R. Samuel bar Isaac said, "*If he is required* to repeat the washing, *how do you claim* it is a matter of choice?

"Or if you want, I may point out you require one to go four miles [in search of water], so *how do you claim* it is a matter of choice!"
C. R. Jacob bar Idi said, "On account of the first [washing of hands], a pig's flesh was eaten; on account of the second [washing of hands], a woman left her house."

"And some say, three souls were killed on her account. [It is not a matter of choice at all.]"

Jacob b. Idi's answer more or less ignores the question. He simply solves the problem by saying the original rule is wrong. You must make both washings. Let us review the whole.

A presents a Tannaitic teaching. B then attempts to explain it. The problem is the meaning of "wash and interrupt." Washing and repeating means that the man does not pour out all the water at once. He washes once, then goes and does it a second time.

If so, doing the act twice can hardly be interpreted as a matter of choice. The man is put to some trouble, and this must mean it is a fixed obligation that the act be done correctly. This seems contrary to the spirit of the rule that one does not have to go to the trouble to find water for washing.

To prove washing is required, Jacob b. Idi then refers to a story of an innkeeper who was selling both properly and improperly slaughtered meat, as well as pork. To whoever washed his hands he gave properly slaughtered (*kosher*) meat. One time a Jew came and did not wash his hands, and the innkeeper thought that he was a gentile and gave him pork.

As to the washing of the hands before Grace after Meals, the allusion is to a story (Babylonian Talmud, Yoma 83b) about Rabbis Judah, Yosé, and Meir who stayed at an inn maintained by a dishonest innkeeper. Judah and Yosé entrusted their purses to him on the Sabbath eve. Meir did not, but put it on the grave of the man's father. Meir retrieved his purse; the others then asked for theirs. The man denied they had deposited money with him. They then took the man to a shop and gave him something to drink. Afterward they saw a residue of lentils on his moustache. They went to his wife and told her that the husband had eaten lentils for lunch—a sign that the innkeeper had confided in them. They then said the husband sent them for the purses. She gave them the money. Outraged, the innkeeper came home and killed the wife: "It is with regard to this that it was taught . . . the 'second washing' killed a person." For had the innkeeper washed his hands after meals and wiped his upper lip, the rabbis would not have known what he had eaten. The man would not have killed his wife.

But Jacob b. Idi's story *should* have the man divorce the wife, for he refers to a woman's leaving home. "Some-say" 's version should have more murders. At any rate this is evidently the main outline of the story to which the vague allusion is made.

A. *Samuel went up to visit Rav. He saw him sitting and eating with* [his hands covered by] *a napkin. He said to him, "How so?* [Did you not wash your hands?]"
He said to him, "I am sensitive."

Samuel seems to suppose Rav did not wash his hands. Rather, he simply covered them with a napkin. He is told the reason has nothing to do with washing the hands. Rav has his private idiosyncrasy.

B. When R. Zeira came up here [to Palestine], he saw the priests eating with a napkin. He said to them, "Lo, this is in accord with the story of Rav and Samuel."

C. R. Yosé bar Kahana came [and said] in the name of Samuel, "One washes the hands for Heave-offering, not for unconsecrated food."

R. Yosé says, "For Heave-offering and for unconsecrated food."

R. Yosah in the name of R. Hiyya bar Ashi, and R. Jonah and R. Hiyya bar Ashi in the name of Rav [said], "They wash the hands for Heave-offering up to the wrist, and for unconsecrated food up to the knuckles."

D. Measha the son of the son of R. Joshua b. Levi said, "If one was eating with my grandfather and did not wash his hands up to the wrist, grandfather would not eat with him."

E. R. Huna said, "Washing the hands applies only for bread."

R. Hoshaia taught, "Whatever is unclean on account of liquid [is protected by washing the hands]."

R. Zeira said, "Even for cutting beets, he would wash his hands."

These stories again illustrate what we observed at the outset, that the deeds of the rabbis, even more than their words, constitute modes of "Torah." You will study Torah not merely by listening to, and memorizing, the masters' words, but also by carefully observing, and preserving the record of, what they actually did.

Samuel (A) thought that since Rav covered his hands with a napkin, he had not washed them. Rav then explained that he had washed them but preferred nonetheless to cover them.

In B Zeira cites this story to account for the behavior of the priests in eating their Heave-offering without washing their hands. So the napkin *is* sufficient protection against the ritual impurity. He concludes that, even in the opinion of both the masters, one still has to wash the hands, for unclean hands render Heave-offering unfit. In C we have the same view; one does have to wash for consecrated food, but not for ordinary food. Yosé differs, presumably an additional "decree" to protect the Heave-offering. Rav then presents the view that one must wash for both, but in the one case more of the hand is to be washed than in the other.

Then in D Measha reports his grandfather, Joshua b. Levi, differed from the ruling of Rav and required washing all the way to the wrist even for unconsecrated food.

In E Huna differs; the washing is only for bread. Hoshaia holds anything which may be mixed with liquid is to be protected by washing the hands. Finally, we have Zeira's view, the most extreme of all. No effort goes into harmonizing these discrete, contradictory opinions. We are left simply with a mere compendium of various rules, but no principles for interpreting, or choosing among them. This is typical of the Palestinian *Gemara*.

A. Rav said, "He who washed his hands in the morning is not required to do so in the afternoon."

B. R. Abina ordered his wine-steward, "Whenever you find water, wash your hands and keep doing so all day long."

C. R. Zeira went up to R. Abbahu in Caesarea. He found him saying, "I shall go to eat."

He gave him a chunk of bread to cut. He [Abbahu] said to him [Zeira], "Let the elder bless."

He [Zeira] said to him [Abbahu], "The host knows the value of his loaf." [You should bless.]

When they had eaten, he [Abbahu] said to him [Zeira], "Let the elder bless."

He said to him, "Rabbi, does the rabbi [you] know R.

Huna, a great man, who would say, 'He who opens [blesses first] must close [and say Grace after Meals]'?"

D. A Tannaitic teaching differs from R. Huna, as it has been taught:

The order of washing the hands in this: With up to five people present, they begin with the greatest. [If] more than this [are present], they begin with the least. In the middle of the meal, they begin with the eldest. After the meal they begin with the one who blesses.

Is it not [done] so that he may prepare himself for the blessing? [So he did not bless at the beginning!]

If you say the one who opens in the one who closes, he is already prepared [having opened the meal].

R. Isaac said, Explain it in regard to those who come in one by one and did not know which one had blessed [at the outset].

A gives Rav's lenient rule. B has a story indicating Abina took the opposite position.

The story in C concerns the etiquette for saying Grace before and after food. Zeira was invited to bless the bread, but advised the host it was proper only for the latter to do so. At the end he cited Huna's view that the man who blessed the bread at the beginning of the meal should also say the Grace at the end.

C presents a challenge to Huna's view. As to passing around water for the final washing, if five people are eating together, you begin with the most important; if there are more than five, you start with the least important person, and continue until five are left. Then you return to the greatest person who is present.

Finally, we are referred to the mixing of the cup at the end of the meal. You mix first for the one who is going to bless. This is interpreted as a means of designating the person to be assigned the honor of saying Grace after Meals.

But that interpretation is rejected. You begin from the one who is going to bless so that he will prepare himself to bless. Now if Huna were right that the one who breaks bread at the outset is the one who blesses at the end, why should he be given a sign to prepare himself for the blessing? He already is prepared from the beginning of the meal. So Huna's view seems contradicted. Isaac says the teaching cited in contradiction of Huna deals with a situation in which people came to the table one by one; they did not sit down all at once. Therefore, you cannot be sure who will bless at the end, since not all were present at the outset. So now they are given a sign to that effect. But this interpretation is hardly implied by the tradition cited earlier.

8:3. The House of Shammai say, "He dries his hands on the napkin and puts it on the table."
And the House of Hillel say, "On the cushion."

We once again are going to look for the reasons behind the Houses' respective rulings. But first, we establish a new definition for the situation.

A. The Mishnah deals with either a table of marble [which is not susceptible of uncleanness] or a table that can be taken apart and is not susceptible of becoming unclean.

The Houses both agree that we are dealing with a table which is *not* going to receive uncleanness! So the issue important in the Babylonian Talmud's analysis of the law is forthwith excluded. The possibility of leaving the napkin on the table is *not* going to be affected by the table's uncleanness, for our table is *not* susceptible to uncleanness.

B. *What is the reason of the House of Shammai?*
So that the liquids which are on the napkin may not become unclean from the cushion and go and render his hands unclean.

The House of Shammai are in the same position as before. That is, we are concerned about the liquids on the napkin. We do not want them to be made unclean by the cushion and then make his hands unclean. The table never was an issue to them. But the House of Hillel's position is going to change.

And what is the reason of the House of Hillel?
The condition of doubt[ful uncleanness] with respect to the hands is always regarded as clean.
Another reason: The [question of the cleanness of] hands does not apply to unconsecrated food [which in any case is not made unclean by unclean hands, unclean in the second degree].

The only principle available to the House of Hillel is this: The hands are *not* going to be made unclean at all! So you may put the napkin on the cushion. The Shammaite reason is based upon false premises. Furthermore, even if the hands are unclean, they will not affect unconsecrated food, but only Heave-offering—just as we noticed in the Babylonian Talmud. But this forthwith raises the question of the Shammaites' opinion on the subject.

C. *And according to the House of Shammai,* does [the question of the cleanness of] hands [indeed] apply to unconsecrated food?
D. *You may interpret* [the tradition] either in accord with R. Simeon b. Eleazar or in accord with R. Eleazar b. R. Saddoq.

We now have to find an opinion which will explain the position of the House of Shammai on the cleanness of the hands and unconsecrated food (not Heave-offering). The first tells us that the question of cleanness of hands most certainly *does* apply to unconsecrated food. The hands then may make such food unclean.

According to R. Simeon b. Eleazar, as it has been taught:
R. Simeon b. Eleazar says in the name of R. Meir, "Hands are in the first degree of uncleanness with respect to unconsecrated food, and in the second degree of uncleanness with respect to Heave-offering."

We may also explain the Shammaites' position in another way. Eleazar b. R. Saddoq says unconsecrated food prepared with consecrated food enters the status of the latter; Therefore, it *may* be made unclean by hands, which are unclean in the second degree. So the original question is neatly dealt with according to one of two opinions.

E. *Or according to R. Eleazar b. R. Saddoq, as we have learned there:*
Unconsecrated food which has been prepared along with consecrated [food] is like unconsecrated food [and subject to the same, less strict cleanness rules].
R. Eleazar b. R. Saddoq says, "Lo, it is like Heave-offering, capable of becoming unclean from [something unclean in the] second degree of uncleanness and to be rendered unfit from [something unclean in] still a further degree of uncleanness."
F. *There we have learned:*
He who anoints himself with clean oil and is made unclean and goes down and bathes [in a ritual pool]—
The House of Shammai say, "Even though he drips [with oil], it [the oil] is clean."
And the House of Hillel say, "It is unclean [so long as there remains enough to anoint a small member]."
And if the oil was unclean in the first place—
The House of Shammai say, "[It remains clean, even after he has immersed himself, so long as there remains] sufficient for anointing a small limb."
And the House of Hillel say, "[So long as it remains] a dripping liquid."

The reason this case is cited is not yet clear. But the problem is going to face the Hillelites. If a person who has anointed himself with clean oil becomes unclean and immerses himself, the House of Hillel say that, if the oil is still dripping, it is regarded as unclean. If the oil was unclean to begin with, of course it will remain unclean. So the House of Hillel do pay attention to the uncleanness of the liquid. Yet in the cases we just cited the House of Hillel seem *not* to care that the moist liquid in the napkin may be made unclean by the cushion.

R. Judah says in the name of the House of Hillel, "So long as it is dripping so as to moisten something else."

The problem will now be pointed out, then solved. The solution is based on a distinction between the two cases, the napkin and the oil. In the case of the napkin, the liquid has been absorbed. Therefore, it is ignored by the Hillelites. In the case of the oil, it is physically present in and of itself. Therefore, it is subject to concern.

G. *The principle of the House of Hillel has been turned around.*
There [in the just-cited law] *they say it is* unclean. *And here* [in our Mishnah] *they say it is* clean.
There it is present. *But here* it is absorbed in the napkin.

How is the foregoing to be put back together? As noted in our discussion of the Tosefta, the Palestinian Talmud takes for granted that the Mishnah deals with a table which is insusceptible to uncleanness. That is why the House of Hillel will allow the man to put the napkin on the table in preference to the cushion. The reason of the House of Shammai is clear: The liquid may be made unclean by the cushion and will go and make the hands unclean.

The House of Hillel are not sure that the cushion really is unclean, or that liquid actually is dripping from the napkin. In matters of doubt concerning the hands, we rule that the doubt is resolved in favor of cleanness. We therefore do not have to take account of the problem of the uncleanness of the cushion *or* of the table. Furthermore, hands will not make unconsecrated food unclean, for they are in the second degree of uncleanness, and something unclean in the second degree makes Heave-offering unfit, but does not make secular, unconsecrated food unclean.

C then raises the necessary query: Do the House of Shammai differ and hold that the unclean hands do make unconsecrated food unclean? If they do *not* hold that position, their opinion here is senseless. The following solution is proposed: The House of Shammai share the opinion of two masters who hold that the hands do indeed render food unclean.

D gives Simeon b. Eleazar's tradition in the name of Meir: the hands are in the *first* degree of uncleanness.

E cites Eleazar b. R. Saddoq, who says that if unconsecrated—nonpriestly—food is prepared in the condition of sanctity appropriate for Holy Things of the Temple, it will be subject to the laws of those Holy Things, which may be made unclean by something unclean in the second degree, such as the hands.

F introduces a new problem. The position of the House of Hillel seems inconsistent with their opinion on a related matter concerning unclean liquids. The case concerns a person who anointed himself with clean oil, was made unclean, and then immersed. The House of Hillel hold that, if so much oil remains on him as to be sufficient for anointing a small limb, the oil is regarded as unclean; but less than that amount of oil is clean. Then what if the oil was unclean to begin with? The Hillelites say if the liquid is enough to moisten the hand, the oil remains unclean.

In the first case, the presence of more oil than the specified quantity will mean the oil, made unclean by the man's uncleanness, remains unclean. Oil remaining on his flesh after the ritual bath is unclean. The oil is not made clean in the bath. If the oil to begin with was unclean, then, when at all moist, it remains unclean.

Now, clearly, the two cases take for granted a person is concerned about the unclean liquid. Yet here, by contrast, the House of Hillel are indifferent to the fact that the small amount of liquid in the napkin may be made unclean by the cushion.

The two cases therefore have to be distinguished from each other. In the present one, the liquid is absorbed into the napkin when the man dries his hands. So we are *not* concerned about its cleanness. But in the other case, concerning oil, the oil is apparent on the man's flesh, so remains unclean.

On several occasions we have examined the problem of why you have to wash your hands before eating. Indeed, so many reasons for doing so are before us that we must wonder whether anyone actually knew what originally was in the minds of the Houses. Notice, we worried about the table—clean or unclean, if unclean, in what degree. We asked about the hands—unclean only in the second degree, therefore not able to make the ordinary food unclean at all; or unclean in the first degree. We wondered about liquid which may or may not be on the napkin, or on the cup, or in the cushion. The simplest answer is Meir's: Hands are unclean in the first degree. But no one agrees with Meir. The arguments in both Talmuds take for granted he cannot be right—or they do not know his opinion to begin with. Then there are the Babylonian Talmud's priests, who are, or are not, assumed to be careful about where they eat.

Now what if cleanness plays no role in the original formation of the Houses' opinions? Perhaps their original rulings about washing the hands and mixing the cup, or about where you lay the napkin, have nothing to do with the laws of cleanness at all! Remember, when we came to cleaning the house and washing the hands, no one suggested that the issue was purity. We worried only about not wasting food. Perhaps here too the opinions of the Houses about the order of washing the hands and mixing the cup and about where you place the napkin were nothing more than matters of ordinary etiquette.

Once you ask the question, you are going to get the answer. But if to begin with is no "question," but merely a procedure with-

out anything more attached to it than "common sense" or cus-
omary behavior, what do we need these answers for?

My suspicion is that both the questions and the answers, which
have occupied us for a long time, are the creation of the later
rabbis, who take for granted some reason lies behind the opinions
of the respective Houses, and who therefore go in search of appropriate reasons and logical issues. That seems to me expressive
of the rabbis' mode of thought. It is not historical. The rabbis do
not look in ancient sources for the social or cultural motive behind
a ruling. Obviously, if the sources give evidence of such a motive,
they take it seriously. But normally the ancient sources in the
rabbis' hands are brief and enigmatic. So they leave it up to the
rabbis themselves to think up reasons for the opaque laws.

Modern men and women like to find historical reasons, perhaps
based upon the economic, or the psychological, or the sociological
realities of the day. The House of Shammai wished to give preference to the hands over the cup because their class in society held
such-and-such an opinion; the Hillelites, representing a lower
class, had the opposite opinion. You put the napkin on the table
because you are rich enough to afford to have a napkin. You put
it on the cushion because if you show it off, you are going to put
to shame the poor man who has no napkin. I do not mean to suggest modern scholars have so interpreted the issues before us, thus
reducing them to another set of values or to a different interpretive
framework from the one important to the law itself. But this is
the sort of reductionist interpretation that gives us a feeling we
truly have understood things.

The rabbis too seek satisfying explanations. To begin with, they
suppose that such explanations are indeed to be found—the most
satisfying conviction of all! Their explanations stress not social
realities, economic interests, psychological preferences, even aesthetic concern, but purity laws. The stress on purity is apt to tell
us more about the rabbis than it does about the original reasons,
if any, of the Houses. And what it tells us we already know. We
need to remind ourselves, however, that the fact in *our* hands is

what the rabbis have to say about the tradition in *their* hands, not about the original intent of the authorities behind the tradition. I should not be surprised to learn that, about a hundred years after the Houses' opinions were formed into little mnemonic lists, no one had a clear picture of the reasons, if any, for the arrangements of opinions, let alone for the abstract and general laws reduced to those arrangements. So everyone has a chance to think out his own interpretation.

8:4. **The House of Shammai say, "They clean the house and afterward wash the hands." And the House of Hillel say, "They wash the hands and afterward clean the house."**
What is the reason of the House of Shammai?
Because of the waste of food.
And what is the reason of the House of Hillel?
If the servant is clever, he removes the crumbs which are less than an olive's bulk, and they wash their hands and afterward they clean the house.

The discussion does not differ from that in the Babylonian Talmud, except that we should expect the crumbs to be an olive's bulk of *larger,* rather than *less.* So the meaning must be "Crumbs [to a size] less than an olive's bulk are removed."

8:5. **The House of Shammai say, "Light, and food, and spices, and Havdalah." And the House of Hillel say, "Light, and spices, and food, and Havdalah." The House of Shammai say, " 'Who created the light of the fire.' " And the House of Hillel say, " 'Who creates the lights of the fire.' "**
A. It was taught:
R. Judah said, "The House of Shammai and the House of Hillel did not differ concerning the [blessing for] the meal, that it comes at the beginning, or concerning Havdalah, that it comes at the end. And concerning what did they differ? Concerning the light and spices, for the House of Shammai

say, 'Spices and light.' And the House of Hillel say, 'Light and spices.'"

R. Ba and R. Judah in the name of Rav [said], "The law is in accord with him who says, 'Spices and afterward light.' [That is, Judah's House of Shammai.]"

B. The House of Shammai say, "The cup [should be] in his right hand, and the sweet oil in his left hand. He says [the blessing for] the cup and afterward says the blessing for the sweet oil."

The House of Hillel say, "The sweet oil [should be] in his right hand and the cup in his left hand, and he says [the blessing for] the sweet oil and rubs it in the head of the servant. If the servant is a disciple of a sage, he rubs it on the wall, for it is not fitting for a disciple of a sage to go forth scented in public."

C. *Abba bar bar Hanna and R. Huna were sitting and eating, and R. Zeira was standing and serving them. He went and bore both of them [oil and cup] in one hand.*

Abba bar bar Hana said to him, "Is one of your hands cut off?" And his [Abba's] father was angry at him.

He [the father] said to him [Abba], "Is it not enough for you that you are sitting and he is standing and serving? And furthermore, he is a priest, and Samuel said, 'He who makes [secular] use of the priesthood has committed sacrilege.' You make light of him.

"I decree for him to sit and you to stand and serve in his place."

The little story is meant to show several things. First, you should not hold the oil and the cup in the same hand. But, second, you have to show respect for the young man. Now the rule is introduced that you should not make secular use of a priest. That is, just as the Temple is reserved for sacred purposes, so the priests of the Temple cannot be employed for other than sacred tasks.

D. How do we know that he who makes use of the priesthood has committed sacrilege?

R. Aha in the name of Samuel said, " 'And I said to them, You are holy to the Lord and the vessels are holy' [Ezra 8:28]. Just as one who makes use of the vessels commits sacrilege, so he who makes use of the priests commits sacrilege."

[The House of Shammai say, " 'Who created . . .' "]

E. According to the opinion of the House of Shammai [one should say as the blessing for wine] "Who created the fruit of the vine" [instead of "who creates . . . ," as actually is said].

The criticism of the Shammaite position is a good one. Why do they take inconsistent positions, on the one hand saying "who creates the fruit of the vine," but on the other, "who *created* the light . . ."?

According to the opinion of the House of Hillel, [one should say] "Who creates the fruit of the vine" [as is indeed the case].

The Shammaites will make a distinction between the two cases.

The Shammaite reply:
The wine is newly created every year, but the fire is not newly created every hour.

This is a fair distinction and satisfactorily lays the objection to rest.

The next set of materials is long but poses no problems. It is first asserted that although the fire and the mule were not actually created during the first six days, they were *thought of* during that time. This point will then be proved by reference to various Scriptures. Thus the subject will run on. How do you know the difference between a mule whose sire was an ass, and one whose sire was a horse? Afterward, the story of Zibeon and Anah, which is alluded to at the outset, will be discussed. Finally, the creation of fire, mentioned in the beginning, is going to be described. Fire came at the very end of the first Sabbath, on Saturday night after the first week of creation.

F. The fire and the mule, even though they were not created in the six days of creation were thought of [entered the Creator's mind] in the six days of creation.

Proof of the mule: "These are the sons of Zibeon: Aiah and Anah; he is the Anah who found the hot springs (HYYMYM) in the wilderness" [Genesis 36:24].

What is the meaning of hot springs (HYYMYM)?

R. Judah b. Simeon says, "Mule." [Greek: *hemiovos.*]

And the rabbis say, "Half-a-horse [Greek: hemi-hippos], half was a horse, half an ass."

And what are the marks [to know whether the father was a horse, the mother an ass, or vice versa]?

R. Judah said, "If the ears are small, the mother was a horse and the father an ass. If they are big, the mother was an ass and the father a horse."

R. *Mana instructed the members of the Patriarchate,* "If *you want to buy a mule, buy those whose ears are small,* for the mother was a horse and the father an ass."

What did Zibeon and Anah do? They brought a female ass and mated her with a male horse, and they produced a mule.

The Holy One, blessed be he, said to them, "You have brought into the world something which is destructive. So I too shall bring upon that man [you] something which is destructive."

What did the Holy One, blessed be he, do?

He brought a snake and mated it with a lizard and it produced a *havarbar*-lizard.

A man should never say to you that a *havarbar*-lizard bit him and he lived, or a mad dog nipped him and he lived, or a she-mule butted him and he lived. We speak only of a white she-mule.

F. As to the fire:

R. Levi in the name of R. Nezira [said], "Thirty-six hours that light which was created on the first day served [the world]. Twelve on the eve of the Sabbath [Friday], twelve on the night of the Sabbath, and twelve on the Sabbath.

"And the First Man [Adam] looked at it from one end of the world to the other. When the light did not cease [from shining], the whole world began to sing, as it is said, 'Under the whole heaven, he lets [his voice] go, and his light to the corners of the earth' [Job 37:2].

"When the Sabbath ended, it began to get dark. Man became frightened, saying, 'This is the one concerning whom it is written, "He will bruise your head, and you shall bruise his heel" [Genesis 3:15].

" 'Perhaps this one has come to bite me.' And he said, 'Let only darkness cover me' " [Psalm 139:11].

R. Levi said, "At that moment the Holy One, blessed be he, prepared two flints and struck them against each other, and the light came forth from them. This is the meaning of that which Scripture says, 'And the light around me be night' [Psalm 139:11].

"And he [man] blessed it, 'Who creates the lights of the fire.' "

Here we have the story of the discovery of fire. Man did not steal it from the god. He was not punished, as was Prometheus, on that account. Fire is a blessing. It was given by God to man to reassure him against the darkness. Fire is a gift of God and so testifies to God's benevolent protection of the fearful man. That is why you thank God for fire and for light—for the darkness is not too dark for God. Samuel will make clear why the blessing for fire comes at *Havdalah,* on the occasion of darkness at the end of the Sabbath.

G. Samuel said, "Therefore they bless the fire at the end of the Sabbath, for that is when it was first created."

H. R. Huna in the name of R. Abbahu in the name of R. Yohanan [said], "Also at the end of the Day of Atonement one blesses it, for the light has rested that entire day."

The comments on Mishnah 8:5 form a sequence of sayings pertinent to the Mishnah's theme, but none is either closely examined or integrated with any other.

A simply cites Judah [b. Ilai]'s tradition on the difference between the Houses and the opinions assigned to each. Rav's saying tells us the law, but not the House to which that law is attributed according to his version of the Houses' dispute.

B introduces further Toseftan materials, again without examination.

Then C tells us a story, somewhat relevant to the Tosefta's rule about having the cup in one hand, the oil in the other; you should not carry them together in one hand. D further augments C.

E brings a challenge to the view of the House of Shammai about using the past tense, *created,* in connection with the light. If creation is completed, then the blessing for wine is rightly, "Who creaed the fruit of the vine." This poses no problem to the Hillelites. The answer is that there is a difference between the creation of wine and that of fire. If you compare this primitive analysis of the Shammaite position with the better developed and more interesting one in the Babylonian Talmud, you see what might have been done on this question.

E then brings in a passage only remotely connected to the foregoing. It refers to the creation of fire and the mule (!). Then the mention of the mule involves us in a long discussion of how various hybrids are created and of how to identify their constituent elements. F brings us back to the fire, and G-H gloss the issue, but not the story.

Nothing before us has been generated by the Palestinian Talmud's editors themselves for the analysis of our Mishnah. Everything derives from some other corpus of materials. We have here a little anthology of pertinent sayings and stories, by contrast to the discussions of the earlier sections of the Mishnah, in which we discern a sustained effort to develop original inquiries.

8:6. **They do not bless the light or spices of gentiles, nor the light or spices of the dead, nor the light or spices which are before an idol. They do not bless the light until they make use of its light.**

A. R. Jacob taught before R. Jeremiah, "They do bless the spices of gentiles."

What is the difference [between this view and the Mishnah's]?

We explain that the latter refers to the gentile's deeds before his own store, [while the Mishnah refers to a banquet].

B. Even though it has not gone out [but burned the entire Sabbath], they may bless [the light of] a lantern [because no prohibited work has been done by its light].

C. As regards a flame in the folds of one's garment, in a lamp, or in a mirror, if one sees the flame but does not make use of its light, or makes use of its light but not see the flame, one may not bless it. [One may bless] only when one may see the flame and makes use of the light.

D. Five things were said in regard to the burning coal, and five with regard to the flame.

1. A coal of the sanctuary is subject to the law of sacrilege, but a flame is neither used for pleasure nor subject to the law of sacrilege.

2. A burning coal used for idolatry is prohibited, but a flame is permitted.

3. He who vows not to have enjoyment from his fellow may not use his burning coal, but may use his flame.

4. He who brings a coal out to the public way [on the Sabbath] is liable, but if he brings a flame, he is not liable.

5. They bless the flame, but not the burning coal.

R. Hiyya bar Ashi in the name of Rav said, "If the coals were flaming, they may bless them."

R. Yohanan of Kerasion in the name of R. Nahum bar Simai [said], "On condition that it was cut off." [That is, the flame was shooting up from the coal.]

A produces a rule contrary to that printed in the Mishnah: One *may* bless the spices of gentiles. The Mishnah is understood to refer to a banquet—just as in the Babylonian discussion—while Jacob's view alludes to the spices belonging to a private person. These are not necessarily used for idolatrous purposes.

B tells us that a flickering lantern which has burned the entire Sabbath may be blessed; nothing forbidden has been done in its light. This is all we have as an equivalent to the Babylonian Talmud's full discussion of whether or not a candle has "rested" on the Sabbath.

C cites the Tosefta, and D is a group of five rules which make the same point about the coal and the flame. The one is material, the other immaterial. The fourth is contradicted in he Babylonian Talmud, which therefore presumably does not know this list; if it did, someone would have remarked on the contradiction.

It was taught:

A. A gentile who kindled [a light from the flame of] an Israelite, and an Israelite who kindled [a light from the flame of a gentile]—*this poses no problems.*

But [the light of] a gentile who kindled [a light from the flame of] an Israelite [may be blessed]. If so, even [the flame of] a gentile who kindled from a gentile [should be allowed].

The problem is the same as that posed in the Babylonian Talmud. What is the reason you may not kindle a flame from one kindled by a gentile from a gentile, if you *may* do so from a flame kindled by an Israelite from a gentile.

It is indeed taught: They do *not* bless [a light kindled by] a gentile from a gentile.

The solution to the problem is no solution at all. It simply reasserts the original proposition.

B. R. Abbahu in the name of R. Yohanan [said,] "As to an alleyway which is populated entirely by gentiles with a single Israelite living in its midst—if the light comes from there, they may bless it on account of that one Israelite who lives there."

Yohanan will now be cited in a saying, which, in concrete terms, repeats the principle already established in general language, that you may say a blessing over something which is used for its normal purpose. But you may not recite a blessing over something which is used for some abnormal purpose—spices used for cleaning clothes, for example.

C. R. Abbahu in the name of R. Yohanan [said], "They do not bless either the spices on Sabbath evenings in Tiberias or the spices on Saturday nights in Sepphoris, or the light or the spices on Friday mornings in Sepphoris, for these all are prepared only for another purpose [cleaning clothes]."

D **Nor over the light or spices of the dead.**

R. Hezekiah and R. Jacob b. Aha in the name of R. Yosi b. R. Hanina [said], "This is what you say: 'When they are placed over the bed of the dead. But if they are placed *before* the bed of the dead, they may be blessd.'

"[For] I say, they are prepared for the purposes of the living."

E. **Nor the light nor the spices of idolatry.**

But is not that of gentiles the same as that of idolatry? [Why repeat the same rule?]

Interpret it as applying to an Israelite idol.

A quotes and examines, then emends, the Tosefta's rule. B gives a law contrary to the Babylonian Talmud's *baraita,* which held a *majority* must be Israelites before the flame may be blessed. Again it seems this rule cannot have been known to the Babylonian editors.

In C we have the same view as above: People in Galilee would use spice for cleaning clothes; therefore, you may not bless the spice at the times at which it is used for that purpose.

D goes back over the law that you have to use a light for its normal purpose, not for the honor of a corpse.

E raises a good problem in literary analysis. The Mishnah seems to repeat itself. The solution is routine.

They do not bless the light until they make use of its illumination.

A. R. Zeira son of R. Abbahu expounded, " 'And God saw the light, that it was good' [Genesis 1:4]. And afterward, 'And God divided the light from the darkness' " [Genesis 1:5]. [That is, first it was seen and used, then comes the *Havdalah.*]

B. R. Berekiah said, "Thus the two great men of the world [age], R. Yohanan and R. Simeon b. Laqish, expounded: 'And God divided—a certain division." [That is, he did so literally.]

R. Judah b. R. Simon said, "They divided for Him."

And the rabbis say, "They divided for the righteous who were destined to come into the world.

"They drew a parable: To what is the matter to be likened? To a king who has two generals. This one says, 'I shall serve by day,' and this one says, 'I shall serve by day.'

"He calls the first and says to him, 'So-and-so: The day will be your division.'

"He calls the second and says to him, 'So-and-so, the night will be your division.'

"That is the meaning of what is written, 'And God called the light day, and the darkness he called night.'

"To the light he said, 'The day will be your province.' And to the darkness he said, 'The night will be your province.' "

R. Yohanan said, "This is what the Holy One, blessed be He, said to Job [Job 38:12], 'Have you commanded the morning since your days began, and caused the dawn to know its place?'

"What is the place of the light of the six days of creation—where was it hidden?"

R. Tanhuma said, "I give the reason: 'Who creates light and makes darkness, and makes peace' [Isaiah 45:7]. When he went forth, he made peace between them."

C. **They do not bless the light until they make use of its illumination.**

Rav said, "They use [spelled with an 'alef]."

And Samuel said, "They enjoy [spelled with an 'ayin]."

He who said "they use" [may draw support from the following]:

"Only on this condition will we consent to you" [Genesis 34:15].

He who said "enjoy" [may draw support from the following]:

"How to sustain with a word him that is weary" [Isaiah 50:4].

There we have learned: "How do they extend (M'BR) the Sabbath limits of cities?"

Rav said, "Add" ['alef].

And Samuel said, "Increase" ['ayin].

He who said it is with an 'alef means they add a limb to it.

He who said it is with an 'ayin means it is [increased] like a pregnant woman.

There we learned, "Before the festivals ('YD) of gentiles."

Rav said, "Testimonies" ['ayin].

And Samuel said, "Festivals" ['alef].

He who said it is with an 'alef [may cite this verse], "For

near is the day of their calamity ['YD]" [Deuteronomy 32:35].

He who said it is with an 'ayin [may cite], "Their testimonies neither see nor know, that they may be put to shame" [Isaiah 44:9].

How does Samuel deal with the reason of Rav? [He may say,] "And their *testimonies* are destined to *shame* those who keep them on the day of judgment."

D. **They do not bless the light until they have made use of its illumination.** [How much illumination must there be?]

R. Judah in the name of Samuel said, "So that women may spin by its light."

R. Yohanan said, "So that one's eye can see what is in the cup and what is in the saucer."

R. Hanina said, "So that one may know how to distinguish one coin from another."

E. R. Oshaia taught, "Even [if the flame is in] a hall ten by ten, they may say the blessing."

R. Zeira drew near the lamp. His disciples said to him, "Rabbi, why do you rule so stringently for us? Lo, R. Oshaia taught, 'One may bless even in a hall ten by ten.' "

The point of A is that Scripture itself implies you must actually use the light before saying *Havdalah*. It refers to God's "saying *Havdalah*"—that is, making a division—only after he had looked at the light.

B then introduces a story about why the light was divided from the darkness.

C is a collection of three examples of disputes between Rav and Samuel, early third-century Babylonian masters, about whether words are spelled with the *'alef* or the *'ayin,* both evidently silent letters in Babylonia, not distinguished from each other in pronunciation. The first concerns the spelling of the word *use* in our Misnah; the difference produces variations in meanings, *use* versus *enjoy*. Each then is given a Scripture in which his spelling of the word appears. The second has to do with extending the Sabbath limits of a city; the *'alef* spelling of the word in question produces the meaning of *increase-by-adding-on,* augment; and the *'ayin* spelling produces the meaning of *increase-from-within,* expand. The final example has to do with the word for festival employed for gentile festivals. The *'alef* spelling yields a play on words, for, spelled with an *'alef,* the word means both "festival" and "calamity"; the *'ayin* spelling means "testimony."

D and E illuminate the rule about using the illumination. How is this to be defined? The answers are routine. Oshaia's interpretation in E is not much different, except that he evidently regards as adequate the light available at a still greater distance from the flame. The story that follows provides a different literary and formal setting for the citation of Oshaia's rule.

8:7. **He who ate and forgot and did not bless—**
The House of Shammai say, "He should go back to his place and bless."
And the House of Hillel say, "He may bless in the place in which he remembered.
"Until when may he say the blessing? Until the food has been digested in his bowels."
A. *R. Yusta b. Shunam said, "[There are] two authorities. One gives the reason of the House of Shammai and the other the reason of the House of Hillel."*

Instead of a debate, we shall have a simple statement of the positions of the respective Houses. But the actual opinions are familiar from the more fully articulated version in the Babylonian Talmud. The Shammaites say you would take some trouble for material things, so you should also take some trouble for the divinity. The Hillelites say you do not put people to too much trouble.

"The one who gives the reason of the House of Shammai [says], 'If he had forgotten a purse of precious stones and

pearls there, would he not go back and take his purse? *So too let him go back to his place and bless?'*

"The one who gave the reason of the House of Hillel [states], 'If he were a worker on the top of the palm or down in a pit, would you trouble him to go back to his place and bless? But he should bless in the place where he remembers [to do so]. *Here too* let him bless in the place where he remembers.' "

B. **Until when does he bless?**

The Mishnah will be defined in concrete terms. How long is a person liable to say a blessing? If he forgets after a certain time, he surely is not going to be expected to say the Grace. The definitions are reasonable.

R. Hiyya in the name of Samuel said, "So long as he is thirsty on account of that meal."

R. Yohanan says, "Until he becomes hungry again."

The "reasons" of A and the definitions of B do not greatly differ from what we have seen in the Babylonian *Gemara*.

8:8. **If wine came to them after the food, and there is there only one cup—**

The House of Shammai say, "He blesses the wine and afterward blesses the food."

And the House of Hillel say, "He blesses the food and afterward blesses the wine."

They answer Amen after an Israelite who blesses, and they do not answer Amen after a Samaritan who blesses until the entire blessing has been heard.

A. R. Ba said, "Because it is a brief blessing, he may forget and drink the wine. But because it is joined to the [blessings for] cup, he will not forget."

B. **After an Israelite they answer Amen,** even though he

has not heard [the Grace]. Has it not been taught, "If he heard [the Grace] and did not answer, he has carried out his obligation [to say Grace]. If he answered [Amen] and did not hear [the Grace], he has not carried out his obligation."

The problem is already familiar. We assume the man has eaten, but has heard only part of the grace. But he has to hear the whole of the prayer if he is to have carried out his obligation to say the Grace after Meals. The solution is simple. As before, we have made the wrong assumption. In fact, the man did not participate in the meal, so is not obligated at all. Yet, we are taught, he still is supposed to respond with *Amen*.

Hiyya the son of Rav said, "[The Mishnah speaks of him who] did not eat with them as much as an olive's bulk."

So to it has been taught: If he heard and did not answer, he has carried out his obligation. If he answered and did not hear, he has not carried out his obligation.

Now Rav is going to refine the foregoing rule.

C. Rav in the name of Abba bar Hanna [said], *and some say Abba bar Hanna in the name of Rav* [said], "And this applies to a case in which he answered at the chapter [paragraph] headings."

D. *R. Zeira asked, "What are these chapter headings?"*

"Praise the Lord, praise the servants of the Lord, praise the name of the Lord" [Psalm 113:1].

Hiyya b. Abba will now explain the rule given at the outset, that merely hearing the Grace after Meals, without answering Amen, is sufficient to carry out one's obligation in that connection.

E. *They asked before R. Hiyya b. Abba, "How do we know*

that, if one heard and did not answer [Amen], he has carried out his obligation?"

Hiyya's answer draws upon the actual deeds of the rabbis of the day.

He said, "From what we have seen the great rabbis doing, so they do in public, for they say this: 'Blessed is he that comes.' And the others say, 'In the name of the Lord.' And both groups thus complete their obligation."

R. Oshaia taught, "A man responds Amen, even though he has not eaten, and he does not say, 'Let us bless him of whose bounty we have eaten,' unless he actually ate."

We have a new tradition—several types of *Amens.* These will be listed, then explained.

F. *It has been taught,* They do not respond with an orphaned Amen, a cut-off Amen, or a hasty Amen.

Ben Azzai says, "If one answers an orphaned Amen, his sons will be orphans. A cut-off one—his years will be cut off. A hasty one—his soul will be cut down. A long one—his days and years will be lengthened with goodness."

What is an orphaned Amen?

R. Huna said, "This refers to a person who sat down to bless, and he answered, but did not know to what [prayer] he answered [Amen]."

G. It was taught: If a gentile who blessed the divine name, they answer Amen after him.

R. Tanhum said, "If a gentile blesses you, answer after him Amen, as it is written, 'Blessed will you be by all the peoples' " [Deuteronomy 7:14].

A gentile met R. Ishmael and blessed him. He said to him, "You have already been answered."

Another met him and cursed him. He said to him, "*You have already been answered.*"

His disciples said to him, "*Rabbi, how could you say the same to both?*" He said to them, "Thus it is written in Scripture: 'Those that curse you will be cursed, and those that bless you will be blessed' " [Genesis 27:29].

The story about Ishmael calls to mind the very different formulation of the same attitude, that Israel is not wholly powerless in the face of the gentiles. God has already decided the relationships between Israel and the peoples of the world. If a gentile blesses you and treats you kindly, it is because God has ordained the peoples will bless Israel. If a gentile curses you ("anti-semitism") or pushes you around, this too has been taken care of by God: That man will be cursed. So whatever happens—in the village as much as in the heavens—reveals the plan and will of God. Nothing that takes place, whether the setting of the sun in the skies or the gesture of good will in the streets, whether in nature or in "history," to use grand, if inappropriate language, falls outside the realm of Torah.

Ba's explanation in A stands all by itself. Without some sort of commentary or explanation, one should have difficulty knowing what point Ba intends to make. The contrast to the Babylonian version of the same explanation is striking indeed. There we see what has led us to this little "explanation." In fact, Ba's saying comes at the end of, and summarizes, a considerable discussion.

The same pattern recurs in B. We are not told the problem, only the solution, given by Hiyya. C-D-E further illuminate the problem of saying *Amen* at the Grace after Meals. F gives three examples of unsatisfactory *Amens,* and G concludes the chapter with a little story.

The difference between the last half of the Palestinian Talmud and the equivalent discussions of the same Mishnahs in the Babylonian Talmud is striking. In some instances the very same issues are raised. But while the Babylonian Talmud spells things out in detail, the Palestinian one supplies only enigmatic sayings.

A still more striking difference is in the failure of the Palestinian Talmud's editors to make much of the materials they do cite. Analyses, critical or otherwise, are few and far between. Normally, the editor simply tosses in a saying pertinent to the Mishnaic law, or at least relevant to its theme, and that completes his *Gemara*.

The Babylonian Talmud not only is tightly organized, but also excludes materials not closely pertinent to the Mishnah. The Palestinian one by contrast includes a wide range of stories and sayings remotely connected to the Mishnah's original concerns.

That is not to suggest the Palestinian Talmud is uninteresting. Its discrete stories reveal the mind of the rabbis who told them. One may learn a good deal about how they imagined the process of the creation of the world, for instance; or about how they envisioned the worldly relationships among imperial authorities. The exegeses of texts show how the rabbis understood Scriptures. The little collections of *'alef-'ayin* wordplays of Rav and Samuel is important evidence about how words were pronounced. In their own context, however, when properly set alongside the Mishnah passages to which they are pertinent, they yield considerable differences in the interpretation of the meaning of the Mishnah's language. Here they do not.

The primary problem for us is whether now one can attempt to enter the discussions of the Palestinian Talmud. The answer clearly is that one cannot. The materials may be elucidated by scholars of exegesis and used by historians. The one thing one cannot do is join the conversation, because, as is already clear, the discussion in the latter part of the chapter lacks a concern for logical inquiry and rational criticism. One can hardly call it a conversation at all. In the Babylonian Talmud and in the first part of the chapter before us, one may attempt to work out and master technicalities, because these provide the wherewithal for understanding something beyond the technicalities. The rest of the Palesinian Talmud just now reviewed consists of little more than details, some charming, some esoteric, but all episodic and none suggestive of anything beyond itself. One cannot regard the materials of the Palestinian Talmud as very "Talmudic" at all.

CHAPTER
VII

Talmudic Thinking and Us

THE TALMUD we have studied records not only laws, but the processes by which laws are uncovered. By describing those processes, the rabbis propose to resolve the tension between ordinary life and logic. Using the data deriving from revealed laws of ritual purity and liturgy, the Talmud engages in the give-and-take of argument about what one is obligated to do and not do in eating a meal. The argument develops its themes through inquiry into fundamental, unifying principles and their application of those to ordinary affairs. Humble matters of where one puts his napkin are shown to reveal such underlying principles. These are then subjected to analysis and produce a search for still more basic, and ultimately unifying conceptions. The primary convictions which generate this search for hidden unities are that God is one, creation derives from the single, omnipotent and omnipresent Creator, and Torah expresses his wholly self-consistent will. We deal, therefore, with the intellectual effects of the fundamental conviction of monotheism.

The conceptions turned up by the rabbis' quest for the principles to guide everyday deeds prove to be highly relative and abstract. For nothing is more abstract than the nonmaterial, or supramaterial, laws of purity and impurity. So even the placing of a napkin at a meal is turned into a sacred discipline for living, a discipline which requires that logic and order everywhere prevail, and demands, as I said, that concerns for a vast world of unseen, well-regulated, and highly principled relationships of sanctity come to bear. Thoughtless action is elevated, sanctified, made worthy of thought, and is shown to bear heavy consequences. Thus, as Judah Goldin says, "Study, interpretation, debate are the discipline for living; without them no right action is likely. . . ."*

The Talmud is a fundamentally nonhistorical document. It does not appeal to the authority of the past. The argument, though unfolding by generations of rabbis, is not about the authority and biography of the ancients, but about their timeless, impersonal reasons for ruling as they do. The participants in the argument sometimes are named, but the most interesting constructions are given anonymously: "What is the reason of the House of Shammai?" "Do not the House of Shammai and the House of Hillel agree with R. Yosé and R. Meir, respectively?" These elegant structures are not assigned to specific authorities, because to the Talmud the time and place, name and occupation of the authority behind an inquiry are of no great interest. Logic and criticism are not bound to specific historical or biographical circumstances. Therefore, the principles of orderly, disciplined, holy life are not reduced to the personalities or situations of the men who laid down or discovered those principles.

Talmudic thinking stands over against historical and psychological interpretation because of its preference for finding abstraction and order in concrete, perennial problems of daily life. What counts is reason, ubiquitous, predominant, penetrating. The object of reason is twofold: first, the criticism of the given by the criterion of fundamental principles of order; and second, the demonstration of the presence within commonplace matters of transcendent considerations. Casuistical controversy over trivialities does not always link up to a transcendent concern for the sacred; but it always is meant to. For the ultimate issue is how to discover the order of

* *The Living Talmud* (N.Y., 1957: Mentor, New American Library), p. 15.

the well-ordered existence and well-correlated relationships; and the prevalent attitude is perfect seriousness (not specious solemnity) about life, man's intentions, and his actions.

The presupposition of the Talmudic approach to life is that order is better than chaos, reflection than whim, decision than accident, ratiocination and rationality than witlessness and force. The only admissible force is the power of fine logic, ever refined against the gross matter of daily living. The sole purpose is so to construct the discipline of everyday life and to pattern the relationships among men that all things are intelligible, well-regulated, trustworthy—and sanctified. The Talmud stands for the perfect intellectualization of life, that is, the subjection of life to rational study. For nothing is so trivial as to be unrelated to some conceptual, abstract principle. If the placing of a napkin or the washing of the hands is subject to critical analysis, what can be remote from the Talmud's rigorous inquiry? But the mode of inquiry is not man's alone. Man is made in God's image. And that part of man which is like God is not corporeal. It is the thing which separates man from beast: the mind, consciousness. When man uses his mind, he is acting like God. That surely is a conviction uncharacteristic of modern intellectuals, yet at the heart of Talmudic intellectuality.

The Talmud's conception of us is obvious: We think, therefore we and what we do are worth taking seriously. We will respond to reason and subject ourselves to discipline founded upon criticism. Our response will consist in self-consciousness about all we do, think, and say. To be sure, man is dual, we are twin-things, ready to do evil and ready to do good. The readiness is not all, though some now think so. Beyond readiness there is mindfulness. As the Talmudic warning about not interrupting one's study even to admire a tree—that is, nature—makes clear, man cannot afford even for one instant to break off from consciousness, to open ourselves to what appears then to be "natural"; to be mindless is to lose touch with revealed order and revealed law, the luminous disciplines of the sacred.

Nor is the ultimate issue of man solely ethical; it is holiness. To be sure, one must do the good, but Torah encompasses more than ethical behavior. The good is more than the moral; it is also the well-regulated conduct of matters to which morality is impertinent. The whole man, private and public, is to be disciplined. Etiquette—who blesses first—is blended with theology—the imitation of God's behavior at the end of the first Sabbath; furthermore with something one might call metaphysics—the composition of the flame; and finally with social law—relationships with sages, on the one side, and idolators, on the other. Other examples of the Talmud would have laid greater stress on different aspects of behavior and belief; monumental discussions of civil obligations, torts and damages, for example, might well have been cited. But these would have produced a picture not much different, except in substance, from the one yielded by the Talmud's investigations into how a meal is conducted. For no limits are set to the methods of exploring reason and searching for order. Social order with its concomitant ethical concern is no more important than the psychic order of the individual, with its full articulation in the "ritual" life. All reality comes under the discipline of the critical intellect, all is capable of sanctification.

The Talmud's single-minded pursuit of unifying truths itself constitutes its primary discipline. But the discipline does not derive from the perception of unifying order in the natural world. It comes, rather, from the lessons imparted supernaturally in the Torah. The sages perceived the Torah not as a mélange of sources and laws of different origins, but as a single, unitary document, a corpus of laws reflective of an underlying ordered will. The Torah revealed the way things should be, just as the rabbis' formulation and presentation of their laws tell how things should be, whether or not that is how they actually are done. The order derives from the plan and will of the Creator of the world, the foundation of all reality. The Torah was interpreted by the Talmudic rabbis to be the architect's design for reality: God looked into the Torah and created the world, just as an architect follows his prior design in raising a building. A single, whole Torah—in two forms, oral and written, to be sure—underlay the one, seamless reality of the world. The search for the unities hidden by the pluralities of the trivial world, the supposition that some one thing is revealed by many things—these represent, as I said, in intellectual form the theological and metaphysical conception of a single, unique God, creator of heaven and earth, revealer of one complete Torah, guarantor of the unity and ultimate meaning of all the human actions and events that constitute history. On that account the Talmud links the private deeds of man to a larger pattern, provides a large and general "meaning" for small, particular, trivial doings.

Behind this conception of the unifying role of reason and the integrating force of criticism lay the conviction that God supplies the model for man's mind, therefore man, through reasoning in the Torah's laws, may penetrate into God's intent and plan. The rabbis of the Talmud believed they studied Torah as God did in heaven; their schools were conducted like the academy on high. They performed rites just as God performed rites, wearing fringes as did he, putting on phylacteries just as God put on phylacteries. In studying Torah they besought the heavenly paradigm revealed by God "in his image" and handed down from Moses and the prophets to their own teachers. If the rabbis of the Talmud studied and realized the divine teaching of Moses, whom they called "our rabbi," it was because the order they would impose upon earthly affairs would replicate on earth the order they perceived from heaven, the rational construction of reality. It is Torah which reveals the mind of God, the principles by which he shaped reality. So studying Torah is not merely imitating God, who does the same, but is a way to the apprehension of God and the attainment of the sacred. The modes of argument are holy because they lead from earth to heaven, as prayer or fasting or self-denial cannot. Reason is the way, God's way, and the holy man is therefore he who is able to think clearly and penetrate profoundly into the mysteries of the Torah and, especially, of its so very trivial laws. In context those trivialities contain revelation.

To the Talmudic way of thinking, man is liberated, not imprisoned, by reason, which opens the way to true creativity, that is, the work of finding, or imposing, form and order upon chaos. The wherewithal of creativity is triviality—that by now is obvious— and what is to be done with triviality is to uncover, within or beyond the simple things of chaos, the order, the complex structure, the coherence of the whole. What is concrete therefore is subordinate to what is abstract. It is the construction of the larger reality that reveals the traits of that reality. And to the Talmudic rabbi, the most interesting aspect of reality is the human and the societal: the village, the home, the individual. Talmudic Judaism, because of its stress on what and how one eats and drinks, has been called a religion of pots and pans. And so it is, if not that alone, for its raw materials are the irreducible atoms of concrete life. But these come at the beginning; they stand prior to what will become of them, are superficial by contrast to what lies beneath them, to what they adumbrate.

What is to be done with these atoms, these smallest building blocks of reality? The answer now is evident: They are to be subjected to control, the man to self-control. All impulses are to be carefully regulated in accord with the divine plan for reality. All are good and may be holy when so ordered, evil when not. The robust sexuality of the Talmudic laws of marital relations testifies to the rabbis' seriousness and matter-of-factness about what today is highly charged material. For one thing, they consistently referred to a couple's having intercourse "all night long" and promised sons and other blessings to those who engaged in sexual relations two (or more) times in succession—the more the better.

So the regulation of impulse was the opposite of its suppression; it was its liberation. But what was done had to be done rightly, had to be sanctified; the nuptial bed was the right circumstance. To be sure, appropriate social and legal regulations brought the couple to their bed; but (in theory at least), if an unmarried man, legally permitted to marry his beloved, engaged in sexual relations with an unmarried woman, the couple thereby consummated a legitimate marriage-union and were regarded as fully and legally married in all respects. It is assumed that a man does not enter sexual relations lightly or licentiously. It is taken for granted that people intend to do the right thing. Again, the time had to be right. The Torah prohibited sexual relations during a woman's menstrual cycle. Then not during that cycle relations are to be encouraged. The circumstances then had to be discussed: Is it better in the light or in the dark? Is it all right in not completely private conditions? The pious would have relations in the dark; the ultrapious would drive away even flies and mosquitoes. So the course of law rolls on, regulating what is natural and enhancing it through good order, bringing to consciousness what is beneath the surface, through the therapy of public analysis and reasoned inquiry legitimizing what otherwise might be repressed. It is not unimportant that the Talmudic tractate on betrothals is called "sanctification."

Certainly, the Talmudic way of thinking appeals to, and itself approves, the cultured over the uncultured, those capable of self-conscious criticism over those too dull to think. "An ignorant man cannot be pious." Fear of sin without wisdom is worthless. The sages encouraged the articulate over the inarticulate: "The shy person cannot learn." For the give-and-take of argument, one cannot hang back out of feigned or real bashfulness. Reason makes men equals and reveals their inequalities. Reason is not a quirk of personality, but a trait of mind, therefore must be shamelessly and courageously drawn out. The ideal is one for intellectuals, devoted to words and the expression, or reduction, of reality to the abstractions constituted by words.

Notice, for example, how few are the simple, declarative sentences we saw in our chapter of the Talmud; the primary mode of expression is those joining-parts of language which link thought to thought, or set thought against thought: "But," "However," "Do you reason so?" "What is the presupposition?" What is Talmudic about the Talmud is expressed in the Aramaic mortar, not in the Hebrew stones. The near-grunts of the uneducated, "I want this," "I do that," "That is my opinion"—these are virtually absent in

the extended discourse. The argument is expressed in terse, apocopated phrases, moving almost too rapidly for the ordinary ear to
grasp.

What is Talmudic, too, is perpetual skepticism, expressed in response to every declarative sentence or affirmative statement. Once
one states that matters are so, it is inevitable that he will find as a
response: "Why do you think so?" or "Perhaps things are the opposite of what you say?" or "How can you say so when a contrary principle may be adduced?" Articulation, forthrightness,
subtle reasoning but lucid expression, skepticism—these are the
traits of intellectuals, not of untrained and undeveloped minds,
nor of neat scholars, capable only to serve as curators of the past,
but not as critics of the present.

Above all, Talmudic thinking rejects gullibility and credulity.
It is, indeed, peculiarly modern in its systematic skepticism, its
testing of each proposition, not to destroy but to refine what people
suppose to be so. As we have seen time and again, the Talmud's
first question is not *"Who* says so?" but "Why?" "What is the reason of the House of Shammai?" In the Talmudic approach to
thought, faith is restricted to ultimate matters, to the fundamental
principles of reality beyond which one may not penetrate. Akabya
warned to try to find out whence one comes and whither one is
going. The answers will yield humility. But humility in the face of
ultimate questions is not confused with servility before the asser-
tons, the truth-claims, of putative authorities, ancient or modern,
who are no more than mortal.

Since the harvest of learning is humility, however, the more one
seeks to find out, the greater will be one's virtue. And the way to
deeper perception lies in skepticism about shallow assertion. One
must place as small a stake as possible in the acceptance of specific
allegations. The fewer vested convictions, the greater the chances
for wide-ranging inquiry. But while modern skepticism may yield
—at least in the eye of its critics—corrosive and negative results,
Talmudic skepticism produces measured, restrained, and limited
insight. The difference must be in the open-endedness of the Tal-

mudic inquiry: nothing is ever left as a final answer, a completed solution. The fruit of insight is inquiry; the result of inquiry is insight, in endless progression. The only road closed is the road back, to the unarticulated, the unconscious, and the unself-conscious. For once consciousness is achieved, a reason spelled out, one cannot again pretend there is no reason, and nothing has been articulated. For the Talmud the alternatives are not faith or nihilism, but reflection or dumb reflex, consciousness or animal instinct. Man, in God's image, has the capacity to reflect and to criticize. All an animal can do is act and respond. And man may be holy or unholy. An animal can only be clean or unclean—a considerable difference.

That is why energy, the will to act, has to be channeled and controlled by law. You are what you do. Therefore, deed without deliberation is not taken seriously. Examination of deeds takes priority over mere repetition of what works or feels good. For this purpose, genius is insufficient, cleverness is irrelevant. What is preferred is systematic and orderly consideration, step by step, of the principles by which one acts. The human problem in the Talmudic conception is not finding the motive force to do, but discovering the restraint to regulate that protean force. In the quest for restraint and self-control, the primal energies will insure one is not bored or lacking in purpose. For the Talmudic mode of thought perceives a perpetual tension between energy and activity, on the one side, and reflection on the other. To act without thought comes naturally, is contrary, therefore, to the fact of revealed discipline. The drama of the private life consists in the struggle between will and intellect, action and reflection. If the Talmud is on the side of the intellect and reflection, it is because the will and action require no allies. The outcome will be determined, ultimately, by force of character and intellect, these together. And the moot issue is not how to repress, but how to reshape, the primal energy.

Yet it is an error to focus so one-sidedly upon the Talmudic mind and so to ignore the other formative force in culture, the community. The Talmud, for its part, fully recognizes the social forces, the pressures to conform and to follow established custom and habit. That is why so much attention centers upon people's doing things together. The Talmudic rabbis exhibit keen awareness that restraint is societal before it is personal; community takes priority over individuality and gives the private person nearly the whole of the structure of symbols and values that render living meaningful. "Give me fellowship, or give me death," said one of them.

The "meal" we analyzed in some detail is assumed to be a public occasion; there is nothing private about it. When people eat, it is taken for granted that they eat together and follow publicly known regulations; that is why there are such regulations. The more important parts of the Talmud, furthermore, deal with civil regulations: What to do if an ox gores another ox? How to divide a disputed prayer shawl? How to litigate a contested will, in which the material results affect the disposition of a palm tree or a tiny bit of land?

The Talmudic rabbis are well aware that society forms the individual. If a person seeks to create a disciplined individual, whose life is regulated by revealed law, he must give priority to the regulation of the society which forms the ground of individual existence. And to regulate society, he must concentrate upon the conflicts among men, the conflicting claims to unimportant things which, all together, will add up to justice and make possible dignity and autonomy. It is through law that you will revise habit, establish good customary behavior. It is through a lawful society that you will create an environment naturally productive of restraint and rational manners. If, therefore, it is correct to claim that what is Talmudic about the Talmud is the application of reason and criticism to concrete and practical matters, then the Talmud is at its core an instrument for the regulation of society in the most humble and workaday sense of the words.

To be sure, to regulate society you must have access to the institutions that exercise and confer legitimate power, and the Talmudic rabbis knew the importance of various sorts of power. They understood, first of all, the intrinsic power of law itself, which rendered unnecessary constant, *ad hoc* intervention of puissant authority into routine affairs. Once law has established how things should be done, the enforcement of the law becomes necessary only in exceptional circumstances. In normal ones the law itself ensures its own enforcement, for most men most of the time are law-abiding.

The Talmudic rabbis, second, actively sought access to the instrumentalities of Jewish autonomous government made available by the authorities of Roman Palestine and Iranian Babylonia. If the imperial regimes were content to have the Jews regulate their own affairs and fundamentally disinterested in meddling in ritual and community regulations, the rabbis were eager to take over the institutions authorized to regulate the people's lives. They worked their way into these institutions, formed by the Patriarch of Palestine and the Exilarch of Babylonia, and made themselves the chief agents for the day-to-day government of the local communities. So far as the state stood behind the Jewish community's officials, the rabbis enjoyed the benefit of state power and therefore mastered the intricacies of politics.

Third, the Talmudic rabbis exercised moral authority sufficient to make people do what the rabbis wanted without the intervention of secular authorities. That moral authority was based upon multiform foundations.

First, the rabbi was understood to have mastery of the divine revelation and unique access to part of it, the Oral Torah handed down from Sinai. So his rule was according to heavenly principles.

Second, the rabbi was seen as himself paradigmatic of the Torah's image of man. Therefore, what he did was revelatory. Common folk who proposed to obey the will of God as the rabbis explained it would not have to be coerced to do what the rabbis said. They might just as well imitate the rabbi, confident that he did what he did in order to imitate Moses "our rabbi" and God, Moses' rabbi. The Talmud we have studied is full of stories of what individuals said and did on specific occasions. In some instances the abstract law is conveyed by such stories. In most others, the point of the story is to show, by relating the rabbi's deed, what the law is, how one should conduct himself. These are not "political" stories, yet they have a pronouncedly political result, for the story influences behavior no less than a court decree shapes action.

Finally, among the rabbis were some who could exercise miraculous and even supernatural powers. A modern anthropologist having spent a few years in Talmudic circles to study the social role of the rabbi might well call his book, "The Lawyer-Magicians of Babylonia." But the exercise of supernatural power, the ability to appeal to the fantasies of ordinary folk—fantasies the rabbis themselves certainly shared—these too constituted a kind of "moral authority." Curiously, it was intellectual achievement that produced theurgical power. The righteous were believed to have the creative power of God: "If a righteous man desires it, he can create a world." And why should the rabbi not have such power, given his knowledge of the Torah, which contained the plan and pattern for God's own creation of this world? Learning reshaped a man into the likeness of God and therefore endowed him with God's powers of creation. In a secular sense, belief in the supernatural consequences of the supernatural power of mastery of Torah traditions and reasoning about them produced a practical power considerably more efficient than political instrumentalities in moving people to do the right thing. The charisma represented by brilliance in reasoning and argument was affective outside of the circle of intellectuals, just as it is today, but with better reason then. This is what I mean in saying that the luminous becomes numinous.

One can hardly refer to politics without alluding, as well, to the construction of the family, the relationship of father to son. Here Talmudic rabbis discerned a tension and resolved it in their own favor. They understood the primacy of the father in the formation of the personality of the child and the shape of the family.

At the same time they claimed they, as masters of Torah, should shape personality and provide the model for the family. They admitted that the father brought the child into this world. But, they quickly added, the sage brings him into the next world, therefore is entitled to the honor owing from the child to the father. The sage is better than the father, above the father, just as God is the ultimate father of the child and giver of his life. If, therefore, a son sees the ass of his father struggling under his load, and at the same time he sees the ass of his sage about to stumble, he helps the ass of his rabbi, then that of his father, for the one has brought him into this world, the other, eternity. Just as the rabbi placed his rule over that of the state and the state's functionaries, the patriarch and exilarch, so he sought to take precedence over the primary component of the community, the family, by laying claim to the position of the father.

In larger terms the effort to replace the father by the rabbi symbolizes a struggle equivalent to the effort to replace the concrete, this-worldly government of ordinary officials by the nonnatural or supernatural authority of the rabbi, qualified by learning of the Torah and capacity to reason about it. The Roman authority and his representative in Jewry ruled through force or the threat of force. The rabbinical figure compelled obedience through moral authority, through the capacity to persuade and to demonstrate, through affective example, what the law required. Both political and familial life thus was to be rendered something other than what seemed natural or normal. Everyone could understand the authority of the gendarme, the priority of the father. But to superimpose the rabbi both in politics and in the family represented a redefinition of the ordinary sense of politics and the plain, accepted meaning of the family. It made both into something abstract, subject to a higher level of interpretation, than an ordinary person might readily perceive. Political life to the rabbi was not merely a matter of the here and now, nor was the family what it seemed. Both were to be remodeled in the image of Heaven, according to the pattern of the Torah. That is to say, they were to be restructured according to the underlying principles of reality laid down by the divine plan as undercovered by rational inquiry. Society was to be made to conform to the heavenly definition of the good community; the family was to be revised according to the supernatural conception of who the father really was: God and his surrogate, the rabbi—man most closely conforming to his image.

The Talmudic stress upon criticism, therefore, produced a new freedom of construction, the freedom to reinterpret reality and to reconstruct its artifacts upon the basis of well-analyzed, thoroughly criticized principles revealed through the practical reason of the sages. Once a person is free to stand apart from what is customary and habitual, to restrain energies and regulate them, he attains the higher freedom to revise the given, to reinterpret established perceptions of reality and the institutions which give them effect. This constitutes, to begin with, the process of the mind's focusing upon unseen relationships and the formation of imposed, nonmaterial and nonnatural considerations.

We recall in this connection the purity laws, which play so considerable a role in the rabbis' regulation of eating (and other fundamental things, for instance, sexual relations). Those laws seem to have comprised and created a wholly abstract set of relationships, a kind of non-Euclidean geometry of the levitical realm. Yet such high abstractions are brought down to earth to determine in what order one washes his hands and picks up a cup of wine, or, as noted, where one puts his napkin. So what is wholly relative and entirely a matter of theory, not attached to concrete things, transforms trivialities. It affects, indeed generates, the way one does them. It transforms them into issues of some consequence, by relating them to the higher meanings (to be sure, without much rational, let alone material substance) associated with the pure and the impure. The purity laws stand at the pinnacle of Talmudic abstraction and ratiocination.

We may supply a social explanation for the intellectuality and abstraction of the Talmudic rabbis' approach to reality. They themselves stood apart from the larger Jewish society, much as the Jews stood apart from the gentile majority. Their intent was to reshape and improve society. But they were different from other men because of their learning and intellect. They lived in this world, but in another too, one in which, for example, the unseen realities and unfelt relationships of purity and impurity were taken so seriously as to determine behavior in the world of material realities and perceived, concrete relationships. They stood apart not because they alone believed in God, for everyone did, or because they alone revered the Torah, for they were not alone, but because they alone conceived it possible for man to elevate himself heavenward through Torah, rationally apprehended. They participated in the history of this world, but were aware of the precariousness and imperfection of this world when perceived and measured by the standard of the next.

Their capacity to criticize therefore derived from their detachment. They knew that what is now is not necessarily whatever was or what must always be. Able to stand apart because of the perspective of distance attained through rational criticism of the practical life, they realized men have choices they themselves may not perceive. There have been and are now other ways of conducting life and living with men, of building society and creating culture, than those the ordinary people supposed were normative. Able to criticize from the perspective of a transcendent perception of the principles of being, the rabbis could evaluate what others took for granted, could see the given as something to be elevated and transcended.

In a word, the Talmud is a document created by the intellect devoted to morality and seeking sanctity. It takes for granted that man's primary capacity is to think; he therefore is to be taken with utmost seriousness. The Talmud endures as a monument to intellectualism focused upon the application of practical rationality to society. It pays tribute, on every page, to the human potential to think morally, yet without lachrymose sentimentality, to reflect about fundamentals and basic principles, yet for concrete purposes and with ordinary society in mind. The good, well-regulated society will nurture disciplined, strong character. The mighty man—"one who overcomes his impulses"—will stand as a pillar of the good society. This is what I understand as the result of the intellectual activity of the moral intellect. Reason, criticism, restraint, and rational exchange of ideas—these are not data for the history of Talmudic literature alone. The Talmud itself testifies to their necessary consequences for the personality and for society alike.

What are we to make of the Talmudic approach to life? How shall we appropriate the Talmud's moral intellectualism for contemporary sensibility?

Perhaps you think I have claimed too much for the Talmudic way, but I fear I have claimed too little. For what the Talmud accomplished in the formation of a specific civilization—that of the Jewish people—was to lay the foundations for a society capable of rational, supple response to an irrational situation. The Jews lived as aliens, so they created a homeland wherever they found themselves. They effectively and humanely governed themselves without the normal instruments of government, lacking much of a bureaucracy, having no consequential power at all. They created not one culture but multiple cultures, all of them quintessentially "Jewish," out of the materials of many languages, societies, sorts of natural environment, histories, and traditions. The Talmud's construction of a world of ideas and sacred principles, corresponding to, but transcendent of, reality is a paradigm of the Jews' capacity to reinterpret reality and reconstruct culture in age succeeding age, their nonmaterial power fully, rigorously, and robustly to live the life of the mind. Beyond the Jews' capacity for fantasy—after all, not unique to them—was their power to reflect, reconsider, stand back from reality, and revise its interpretation. This, it now is clear, is the end result of a society which trained its young in the Talmud and rewarded its mature and old men alike for lifelong devotion to its study.

It was the rationality and intellectuality of the Jews' culture which led them to a way of living with one another not in perfect harmony—they were flesh and blood—but in mighty restraint and mutual respect. The inner life of the Jewish community was so organized that the people might conflict with one another, yet not through the totally free expression of the impulse toward mutual annihilation. Renunciation of brute power, affirmation of the force of ideas and reason—these represented the Jews' discovery. They cannot claim to have uncovered these principles, but they most rightly do claim meaningfully to have effected them in the formation of their community life and the establishment of their protean culture. Reason applied to practical affairs through the acute inquiry of Talmudic argument—this I think accounts for the Jews' capacity for so many centuries to accommodate themselves to a situation of worldly powerlessness. For they knew ideas could be powerful; criticism could constitute a great force in society; and, in the end, the sword, once sheathed, could change nothing, but an idea, once unleashed, could so persist as to move men to move the world.

The Talmud lays the foundation for the rational, therefore the moral culture. I refer to Philip Rieff,* who speaks of the functions of culture: "(1) to organize the moral demands men make upon themselves in a system of symbols that make men intelligible and trustworthy to each other, thus rendering also the world intelligible and trustworthy; (2) to organize the expressive remissions by which men release themselves, in some degree, from the strain of conforming to the controlling symbolic, internalized variant readings of culture that constitute individual character." Clearly, the Talmud exhibits the capacity to organize "the moral demands" of men into a system of orderly, integrated symbols. These take the form of actions to be taken, others to be rejected. The degree of order and integration depends upon the rabbis' success in locating the fundamental principles which draw together and show the interrelationships among discrete actions.

* The Triumph of the Therapeutic. Uses of Faith after Freud (N.Y., 1966: Harper & Row), p. 232.

But what is the form of the "expressive remissions"? How does the Talmud make room for individual character? The answer lies in the Talmud's stress on the reasons for its rules. Once the reason is made known, one makes room for contrary reason, for reason to reject or revise the established rule. Not only does the individual have the place to differ, but he also has the power through criticism to move the entire community to appropriate what to begin with expressed his private judgment, his individuality. This I think is not only to the advantage of the individual, but also fundamentally therapeutic for the community as a whole.

Now for contemporary man the Talmud presents formidable criticism, for by it the value, "follow your own impulse"—utter subjectivism in all things—is rejected. The Talmud gives contrary advice. "Tame your impulse," regulate, restrain, control energies through the self-imposition of the restraining rule of law. At the same time, the Talmud demands that a person *not* do "his own thing" alone, but persuade others to make what is his own into what is to be shared by all. The Talmud therefore subjects the individual to restraints on his pure individuality, while opening for individuality the possibility of moral suasion of the community at large. "Unrestrained" and "individualism" therefore are set over against "regulated" and "rationality," for it is rationality which overcomes the isolation of the individual, connecting one mind to another through the mediating way of reason. Through the imposition of rational, freely adopted rules, one restrains those destructive elements of the personality which potentially are damaging for both the individual and the community.

To be sure, the supernatural framework of Talmudic religion cannot claim a serious hearing among Jews who stand at a distance from the traditional world of faith, let alone among gentiles. But the Talmud serves a good purpose nonetheless, for it contains within its pages a detailed demonstration of how practical reason may be applied to humble affairs. As a whole document within the multiform historical civilizations of the Jewish people, it testifies to the concrete possibilities of rational and critical approaches to human affairs. This it does not only in generalities, but in strikingly trivial details. The course of the Talmudic argument shows it is possible committedly, involvedly, to argue about changing hypotheses, to pay serious attention to culturally neutral matters, and to find important principles in ordinary affairs. In a way, the Talmudic rabbi takes a clinical attitude toward his own ideas, and certainly toward those of his fellows. They are there for analysis, not for either gullible acceptance or utter rejection. The purpose of the analysis, moreover, is not final commitment to some one conclusion, but provisional decision for laying the way open to further inquiry.

The open-ended character of the Talmudic argument impressed us earlier. Now its very contemporary pertinence becomes clear. Since one expects no final solutions, man is prepared for a succession of intermediate, provisional ones. He learns, therefore, the discipline of commitment within open-mindedness, the capacity to hold conviction loosely, to refrain from imposing on the other person the task of verifying, by assenting to, one's own deeply held convictions. It is the undogmatic quality of Talmudic discourse which contemporary men might well learn to emulate. They will do so when their commitment is to method, rather than to its results, and when the method, or mode, of thought recovers the form prefigured in the Talmud: above all, skepticism, criticism, easy and free movement.

The tradition of Talmudic learning prepared the Jews for the modern situation and even in premodern times carried within itself the qualities we now associate with modernity. So far as modernity requires man to take this world seriously, the Talmud met the requirements of modernity. So far as modernity is characterized by cosmopolitanism and the relativity of values, the Talmud, which could be both studied and realized in many countries and various cultures, prepared the Jews for the modern situation. By its stress on the unfolding possibilities of reason and by its relentless testing of all propositions against the measure of skeptical reason, the Talmud prepared the Jews to recognize the relativity of successive truth claims, the probability that each would in its term have to give way to the next. A trait of modernity is the denial of the ultimacy of any values. To be sure, the Talmud affirmed the Torah and the final truth of all contained therein. But so far as the ideas were perceived as human, not divine, the Talmud spurned the claim that any insight might endure beyond its capacity to be shown to be reasonable. Later, when *all* ideas were perceived as human, the Talmud's fundamental attitude was simply extended to areas where it formerly had been absent. The Talmud's persistent dubiety disciplined the Jewish intellectual to speculate about the unthinkable—"Perhaps things are the opposite of what they seem?"—to investigate the forbidden, to reconsider the commonplace, and so to reshape reality.

The Talmud thus taught its disciples to deny the need they must have felt, the need to judge all values, all assertions, all theories by their own, particular, self-authenticating system of thought. The Talmud prepared its students to see as merely transitory and useful artifacts and ideas the world understood to be absolute and perfected. The Talmud disciplined its devotees to preserve a thoroughly skeptical attitude toward the perfections of the hour. It imparted the view that reality—the immutable truths of others—was something to be criticized, and imparted the humility likewise to perceive one's own.

So, in the end, the Talmud raised abiding skepticism about what people offered as salvation, as final solutions to the problems of the human condition. The Talmudist did not expect final solutions, was trained to ask simple, therefore devastating questions about their finality. So the Talmud readied the Jews for the modern situation of doubt, of provisional truths and hypotheses subject to testing and revision. True, the Talmud did come to decisions. But these were in matters of detail. No one ever resolved any of the really interesting questions of logic and skeptical reasoning. The Talmudic rabbi remained open to the good insights that might come, denying at the same time the finality of what was already present. This gave him the freedom to criticize the Mishnah, the

Gemara, Rashi, and whatever was to come thereafter. The Talmudist could deny the present achievements of the mind because he hoped for ultimately better ones.

The Jew, disciplined in the Talmud's mode of thought, could accommodate himself to the modern world's relativization of values precisely because he had already seen the vision of greater perfection than what was originally present. The Talmud produced an activist tradition of men interested in daily affairs and in their proper regulation, a tradition which told men they were partners in the task of perfecting the world under the dominion of God. If the world is perceived to be insufficient and incomplete, it is man's task to help complete it. If men saw values as in a measure relative to the situation of specific men and groups, if they understood reason to be something provisional and transitory, the Talmud taught the Jews their duty was to criticize and purify their ideas by skeptical criteria, at once most ancient and still not wholly realized.

Finally, the Talmud taught the Jews not to be terrified by the necessity to face, and to choose among, a plurality of uncertain alternatives in an insecure world. The Talmud testified that men must choose, if tentatively and for a time only, among competing interpretations, so that the law might in fact be applied, and the ordinary man might know what to do. So the Talmud forced choices, in a tentative and austere spirit, among the many truths available to reasonable men. It insisted one cannot be paralyzed before contrary claims and equally persuasive reasons. The House of Shammai and the House of Hillel both laid claim to sound law and excellent reasoning; neither party could be shown inferior to the other in critical acumen. But a choice had to be made. If heaven had to resolve the formidable problem of choice, it set a good example and did not have to intervene again.

The Talmud taught that men must end up doing some one thing when faced with conflicting choices. Values may be relative, but men must choose some ideal by which to guide their lives. Men could not endure in indecision. They have to decide to be more than nothing in particular, for their capacity for rational thought is insufficient without an equivalent ability to make and carry out rational decision. The best proof of the duty to make reasonable decisions among unreasonable alternatives was the Jews themselves, who, because of their international character and their memories of many lands and empires, saw the world in all its complex plurality. But they also chose to form the most vivid and intense of all groups, to sustain what is, after all, one of the most particular of all literary traditions, the Talmud itself. Yet they did so in full knowledge that their group was not coextensive with society, and that their Talmudic tradition did not contain everything worth knowing about the right way of living life.

So the Talmud imparted the lesson that men may face a relativity of values, but in the end, must choose life in some specific place, among some particular group of people. In the end you do put your napkin on the cushion—or the table. The values that shape those lives are not relative to the conditions in which they are lived. When all values are seen to be relative and all reasons may be criticized with equally good reason, that is when men most need the fellowship produced by access to a common, deeply held and widely shared, discipline of thinking. The conclusions will vary; the mode of thought and argumentation must then be constant and enduring.

Having emphasized the priority of making difficult choices, we come to the final, peculiarly modern, trait of the Talmudic mind, one that has recurrently impressed us: its pragmatism. In offering Talmudic pragmatism as peculiarly modern, I do not mean to suggest that, because it is modern, the Talmud is therefore vindicated. I mean the very opposite. What makes it possible for contemporary men and women to reach out to the Talmud's power to transcend and reconstruct reality is their pragmatism and willingness to cope with details and to take seriously the trivialities of ordinary life. Because of the very secularity, the seriousness about worldly things, characteristic of our own day, we are able to understand the importance of the Talmud's lessons about the criticism and regulation of worldly things. What shall we say of a tradition of thought that laid greatest emphasis upon deed, upon a pattern of actions and a way of living, but that it is pragmatic? What shall we say of a perspective upon the world that focused on practical reason, but that it is worldly? What shall we conclude of a religious language that called honesty or charity a *kiddush hashem*, a sanctification of God's name, but that it is deeply secular? A legal system whose deepest concerns were for the detailed articulation of the this-worldly meaning of love for one's fellow man here and now is one which long ago brought the Jews into the pragmatic, this-worldly framework of modernity.

That is why the Talmud not only relates to the contemporary world, but may stand in judgment of it. And it surely will judge a world willing to reduce man to part of himself, to his impulses and energies. It will judge an age prepared to validate the unrestrained expression of those energies as the ultimate, legitimate adumbration of what is individual about the person, as though he had no mind, no strength of rational thought. It will condemn a world of enthusiasts who make an improvement and call it redemption, come up with a good idea and, without the test of skeptical analysis, pronounce salvation. The Talmud shows a better way: It demonstrates that men have the capacity to assess the unredemption of the world, to perceive the tentativeness of current solutions to enduring problems, and at the same time to hope for sanctification and work for salvation. It is this unfulfilled yet very vivid evaluation of the world, the power to take the world so seriously as to ask searching questions about its certainties, which, I think, explains the Jew's capacity to love so much, and yet to doubt; to hold the world very near and close, with open arms. The Jew has been taught by the Talmud to engage realistically in the world's tasks, to do so with a whole heart, yet without the need, or even the power, to regard completion of those tasks as the threshold of a final and completed fulfillment of history.

Because of its mode of thinking, the Talmud teaches men to take seriously the wide range of worldly problems without expecting that in solving them—provisionally, let alone finally—they might save the world. If the Jew has found the modern situation congenial and congruent to his perception of humanity, it is because the Talmud, writ large across the traditional culture of the Jewish people, had uniquely prepared him for the conditions of modernity, readied him not only to participate in those conditions, but deeply and unstintingly to criticize them, and, finally, in full rationality to reform them.

But to undertake reform through Talmudic modes of thought and analysis, we have, to begin with, to reconsider what makes those modes more than merely an expression of practical reason, but an expression of the transcendent which is in ourselves. We cannot ask the Talmud to vindicate itself by our standards. We have to bring to bear upon our perceptions of ourselves the Talmud's critique, *its* sacred image of us. To begin with it asks, What say you of the human condition? What is man, but that God is mindful of him? If all we are and ever shall be is here and now, if our minds are merely useful and our capacity to think entirely a secular virtue, then the Talmudic mode of reform is unavailable to us. If through our strength of reason we pursue the profound rationality which underlies, gives unity, and imparts meaning to existence, and if through our power of reflection we then undertake the reconstruction of reality, the interpretation of what is in terms of what can and should be, then we shall have already entered into the Talmudic situation. But when we do, we shall thereby have undertaken all the Talmud knows as the discipline of the sacred. We shall, in other words, have renewed the experience of sanctification both *through* the intellect and *of* the intellect. That experience is open when the pages of the Talmud lie before us, but becomes consequential when the Talmud's perceptions of life and interpretations of society come to possess us. I therefore speak, without shame, of religious experience, indeed of the turning toward God which the sages called *teshuvah,* insufficiently translated as repentance, but truly meaning, *turning.* The way of Talmudic piety and spirituality has been the path of saints, a path each chose—and may choose again—in full rationality, at life's turning.

BIBLIOGRAPHICAL SUPPLEMENT

"Go, Study"

Two SORTS of further study may be undertaken. First, you may wish to examine other speciments of Talmudic literature. Second, you certainly will want to consider how the Talmud and related rabbinic collections have been used for the study of the history of Judaism and of the Jewish people in late antiquity. The answer is found in the systematic scholarly reconstructions, based upon Talmudic sources, of that history. I shall first of all propose some next steps in the study, in English, of Mishnah and Talmud, then provide an introductory bibliography through which the reader may find counsel for further studies.

Further Texts

Certainly, the next Talmudic text should be *Avot* (The Fathers), in the translation and commentary of Judah Goldin, *The Living Talmud* (N.Y., 1957: Mentor, New American Library). Along with *Avot* should go its *Gemara, The Fathers According to Rabbi Nathan* (New Haven, 1955: Yale University Press), translated by Judah Goldin. These two texts do not exhibit the sort of closely reasoned argument we have examined. But they do provide a comprehensive account of the religious and intellectual ideals of the Talmudic rabbis, in Goldin's masterly translation of the Talmudic language and idiom.

Further tractates of Mishnah to be studied in English might well include the whole of *Berakhot* (Blessings), Chapter One of *Peah* (Gleanings), all of *Bikkurim* (First Fruits), Chapter Ten of *Pesahim* (Passover), Chapter Eight of *Yoma* (The Day of Atonement), Chapter Nine of *Sotah* (The Suspected Adulteress), Chapter Six of *Gittin* (Divorces), Chapter One of *Bava Qamma* (The First Gate; civil damages), Chapter Ten of *Sanhedrin* (on those who have a portion in the world to come), Chapter Three of *Avodah Zarah* (Idolatry), all of *Tamid* (The Daily Whole-Offering), Chapter Twenty-four of *Kelim* (Vessels Susceptible of Receiving Uncleanness), Chapter Two, paragraphs 2–7, of *Tohorot* (Cleannesses), Chapter Four of *Yadaim* (Unclean Hands). These chapters illustrate both the varieties of legal topics and themes, and some of the types of literary forms used for the formulation of Mishnaic law. The best translation of the Mishnah is in the Soncino Talmud (cited below), because the notes are copious and helpful.

A felicitous translation of a complete, and not too difficult, tractate is Henry Malter, *The Treatise Ta'anit of the Babylonian Talmud* (Philadelphia, 1928: Jewish Publication Society). The reader who wishes to study an entire tractate on his own, in English, may start here.

Jewish History and Religion in Talmudic Times

The place to begin is with Judah Goldin, "The Talmudic Period," in Louis Finkelstein, ed., *The Jews: Their History, Culture, and Religion* (Philadelphia, 1960: Jewish Publication Society); and Gerson D. Cohen, "The Talmudic Age," in Leo Schwarz, ed., *Great Ages and Ideas of the Jewish People* (N.Y., 1956: Random House). The essays by Menahem Stern, "The Hasmonean Revolt and Its Place in the History of Jewish Society and Religion," E. E. Urbach, "The Talmudic Sage—Character and Authority," and S. Safrai, "Elementary Education, Its Religious and Social Significance in the Talmudic Period," in *Journal of World History* XI, 1–2, 1968: *Social Life and Social Values of the Jewish People,* are concise and informative.

For an introductory account of the religious history of Babylonian Jewry in Talmudic times, this writer's *There We Sat Down. Talmudic Judaism in the Making* (Nashville, 1972: Abingdon) is available. An analysis of the sources on pre-70 Pharisaic Judaism and an effort to construct a critical account are in his *From Politics to Piety: The Emergence of Pharisaic Judaism* (Englewood Cliffs, 1973: Prentice-Hall). His Haskell Lectures for 1972–1973 closely relate to the legal materials reviewed in this book. They are published as *The Idea of Purity in Ancient Judaism* (Leiden, 1973: E. J. Brill).

After reading the suggested essays and introductions, you will have formed your own inquiries. To find out how to pursue them, you will want to consult bibliographical guides, the best of which is Judah Goldin, "Judaism," in Charles J. Adams, ed., *A Reader's Guide to the Great Religions* (N.Y., 1965: The Free Press), pp. 191–228. Goldin gives a careful and responsible account of the scholarly literature before 1960. He surveys the state of knowledge and is the most judicious and sage master of the subject.

The Study of Judaism. Bibliographical Essays (N.Y., 1972: Ktav for Anti-Defamation League of B'nai B'rith) contains two papers of importance for our topic, Richard Bavier, "Judaism in New Testament Times," and John T. Townsend, "Rabbinic Sources." The former is a guide, by a student, for beginners in the study of ancient Judaism. The latter is an extraordinary account of the manuscripts, printed editions, translations, concordances, and major studies of ancient Jewish literature, translations of the Scriptures into Aramaic (Targumim), the Mishnah, Tosefta, Palestinian and Babylonian Talmuds, extracanonical tractates, and the like. Townsend's bibliography is, for its subject, without peer.

Moses Mielziner, *Introduction to the Talmud,* with a new bibliography, 1925–1967, by Alexander Guttmann (N.Y., 1968: Bloch Publishing Co.), contains helpful lists of books arranged according to various topics.

The Mishnah in English

Herbert Danby, *The Mishnah. Translated from the Hebrew with Introduction and Brief Explanatory Notes* (London, 1933: Oxford University Press) is a painstaking and, on the whole, accurate version. The notes do not offer much help to the beginner. Danby's translation of *The Code of Maimonides. Book Ten. The Book of Cleanness* (New Haven, 1954: Yale University Press. Yale Judaica Series, Vol. VIII) also should be mentioned. Maimonides presents the Talmudic purity laws with unparalleled thoroughness and clarity. The task of translation was challenging because of the complexity of the laws; it occupied Danby for more than five years.

Somewhat fuller notes and a good translation of the Mishnah, along with the Hebrew text, are provided by Philip Blackman, *Mishnayoth* (N.Y., 1965, Third Edition: The Judaica Press, Inc., Vols. I–VI). Knowledge of Hebrew is advantageous in using this translation, all the more so the commentary.

The Talmud in English

The Palestinian Talmud has never been translated into English. A French translation, Moise Schwab, *Le Talmud de Jérusalem* (Paris, 1871–1889, reprinted 1960: Editions G.-P. Maisonneuve), is in no way satisfactory.

A complete and reliable English translation of the Babylonian Talmud was executed in Britain under the general editorship of Isidore Epstein and published by the Soncino Press, London, between 1935 and 1948 in thirty-five volumes. An eighteen-volume edition was issued in 1961. The translation is accompanied by brief and helpful notes. Some volumes of a bilingual edition have appeared. I wonder whether a person not already familiar with Hebrew and Aramaic and without a Talmudic text before him will fully follow the excellent work of the Soncino translators, for, being close to the original, it also is somewhat concise and preserves the Talmud's exceptional terseness. Often, too, the thrust of argument will not be wholly clear. But one may make considerable progress with the Soncino Talmud, a work of painstaking care and admirable intelligence.

An English translation, with extensive commentary, of selected chapters of the Talmud under the general editorship of A. Ehrman is being issued in fascicles by El-Am-Hoza as Leor Israel (Jerusalem and Tel Aviv, beginning in 1965) and the National Academy for Adult Jewish Studies of the United Synagogue of America (N.Y.). The commentary includes three parts. First come "realia," explanations, frequently not very scholarly, of the practical laws. These explanations are written in a pseudocritical spirit and exhibit a strong homiletical interest. Second, biographical notes are supplied, consisting of compilations of Talmudic allusions to various authorities mentioned in the text. The main commentary, third, is a wordy and prolix paraphrase and expansion of the translation of the Mishnah and *Gemara.* At some other points a commentary on the practical law is supplied.

A sixteen-page fascicle may cover a single folio-page of the Talmud; so far, there are twenty-five fascicles for tractate Blessings (*Berakhot*), reaching folio 17b; twenty fascicles of tractate on Betrothals (*Qiddushin*), for twenty-eight folios; and twenty fascicles for two chapters of *Bava Mesi'a'* (the Middle Gate, civil law), covering folios 33b through 57b. I think the English reader will find it difficult to use this "popular" translation, because he will need a score card to dope out the four English sections on a given page. The actual Talmud on a page is brief and truncated. One has to keep in balance a whole mass of information—the translation of the Talmud, various notes strung out along the sides; an extended, not particularly illuminating commentary, which is full of Hebrew words and therefore not entirely helpful to the English reader. And each section of a page will continue on the next, without regard to where the other columns of type have left off, so one may end up reading three or four pages at once, going back and forth. In the balance, the Soncino Talmud is much preferable.

B. Elizur-Epstein, *A Chapter of the Talmud* (Jerusalem, 1963) translates the ninth chapter of Bava Mesiʻa' with brief explanatory comments. The work seems competent, especially helpful for those who already know some Aramaic and Hebrew.

Anthologies

Three anthologies of Talmudic materials arranged according to topics such as the law, divine mercy, hope and faith, and the like, may be mentioned. The best is C. G. Montefiore and H. Loewe, *A Rabbinic Anthology* (Cleveland and New York, 1963: Meridian Books. World Publishing Co.; and Philadelphia: Jewish Publication Society of America). This indeed is the finest anthology of materials pertinent to the study of Judaism of any period. Montefiore and Loewe do not merely collect and arrange interesting passages; they comment on them, cross-reference and rework them. The reader has a pair of reliable, urbane guides through thoughtfully selected and lucidly presented materials.

The other anthologies are A. Cohen, *Everyman's Talmud* (N.Y., 1949: E. P. Dutton & Co.), and Louis I. Newman with Samuel Spitz, *The Talmudic Anthology. Tales and Teachings of the Rabbis. A Collection of Parables, Folk-Tales, Fables, Aphorisms, Epigrams, Sayings, Anecdotes, Proverbs, and Exegetical Interpretations* (N.Y., 1945: Behrman House). Cohen strings together allusions to Talmudic and related texts; but the texts are not fully translated. Newman's compendium of "tales and teachings" is arranged to serve preachers looking for stunning sayings. It will not meet any other purpose.

Talmudic Lore

A magnificent compilation of Talmudic and later legends, both Jewish and Christian, about biblical history and biography is presented by Louis Ginzberg, *The Legends of the Jews* (Philadelphia, 1947: Jewish Publication Society, Vols. I–VII). Ginzberg paraphrases the stories and arranges them according to the order of the biblical narrative. The stories are not distinguished as to their approximate time of origin, who told them, the texts in which they occur, and the like, so the collection as a whole is of limited historical utility. But the notes, in Vols. V–VI, are thorough and contain numerous important points. A one-volume summary is Louis Ginzberg, *Legends of the Bible* (Philadelphia, 1956: Jewish Publication Society) with a brilliant introduction by Shalom Spiegel, the master of Jewish lore. Spiegel's introduction constitutes an illuminating explanation for Jewish folklore and legend. A still better specimen of Talmudic and later folklore is Shalom Spiegel, *The Last Trial. On the Legends and Lore of the Command to Abraham to Offer Isaac As a Sacrifice: The Akedah. Translated from the Hebrew with an Introduction by Judah Goldin* (N.Y., 1967: Pantheon Books). Spiegel carries the biblical story through Talmudic and medieval times in a wide-ranging and highly literate account.

Talmudic Methodology

Little is available in English to delineate the method of Talmudic logic and the traits of the Talmud as literature. In general, Talmudists tend to neglect systematic presentation of such matters as the structure of Talmudic discussions and the formulation of arguments. An essay in these questions, admittedly not a complete guide but an important beginning, is Louis Jacobs, *Studies in Talmudic Logic and Methodology* (London, 1961: Vallentine, Mitchell). It is a sophisticated account of four logical and six literary questions, a model for further research.

Midrash

Midrash, from the root *darash*, "to seek," comprises the Talmudic interpretation of biblical literature. Midrashic literature dating from

Talmudic and medieval times has been translated in the following works (among others): *Mekilta de Rabbi Ishmael,* by J. Z. Lauterbach (Philadelphia, 1933: Jewish Publication Society, Vols. I–III); *Midrash Sifré on Numbers,* by P. P. Levertoff (London and N.Y., 1926: Macmillan); *Midrash Rabbah, translated into English with Notes, Glossary, and Indices,* under the editorship of H. Freedman and Maurice Simon (London, 1939: The Soncino Press, Vols. I–X); *The Song at the Sea, being a Commentary on a Commentary in Two Parts,* by Judah Goldin (New Haven, 1971: Yale University Press), covering tractate Shirta of Mekhilta; *The Midrash on Psalms,* by W. G. Braude (New Haven, 1959: Yale University Press, Vols. I–II); *Pesikta Rabbati. Discourses for Feasts, Fasts, and Special Sabbaths,* by W. G. Braude (New Haven, 1968: Yale University Press, Vols. I–II); and the same translator's *Pesikta deRav Kahana* is underway.

For the spirit of Midrashic inquiry, the best introduction is Maurice Samuel, *Certain People of the Book* (N.Y., 1955: Knopf). For the history of midrashic traditions, the seminal work is Geza Vermes, *Scripture and Tradition in Judaism* (Leiden, 1961: E. J. Brill).

History

E. Schürer, *History of the Jewish People in the Time of Jesus Christ* (Edinburgh, 1886–1890: T. & T. Clark), will reappear shortly in a revised and updated edition by Geza Vermes and Fergus Millar. It remains the standard account of Palestinian Jewry down to 70. We have in English no satisfactory history of that community from 70 to the end of its corporate existence in 425. For the Jews in the Roman Empire, the definitive account is Jean Juster, *Les juifs dans l'empire romain* (Paris, 1914; Vols. I–II). There is nothing like it in English. For Babylonian Jewry, one may find helpful this writer's *History of the Jews in Babylonia* (Leiden: E. J. Brill). *I. The Parthian Period* (1970, Second Edition); *II. The Early Sasanian Period* (1966); *III. From Shapur I to Shapur II* (1968); *IV. The Age of Shapur II* (1969); and *V. Later Sasanian Times* (1970). A supplementary study is *Aphrahat and Judaism. The Christian-Jewish Argument in Fourth-Century Iran* (Leiden, 1971: E. J. Brill).

On the Pharisees before 70, you may consult this writer's *The Rabbinic Traditions about the Pharisees before 70* (Leiden, 1971: E. J. Brill). *I. The Masters; II. The Houses; III. Conclusions;* this work is summarized in *From Politics to Piety.*

Talmudic Religion

Morton Smith, the great historian of religions in late antiquity, writes, "A gift for systematic theology . . . is a great handicap in the study of rabbinic literature." The reason is that systematic theology requires the imposition of an artificial construct, such as "the rabbis" or "the rabbinic mind," upon sayings and stories which derive from a great many discrete and unsystematic authorities, living in various countries, over a period of seven centuries and more. Consequently, it is misleading to systematize what to begin with derives from authorities whose sayings never were meant to be systematized. Still, we have valuable accounts of rabbinic theology, and, while subject to further refining and improvement, these works are illuminating. Foremost among them are the following: S. Schechter, *Some Aspects of Rabbinic Theology* (N.Y., 1936: Behrman House); George Foot Moore, *Judaism in the First Centuries of the Christian Era. The Age of the Tannaim* (Cambridge, 1954: Harvard University Press, Vols. I–III); Max Kadushin, *Worship and Ethics. A Study in Rabbinic Judaism* (Evanston, 1964: Northwestern University Press); Jacob Z. Lauterbach, *Rabbinic Essays* (Cincinnati, 1951: Hebrew Union College Press); and Louis Ginzberg, *On Jewish Law and Lore* (Philadelphia, 1955: Jewish Publication Society). The last-named work contains classic essays introducing the Palestinian Talmud (pp. 3–60) and on the allegorical interpretation of Scripture (pp. 127–152), among others.

Jewish mysticism, with roots in Talmudic Judaism, is masterfully laid forth in Gershom G. Scholem, *Major Trends in Jewish Mysticism* (N.Y., 1954: Schocken), one of the most important works in the study of the history of Judaism.

For the bearing of archaeological discoveries on the study of ancient Judaism, I recommend Erwin R. Goodenough, *Jewish Symbols in the Greco-Roman Period* (N.Y., 1953 et seq., Bollingen Foundation, Vols. I–XIII).

By the Same Author

In addition to *History* and *Pharisees,* this writer's studies of Talmudic Judaism include the following: *A Life of Yohanan ben Zakkai* (Leiden, 1970, Second Edition, Completely Revised: E. J. Brill); *Development of a Legend. Studies on the Traditions Concerning Yo-*

hanan ben Zakkai (Leiden, 1970: E. J. Brill); *Eliezer ben Hyrcanus. The Tradition and the Man* (Leiden, 1973: E. J. Brill, Vols. I–II); and *The Idea of Purity in Ancient Judaism* (The Haskell Lectures for 1973) (Leiden, 1973: E. J. Brill). In connection with the study of Talmudic literature and history, he has edited *The Formation of the Babylonian Talmud. Studies in the Achievements of Late Nineteenth and Twentieth Century Historical and Literary-Critical Research* (Leiden, 1970: E. J. Brill); and *The Modern Study of the Mishnah* (Leiden, 1973: E. J. Brill); as well as *A Soviet View of Talmudic Judaism. The Work of Yu. A. Solodukho* (Leiden, 1973: E. J. Brill).

For beginners, the following textbooks may prove helpful: *Way of Torah: An Introduction to Judaism* (Encino, 1974: Dickenson Publishing Co.), with its accompanying reader, *The Life of Torah* (Encino, 1974: Dickenson Publishing Co.); for an anthology of Jewish theology, *Theology of Judaism: Classical Issues and Modern Perspectives* (N.Y., 1973: Ktav Publishing House), and *Understanding Rabbinic Judaism* (N.Y., 1974: Ktav Publishing House); and, for rabbinic Judaism in modern times, *American Judaism: Adventure in Modernity* (Englewood Cliffs, 1972: Prentice-Hall).

Index of Biblical
and Talmudic Passages

Index of Names and Subjects